# A THEORY OF THE APHORISM

# A Theory of
# the Aphorism
## From Confucius
## to Twitter

Andrew Hui

**PRINCETON UNIVERSITY PRESS**

PRINCETON AND OXFORD

Published by Princeton University Press
41 William Street, Princeton, New Jersey 08540
6 Oxford Street, Woodstock, Oxfordshire OX20 1TR

press.princeton.edu

Library of Congress Control Number: 2018950885
ISBN: 978-0-691-18895-9

British Library Cataloging-in-Publication Data is available

Editorial: Anne Savarese and Thalia Leaf
Production Editorial: Ellen Foos
Jacket Design: Chris Ferrante
Production: Erin Suydam
Publicity: Jodi Price
Copyeditor: Daniel Simon

This book has been composed in Adobe Text and Gotham

Printed on acid-free paper. ∞

Printed in the United States of America

10 9 8 7 6 5 4 3 2 1

*To Julia, our little book of aphorisms*

# CONTENTS

# A THEORY OF THE APHORISM

# Introduction

## A LINE

This is a short book on the shortest of genres—the aphorism. As a basic unit of intelligible thought, this microform has persisted across world cultures and histories, from Confucius to Twitter, Heraclitus to Nietzsche, the Buddha to Jesus. Opposed to the babble of the foolish, the redundancy of bureaucrats, the silence of mystics, in the aphorism nothing is superfluous, every word bears weight.

Its minimal size is charged with maximal intensity. Consider Heraclitus' "Nature loves to hide"; Jesus' "The kingdom of God is within you"; Pascal's "The eternal silence of these infinite spaces terrifies me"; or Nietzsche's "If a temple is to be erected, a temple must be destroyed." These aphorisms have an atomic quality— compact yet explosive. Yet in comparison to the rich theories and thick histories of the novel, lyric, or drama, the aphorism—this most elemental of literary forms—has been curiously understudied, a vast network of literary and philosophical archipelagos that has so far been thinly explored. At a time when a presidency can be won and social revolutions ignited by 140–character posts (now 280), an analysis of the short saying seems to be as crucial as ever.

This book's focus, however, will not be on the political rhetoric of the aphorism (though I will touch upon it in the epilogue). It will rather take a step back from the noise of digital minutiae and explore the deep life of the aphorism as a literary form.

The theory this book advances is that aphorisms are before, against, and after philosophy. Heraclitus comes before and against Plato and Aristotle, Pascal after and against Descartes, Nietzsche after and against Kant and Hegel. The philosopher creates and critiques continuous lines of argument. The aphorist, on the other hand, composes scattered lines of intuition. One moves in a chain of discursive logic; the other by arrhythmic leaps and bounds. Much of the history of Western philosophy can be narrated as a series of attempts at the construction of systems. My theory proposes that much of the history of aphorisms can be narrated as an animadversion, a turning away from grand systems through the construction of literary fragments. I will shortly offer definitions of the aphorism, the fragment, and the system, but for now, let us heed the German Romantic philosopher Friedrich Schlegel's elegant formulation: "A fragment ought to be entirely isolated from the surrounding world like a little work of art and complete in itself like a hedgehog" (*Athenaeum Fragments* §206).

As aphorisms have been for millennia anthologized and de-anthologized, revived and mutilated, quoted and misquoted, they constitute their own cultural network. As such, a philological understanding of aphorisms is as necessary as a philosophical one: that is to say, one must examine not only their internal meaning but also the circumstances of their material production, transmission, and reception in history. It is no accident that when Schlegel compares an aphorism to a hedgehog (*ein Igel*), the most famous hedgehog in Western thought comes from nowhere else but that fragment of Archilochus: "The fox knows many things, but the hedgehog knows one big thing" (fr 201 West). In Schlegel's Germany, the poetic production of modern fragments went hand-in-hand with the scholarly editions of ancient fragments. As we shall see, the aphorisms of the ancients are some of the most problematic—but also the most generative—specimens in the laboratory of textual criticism.

Though an aphorism by definition is succinct, it almost always proliferates into an innumerable series of iterations. By nature the aphorism—like the hedgehog—is a solitary animal. Striving to cut out all verbiage, its not-so-secret wish is to annihilate its neighbor so that its singular potency would reign supreme. Yet aphorisms also have a herd mentality. Indeed, from the wisdom literature of the Sumerians and Egyptians onward, they find strength in the social collective of anthologies. Each aphorism might very well be "complete in itself," as Schlegel claims, but it also forms a node in a network, often a transnational one with great longevity, capable of continuous expansion. And the best modern aphorists never wrote just one aphorism but almost always a great many—La Rochefoucauld, Goethe, and Lichtenberg had notebooks upon notebooks filled with them and often had trouble finishing them. So I find it ironic that although a *single* aphorism may be a hegemonic hedgehog, a *collection* of aphorisms tends to morph into a multitude of cunning little foxes.

At the same time, the very minimal syntax of an aphorism gives it a maximal semantic force. The best aphorisms admit an infinitude of interpretation, a hermeneutic inexhaustibility. In other words, while an aphorism is circumscribed by the *minimal* requirements of language, its interpretation demands a *maximal* engagement. Deciphering the gnomic remarks of the early Greek thinkers, Jesus, or Confucius marks the birth of hermeneutics. For Friedrich Schleiermacher, a friend of Schlegel and a founder of modern hermeneutics, interpretation is "an infinite task," because there is "an infinity of past and future that we wish to see in the moment of the utterance" (*Hermeneutics and Criticism*, 23). The interpretation of one aphorism thereby opens a plurality of worlds. This is what I mean when I say that an aphorism is "atomic": it is without parts, but its splitting causes an explosion of meaning. The hedgehog must be dissected.

These three methodologies, then—the philosophical, the philological, the hermeneutical—will be the intersecting vectors that guide this book. Taken together, my theory reveals that the aphorism is at times an ancestor, at times an ally, and at times an antagonist to systematic philosophy.

## Toward a definition

Now let us try to define the aphorism. Turn to any reference work and it would read something like "a concise expression of doctrine or principle or any generally accepted truth" (here, the *Encyclopaedia Britannica*). This formulation is problematic. First, it presupposes that an aphorist has a "doctrine" behind such concision. Much of this book will be spent trying to figure out whether such intellectual systems exist or not. Second, most of the aphorisms I'm concerned with are not "generally accepted truth," for they are often enigmatic statements that defy convention.

There are many names for the short saying: *gnōmē, paroimia, proverb, sententia, precept, maxim, commonplace, adage, epigram, apothegm, apophthegm*. Their meanings vary across languages and histories. Sometimes they overlap. "Generally accepted truths" should be more properly called *proverbs* or *sententia*, and they are usually anonymous. Thus "there's no place like home" is a proverb, whereas Kafka's "A cage went in search of a bird" (*Zürau Aphorisms* §16) is not. And for every proverb there is an equal and opposite proverb: "out of sight out of mind," "absence makes the heart grow fonder." An *epigram* contains something clever with a sarcastic twist and is associated with great wits such as Alexander Pope or Oscar Wilde. Here is one from Martial, the Ogden Nash of antiquity: "A work isn't long if you can't take anything out of it, / but you, Cosconius, write even a couplet too long" (2.77). A *maxim* is usually a pithy moral instruction, such as those inscribed in the Temple of Delphi: "Nothing in excess" or "Know thyself." La Rochefoucauld's *Maximes*, however, are more reflections on human nature than prescriptions on how to live: "Mediocre minds usually [*d'ordinaire*] condemn what they don't understand" (V:375).[1] For Kant, the maxim assumed a metaphysical reach: "Act only according to that maxim [*Maxime*] whereby you can, at the same time, will that it should become a universal law [*allgemeines Gesetz*]" (*Grounding for the Metaphysics of Morals*, 30). Whereas the German philosopher is binding and absolute, the French moralist loves exceptions: "most often," "most men," "few people," "usually" (*le plus souvent, la plupart des hommes, peu de gens, d'ordinaire*) are his favorite qualifiers.

Next let us plot the numerous terms for short sayings along various points on a spectrum: proverbs, folk wisdom, platitudes, and bromides are close to the banal extreme; maxims and epigrams are somewhere in the middle; the aphorism is close to the philosophical or theological end. The first class is easy to understand ("Absence makes the heart grow fonder"); the second contains a sharp aperçu ("An almost universal fault of lovers is failing to realize when they are no longer loved," La Rochefoucauld, V:371); the third is more recondite ("If Cleopatra's nose had been shorter, the whole face of the earth would have been different," Pascal, *Pensées* §32, Sellier ed.).

These categories, of course, are fluid. For instance, folk proverbs in some cultures are opaque and even have magical powers. Before he became the editor of the leading journal of French intellectual life, *La Nouvelle Revue Française*, Jean Paulhan stayed in Madagascar from 1908 to 1910 to study its oral culture. He observes that the everyday proverb of the Malagasy, *hain-teny*, "is rather like a peculiar secret society: it does not hide, it operates publicly, and its passwords—unlike other magic words—are banalities. Nonetheless, it remains secret, and everything takes place as if an undefinable difficulty, providing sufficient defense against indiscretion, would protect the proverbs" ("Sacred Language," 308).[2] Conversely there are also aphorisms by rarified authors that are completely crystalline and understood instantaneously. To explain their wit is only to state the obvious. For my purposes, however, I define the aphorism simply as *a short saying that requires interpretation*.

———

The aphorism condenses. It is the *punctum*, the monad, the *kairos* that arrests the welter of our thinking. Italo Calvino writes, "I dream of immense cosmologies, sagas, and epics all reduced to the dimensions of an epigram" (*Six Memos for the Next Millennium*, 51). Joseph Joubert is even more concise: an aphorist must put "a whole book into a page, a whole page into a phrase, and a phrase into a word" (*Carnets*, 2:485). Conversely, interpretation must dissolve this atomic density. To understand the aphorism, one must translate the figural, witty, and intuitive into the logical, explicable, and demonstrable. One must unfold its multidimensional complexes into the flat plane of clarity, render its fulgurating blot (or rather bolt!) into lucid insight. A philological exegesis would carefully examine the authorship, text, language, culture, sources, and receptions of the aphorism; a philosophical analysis would evaluate its logical or normative truth claims; an ethical reading would end in action; a spiritual meditation would lead to an apophatic epiphany, an emptying of words. "People find difficulty with the aphoristic form," Nietzsche writes; "this arises from the fact that today this form is *not taken seriously enough*. Aphorism, properly stamped and molded, has not been 'deciphered' when it has simply been read; rather, one has then to begin its *exegesis*, for which is required an art of exegesis" (*On the Genealogy of Morals*, preface §8, emphasis in the original). The irony is that the aphorism—this shortest of forms to read—actually takes the longest time to understand.

## A short history of the short saying

Aphorisms are transhistorical and transcultural, a resistant strain of thinking that has evolved and adapted to its environment for millennia. Across deep time, they are vessels that travel everywhere, laden with freight yet buoyant. Terse sayings form a rich constellation in the Sanskrit, already found in the *Rig-veda* and the *Brāhmaṇas*.[3] Didactic wisdom literature in Egypt extends from the Old Kingdom to the Ptolemaic period. The fragments or the entirety of some seventeen anthologies survive. It is well attested that the Hebrew Book of Proverbs derives in form and content from the New Kingdom *Instruction of Amenemope* (ca. 1000 BCE).[4] We are told that Solomon "spoke three thousand proverbs" (1 Kings 4:32).

How and why did the aphorism develop and mutate under certain cultural conditions? How did it acquire such longevity? Spherical and solitary, the hedgehog is believed to have been around for fifteen million years, making it one of the oldest mammals on earth. Friendlier and smaller than the porcupine, rather than shooting quills when threatened, this teacup-sized creature rolls up into a ball. The tiny aphorism is also one of the oldest and smallest literary genres on earth. What "affordance," to employ a term from design theory that Caroline Levine has recently used to rethink literary forms, does the aphorism offer? For Levine, affordance is "used to describe the potential uses or actions latent in materials and designs ... allow[ing] us to grasp both the specificity and the generality of forms—both the particular constraints and possibilities that different forms afford, and the fact that those patterns and arrangements carry their affordances with them as they move across time and space" (*Forms,* 6). My theory is that at least in Chinese and European cultures, the aphorism's affordance developed alongside philosophy, either in anticipation of it, in antagonism with it, or in its aftermath. As such, it oscillates between the fragment and the system.

In early China, the teachings of charismatic "masters" (*zi,* 子) circulated in oral traditions long before their establishment as eponymous texts. Though Confucius, Laozi, and Zhuangzi are considered the ancestors of Chinese philosophy, their received doctrines seem to resemble gnomic wisdom and parables more than well-developed doctrines.[5] The *Analects*, for instance, is an assemblage of textual units gathered from a variety of sayings and anecdotes that range from the fifth century BCE to possibly even as late as the first century CE. In the Warring States and Qin periods, the compilation of fragmentary texts began as opposition to the state. By the Han period, however, the systematization of the Confucian canon served as the foundation of imperial authority. Hence the individual "masters" became collective "schools" that required voluminous commentary (chapter 1).

Before the birth of Western philosophy proper, there was the aphorism (chapter 2). In ancient Greece, the short sayings of the Presocratics, known as *gnōmai*, constitute the first efforts at philosophizing and speculative thinking, but they are also something to which Plato and Aristotle are hostile because of their deeply enigmatic nature. (*Gnōmē*, cognate with *gnosis*, "knowledge," ironically became *gnomic* in English—obscure, impenetrable, difficult, with even the connotation of *un*knowable—by way of Anglo-Saxon riddles and kennings.[6]) The *dicta* of Anaximander, Xenophanes, Parmenides, or Heraclitus often elude discursive analysis by their refusal to be corralled into systematic order. No one would deny that their pithy statements are philosophical; but Plato and Aristotle were ambivalent about them, for they contain no sustained ratiocination, just scattered utterances of supposedly wise men.

One account of the history of ancient philosophy might divide it into three ages: first, a brilliant, motley group of speculative thinkers around 585 to about 400 BCE inquired into the origins and nature of things.[7] Then came the grand schools of Plato and Aristotle as well as the Epicureans, Stoics, and Skeptics, in which architectonic arguments arose. The last period, after 100 BCE, might be characterized as a derivative, epigonic era: anthologies, handbooks, and exegeses summarized and elucidated the achievements of the past. One of our largest sources of the Presocratic writings, for instance, survives in the assiduous commentaries of Simplicius, a sixth-century CE late Platonist.[8] In other words, the first age creates aphorisms; the second age argues with and against them; the third age preserves them.

Though the sayings of Jesus are best known from his New Testament sermons and parables, in the early years of the Common Era there existed a genre of *logoi sophon,* "sayings of the sages," that circulated from Jewish wisdom literature to the Nag Hammadi writings (chapter 3). Biblical scholars posit that one collection of Jesus' sayings—dubbed Q—were the basic, oral units of tradition that served as the source text for Matthew and Luke. Eventually Mark, Matthew, Luke, and John were sanctioned as the orthodox Gospels by the early church fathers, but beneath their continuous narratives there still remain the vestiges of Jesus' primitive aphorisms.

The *sententiae* (brief moral sayings) of late antiquity and the Middle Ages were the distillations of biblical truths and theological doctrine.[9] The church fathers urged the faithful to ruminate on the verses of scripture like morsels of spiritual food. The ascetic virtues of the Desert Fathers—self-control, devotion, hospitality, obedience, charity—circulated widely in anecdotal sayings (*Apophthegmata Patrum*). The Eastern Orthodox collection *Philokalia* contains the "Gnomic Anthology" of Ilias the Presbyter. The *Distichs of Cato*, a collection of ancient proverbs, were the basis of the Latin schoolboy curriculum. Both Isidore of Seville and Peter of Lombard composed *Libri sententiarum,* compendia of quotations from scripture and the church fathers. Vincent de Beauvais' *Speculum Maius* sought to encapsulate the known world's knowledge in the form of a mosaic of quotations from Greek, Latin, Hebrew, and Arabic in 3,718 chapters. These massive assemblages—the many made one—became the textual pillars that supported the mighty architectonics of the Christian faith.[10]

It is no exaggeration to say that during the Renaissance, commonplaces constitute the very synapses of the humanist mind (chapter 4). In retrieving the fragments of antiquity, the humanists shattered the well-ordered medieval cosmos by their new philological science. In reconstituting the corpus of classical and Christian aphorisms, they forged new epistemological galaxies—the one became the many again. Philologists like Polydore Vergil, Filippo Beroaldo, and Erasmus collected Greek and Latin adages. Guicciardini and Gracián offered their instruction manuals in the form of maxims to help the courtier navigate the vicissitudes of political life. The plays of Shakespeare, Jonson, Calderón, and Ariosto would be unthinkable without *sententiae*. I call the "Polonius Effect" uttering wise words without knowing what they really mean; I call the "Sancho Panza Effect" uttering wise words at the wrong place and the wrong time. Marlowe's Doctor Faustus in the eponymous play brags to himself: "Is not thy common talk sound aphorisms? / Are not thy bills hung up as monuments?" (1.1.19–20). Matteo Ricci attempted to engage in intercultural East/West dialogue by composing a treatise on friendship (*jiaoyou lun,* 交友論) in one hundred maxims and also translated the *Enchiridion* of Epictetus into Chinese.[11] Francis Bacon wrote his *Novum organum* announcing the birth of a new science in aphorisms.

In seventeenth-century France, the famed moralists' concision was chiseled on the Cartesian foundations of clarity. La Rochefoucauld, Madame de Sablé, Pascal, La Bruyère, and Dufresny all diagnosed the human condition by means of *le bon mot*. Alain Badiou observes that La Rochefoucauld had the ability to "fuse the aphorism and to stretch the electric arc of the thought between poles distributed ahead of time by syntactic precision in the recognizable symmetry of French-style gardens" ("French," 353). Yet Pascal ultimately rejected this classical insistence on order: for the author of the *Pensées*, it is the halting, broken fragment, not the elegant green enclosures of Versailles, that is the only viable form of expression for a philosophy that grapples so deeply with an absent God (chapter 5). For Pascal, the aphorism is instead the tightrope flung between the "two abysses of the infinite and nothingness" (Sellier §230). The aphorism becomes not so much a distillation of doctrine as an expression of the impossibility of any formal systems.

The dialectic between aphorisms and philosophy reaches its apex in eighteenth-century Germany. As Philippe Lacoue-Labarthe and Jean-Luc Nancy argue in their seminal *The Literary Absolute*, the production of the self-conscious fragment of the Jena circle is a response to Kant's relentless system-building (27–58). On one hand, as an *Athenaeum Fragment* holds, "All individuals are systems at least in embryo and tendency" (§242). On the other, "a dialogue is a chain or garland of fragments" (§77). Hence, "it's equally fatal for the mind to have a system and to have none. It will simply have to decide to combine the two" (§53).

In the struggles against German idealism, Schlegel, Schopenhauer, and Nietzsche all used the microform to grapple with how to do philosophy after Kant. "I mistrust all systematizers and avoid them. The will to a system is a lack of integrity," Nietzsche declares (*Twilight of the Idols,* "Maxims and Arrows" §26). "The aphorism, the apothegm, in which I am the first master among Germans, are the forms of eternity. My ambition is to say in ten sentences what everyone else says in a book—what everyone else *does not* say in a book" (*Twilight of the Idols,* "Expeditions of an Untimely Man" §51). His aphorisms, then, from the middle-period *Human, All Too Human* to the late *Ecce Homo*, become his way of training readers not to subscribe to a particular Nietzschean program but rather to craft their own philosophy of life (chapter 6).

Indeed, at the end of one account of Western philosophy, it is Wittgenstein's suspicion of philosophy as dogma that causes him to employ the aphoristic form in both his early and late works. While his early *Tractatus Logico-Philosophicus* follows the logic of propositions, there are also many moments when his remarks are completely unconnected to their surrounding argument. Its last dictum, "Whereof one cannot speak, thereof one must be silent," is oft repeated. In the posthumous *Philosophical Investigations*, he writes in the preface, "I have written down all these thoughts as remarks, short paragraphs, of which there is sometimes a fairly long chain about the same subject, while I sometimes make a sudden change, jumping from one topic to another" (viii).[12] Meanwhile, Simone Weil's *Gravity and Grace,* E. M. Cioran's *Syllogismes de l'amertume* (punningly translated by Richard Howard as *All Gall Is Divided*), and Theodor Adorno's *Minima Moralia* are attempts to write *petite prose* during and after Auschwitz.

## Fragments and systems

Central to my theory, then, is that the aphorism is a dialectical play between fragments and systems. This is inspired by Schlegel's opposing statements that "aren't there individuals who contain within themselves whole systems of individuals?" (*Athenaeum* §77) and "even the greatest system is merely a fragment" (*Literary Notebooks* §930). The first definition is found in the *Athenaeum,* a journal founded by Schlegel, his brother August, Novalis, and Schleiermacher. In a series of dazzling essays, reviews, dialogues, and manifestos published over just three years— 1798 to 1800—the *Athenaeum* established German Romanticism as a unified aesthetic reaction and a viable philosophical alternative to German idealism. The fault lines between Romanticism and idealism can be ascribed to the differences between their understanding of "fragments" and "systems."[13]

In the section "Transcendental Doctrine of Method," a methodological reflection in the final, hard-won parts of *The Critique of Pure Reason,* Kant writes: "By an *architectonic* I mean the art of systems. Since systematic unity is what first turns common cognition into science, i.e., turns a mere aggregate of cognition into a system, architectonic is the doctrine of what is scientific in our cognition as such; and hence it necessarily belongs to the doctrine of method.... Now the system of all philosophical cognition is *philosophy*" (A832/B860; A838/B866). The notion of a system for Kant forms the foundation of scientific knowledge. Indeed, it is this "systematic unity" that makes knowledge possible at all, and such a system would necessarily exclude aphorisms. In the closing pages of the first *Critique,* Kant narrates the history of

Western philosophy from Plato to Aristotle to Locke to Leibniz to himself as a series of attempts to construct such architectonic systems (A854/B882).

What about the fragment? It is from the Latin *fragmen,* which comes from *frangō:* to break, shatter, defeat. In Greek it is *klasma, apoklasma,* or *apospasma,* a potsherd or bits of things, and related to the violent senses of *sparagmos*—convulsion, dislocation, dismemberment. According to A. C. Dionisotti, *fragmenta* in antiquity almost exclusively referred to material objects, not texts ("On Fragments in Classical Scholarship," 1). And if one were to define classical philology as "the systematic search through the works by those authors that survive and information about them and their authors with the aim of reconstructing these latter as far as possible," then, as Glenn Most argues, this scholarly practice in antiquity is "virtually nonexistent" ("On Fragments," 13).

For our purposes, it is crucial to draw a tight nexus between aphorisms, fragments, and classical scholarship. So many of the material remains of antiquity are frustratingly incomplete, and the works of so many Greek and Latin authors (say, Sappho or Publilius Syrus) and the voluminous anthologies and florilegia of late antiquity (Aulus Gellius' *Attic Nights,* Athenaeus' *Deipnosophistae,* or the fourteenth-century *Palatine Anthology*) are aphoristic and epigrammatic. Much of classical scholarship in nineteenth-century Germany, from Schleiermacher to Boeckh to Nietzsche to Diels, was devoted to gathering the remains of the early Greek thinkers. My point is that the genre and its fragmentary state of transmission cannily reflect and refract each other.

The Romantic cult of the fragment is a confluence of the classical philology, poetic spirit, and philosophical idealism of the time: "Many of the works of the ancients have become fragments. Many modern works are fragments as soon as they are written," *Athenaeum Fragments* no. 24 states. This distinction began as early as the fourteenth century when Petrarch, arguably the first modern poet, entitled his poetic collection *Rerum vulgarium fragmenta* and wept as he encountered for the first time the mutilated manuscripts of Quintilian, likening them to a dismembered body. Textual criticism's greatest desire is the reconstitution of the whole, yet as I have argued elsewhere, the wholeness of an artifact—whether it be a text, painting, sculpture, or building—is in fact nothing but a fantasy.[14] For Kant, a "mere aggregate" of aphorisms would not a coherent unity make.

Thus the aphorism is against the architectonic systems of philosophy. Confronted with the problem of *Darstellung*—how to construct an adequate representation of transcendental knowledge—the Romantics insist that the only possible manner of doing so is in parts, hence the apotheosis of the fragment as a privileged genre.[15] The fragment (the thing) and fragmentation (the process) are what enable Schlegel to realize the idea of the absolute in a singular, individual object (hence the hedgehog, the self-sufficient work of art). "The fragment," Lacoue-Labarthe and Nancy write, "functions as the exergue in the two senses of the Greek verb *exergazōmai*; it is inscribed outside the work, and it completes it. The Romantic fragment, far from bringing the dispersion or the shattering of the work into play, inscribes its plurality as the exergue of the total, infinite work" (48). In other words, the fragment's incompletion expresses an impossible desire for endless signification. In this sense the fragment is both a philological contingency of history as well as a philosophical exigency of the system.

In light of this discussion, we can now reread the aphorism of Schlegel that launches this book: "A fragment ought to be entirely isolated from the surrounding world like a little work of art and complete in itself like a hedgehog" (*Ein Fragment muß gleich einem kleinen Kunstwerke von der umgebenden Welt ganz abgesondert und in sich selbst vollendet sein wie ein Igel*). Encapsulated in the modal *muß* is the tension between the poles of German Romanticism: on one hand, the notion of aesthetic unity, expressed in almost every word: *kleinen Kunstwerke, umgebenden Welt, ganz abgesondert, in sich selbst, vollendet*; and on the other, the insistence that any aesthetic work is but part of a larger whole, expressed simply by the subject itself: *Ein Fragment*. Art is a repository of the world that gave birth to it—but it must be severed from it to achieve autonomy. In this act of rupture the fragment comes into being.

One can now easily see how this is related to another aphorism we've seen: "Many of the works of the ancients have become fragments. Many modern works are fragments as soon as they are written" (*Athenaeum Fragments* §24). The Romantics distanced themselves from Winckelmann's famed idealization of classical art as the apotheosis of "noble simplicity and quiet grandeur" and stressed instead the obsolescent grandeur of antiquity and all its estrangement and ruination and decay. On one hand, the recovered fragments of antiquity express the pathos of historical distance; on the other, the invented fragments of Romanticism express the pathos of aesthetic impossibility. That is to say, no work of art can ever be finished—its perfection lies in its imperfection.[16] And the fact that Schlegel composed these two perfectly polished fragments on the nature of the fragment bespeaks the metapoetic self-consciousness of his project.

How then does one adduce meaning from an aphoristic fragment? For the Romantics, the disciplines of philosophy and philology must converge in order to construct a totality of knowledge. Schleiermacher, who contributed to Schlegel's *Athenaeum* journal as well as translated Plato and produced an exegesis of the New Testament, states that whereas *criticism*, "the art of judging correctly and establishing the authenticity of text," should come to an end, *hermeneutics*, the "art of understanding particularly the written discourse of another person correctly," is endless (*Hermeneutics and Criticism*, 3–4).[17] In August Boeckh's conception, philology is "an infinite task of approximation.... The philologist's task is the historical construction of works of art and science, the history of which he must grasp and represent in vivid intuition" (Güthenke, "Enthusiasm Dwells Only in Specialization," 279–80).

In this Nietzsche follows the tradition of Schleiermacher and Boeckh. For him, philology is above all "that venerable art which demands of its votaries one thing above all: to go aside, to take time, to become still, to become slow—it is a goldsmith's art and connoisseurship of the *word* which has nothing but delicate, cautious work to do and achieves nothing if it does not achieve it *lento*" (*Daybreak,* preface §5).

## Hippocratic horizons

Etymologically, "aphorism" is composed of the Greek *apo-* "from, away from" + *horizein* "to bound." A horizon is defined as "*a*: the apparent junction of earth and sky; *b*: the great circle on the celestial sphere formed by the intersection of the celestial sphere with a plane tangent to the earth's surface at an observer's position" (*Merriam-Webster*). You can't ever arrive at the horizon; it is infinitely receding, both immanent and imminent. Ever transcendent, as a line it is without beginning or end, cutting the visible and invisible.

The horizon beckons the promise of hope. It guides and orients us. In the authoritative Greek lexicon of Liddell and Scott, the connotations of *aphorizô* lean toward limiting, end-stopping, pronouncing a halt. An aphorism makes a definitive statement, sets boundaries, establishes property. Yet any good definition is aware of its own limits, what is within and without. To *define* anything, after all, is to *delimit* it. The curvature of the globe, like the shape of thinking, means that there is always a limit to our field of vision. An aphorism, in this sense, is a mark of our finitude, ever approaching the receding horizon, always visible yet never tangible. It pushes us to the edge of what can be grasped; it reaches for the *je ne sais quoi*. Beyond the horizon of language, thinking can go no further. A vector that simultaneously points within and without the boundary—*horos*—of discourse, the short saying limns the very boundaries of thinking itself.

The Greek origin of aphorisms surely predates even Homer, though he did not use the word as such. In the epics, precepts are often doled out for life's myriad experiences.[18] But the first attestation of the word *aphorismos* is actually from the title of the Hippocratic corpus (430–330 BCE). Comprised of some 457 pithy sayings, the *Aphorisms* open as follows:

> Life [βίος] is short, science [τέχνη] is long; opportunity [καιρὸς] is elusive, experiment [πεῖρα] is dangerous, judgment [κρίσις] is difficult. It is not enough for the physician to do what is necessary, but the patient and the attendants must do their part as well, and circumstances must be favorable. (I.1)

As far as insights go, this first aphorism contains some basic truisms, and today they seem somewhat clichéd. Yet as the *incipit* of a medical treatise, its parallel syntactic constructions are remarkable for the precision and intensity of their expressive force. All the subjects of the opening sentence are major keywords of Greek thought that admit of inexhaustible glosses: *bios, tekhnê, kairos, peira, krisis.* As soon as Hippocrates praises human science (*tekhnê*) in opposition to human life (*bios*), he undercuts it: biopower, as it were, is marred by the same contingencies as the thing that it tries to control.

Yet as the Hippocratic aphorisms unfold one by one, they reveal their epistemological functions: "Desperate cases need the most desperate remedies" (I.6, ethical); "Menstrual bleeding which occurs during pregnancy indicates an unhealthy foetus" (III.60, diagnostic); "Dysuria is cured by bleeding and the incision should be in the inner vein" (VI.36, prescriptive); "Hard work is undesirable for the underfed" (II.16, commonsensical); "Everything is at its weakest at the beginning and at the end, but strongest at its height" (II.33, theoretical and observational). In medicine—as in any scientific inquiry—there must be at least some sort of stable correlation or correspondence between theory and observation. To diagnose a disease, a doctor must believe that phenomena are repeatable, predictable, and ultimately rational. Moreover, since it is not possible to observe the operations of the inner body, one must draw inferences from external symptoms.[19] The doctor is above all an interpreter of maladies: "The power of exegesis is to make clear (*saphê*) everything that is unclear (*asaphê*)," writes Galen in his *Commentary on Hippocrates' On Fractures* (18b318).

As exercises in probing the invisible through the visible, ancient medicine posits the epistemic values of aphorisms—bounded, finite words—in circumscribing the endless permutations of the somatic body.

## What I am doing

My interest in aphorisms grew from my first book, *The Poetics of Ruins in Renaissance Literature*. From ruins I started to think about fragments, and fragments led me to think about aphorisms. I then became interested in the architectonics of culture and how literary texts were transmitted through time. I am now interested in the dissolution of architectonic thought and its atomization in a literary form. In other words, how systems dissolve into fragments.

Not every aphorism, of course, can be pinned down to my theory that it comes before, against, and after systematic philosophy. It is too elastic to be captured this neatly. But in what follows I show how this framework can be applied to the short sayings of Confucius, Heraclitus, Jesus, Erasmus, Bacon, Pascal, and Nietzsche. These canonical figures anticipate the pivotal stages of epistemic development or reflect on their aftermath. Their aphorisms constitute a constellation of thoughts, all the while resisting the architectonic impulse of systems. For all their irreducible differences, each author uses aphorisms not to disseminate a closed doctrine but rather to open up fresh lines of inquiry.

In chapter 1 I explore how the *Analects* of Confucius is an assemblage of the master's sayings that, while not offering a systematic account of the good, virtue, or just governance, nevertheless propelled the commentarial tradition of China that sought to codify it. In chapter 2, Heraclitus' insistence on the primacy of the *logos* anticipates the philosophizing of Plato and Aristotle, who nonetheless reject their predecessor on account of his enigmatic style. Chapter 3 explores how the *Gospel of Thomas*, like the *Analects*, is also the posthumous collection of a charismatic teacher. Obscure like Heraclitus, its apocryphal fragments rub against the smooth narratives of the sanctioned Gospels. Taken together, the first part of the book shows that the open-ended nature of the charismatic teacher's sayings inspires readers to take a multitude of interpretive approaches.

Whereas the first three chapters are on antiquity, the latter three are on modernity. The Renaissance serves as the Janus-faced turning point. Chapter 4 investigates how Erasmus looks backward in retrieving the fragments of classical culture; Bacon looks forward in forging a modern system of natural history. In chapter 5, Pascal, standing at the threshold of early modernity, rejects the system of Cartesian philosophy and embraces a Christian poetics of the fragment. Chapter 6 argues that in the aftermath of the soaring systems of Kant and Hegel, Nietzsche clears the rubble from the ruins of German idealism by composing sharp aphorisms that puncture the very soul of European philosophy. Method, order, and systems are basically anticoncepts for Bacon, Pascal, and Nietzsche. The aphorism captures the contingent truths and elusive experiences of modernity.

If in Buddhist metaphysics "form is emptiness and emptiness is form," in the aphorism form is content and content is form. There are thematic similarities across the authors I study: *A deep concern for the hidden*: in Heraclitus nature loves to hide; in *Thomas*, God is hidden; in Bacon nature has secrets; in Pascal, God is also hidden; in Nietzsche our deepest impulses are hidden from ourselves. *The infinite*: either the aphorism's meaning is inexhaustible or its subject of inquiry—be it God or nature or the self—is boundless. The finite words of Confucius and Jesus convey infinite meaning. For Heraclitus, *logos* is so deep that "You could not in your going find the ends of the soul, though you traveled every road." For Pascal, man is "nothing compared to the infinite." For Nietzsche, "there is nothing more awesome than infinity." Because what aphorisms talk about is often concealed or interminable, by the principle of transference, they themselves take on the quality of obscurity, thus the necessity for hermeneutics. "All aphorisms must therefore be read twice," Deleuze advises (*Nietzsche and Philosophy*, 31).

They also share certain morphological similarities. *The discontinuous as condition of the work*: Fragmentary aphorisms—either by design or accident—obviously mean a lack of structure, links, connectives. The disconnected affords more fluid and expansive hermeneutic possibilities. In a way, it is the necessary interval between a dialogue—the author's silence can filled by the reader's voice. Nietzsche writes that "an aphorism [*eine Sentenz*] is a link in a chain of thoughts; it demands the reader to reconstruct this chain on his own: this is a lot to ask" (*Kritische Studienausgabe* 8:361). Floating free of any continuous discourse, interpretations of fragments and configurations of their collection can therefore be potentially unlimited. *A high degree of repetition:* In trying to compress the maximal into the minimal, aphoristic writing can become a recursive exercise of saying the same thing in many different ways. Its concision invites repetitions and modulations. But this repetition is never sterile—as Deleuze would argue in *Difference and Repetition*, it functions as an intensification of the problems at hand, affording discovery and experimentation.

Finally, *the aesthetics of the unfinished:* Bacon's *Instauratio magna*, Pascal's *Apology for the Christian Religion,* Nietzsche's alleged *Will to Power* are all incomplete. Erasmus' catalog of the *Adages* can go on forever. The reason for this seems to be less due to the author's limitations than the ambitious nature of their projects—their fragments resist containment into a final system.

"There are also many other things that Jesus did; if every one of them were written down, I suppose that the world itself could not contain the books that would be written" (John 21:25). The discontinuous, the repetitious, the unfinished—these all express the ever iterative process of infinite becoming.

———

In our short-attention-span age of tweets, memes, and GIFs, the aphorism is the most enduring microform of all. For all the ubiquity of the aphoristic form as a medium of communication and method of thinking—or precisely because of its pervasive presence—the genre has escaped sustained critical attention. The existing scholarship, which is substantial, either consists of descriptive surveys or is very narrow (see my bibliographic essay at the end of the book). There are simply very few unified theories of the aphorism out there. And a history of the aphorism (which this book is not) would be long and tedious. Some might even say that it is too protean, too amorphous to write coherently about. Or perhaps to explain an aphorism evacuates its pungency or mystery: "We undermine any idea by entertaining it *exhaustively*; we rob it of charm, even of life," E. M. Cioran says (*All Gall Is Divided*, 31). For Paul Valéry, "Obscurity, a product of two factors. If my mind is richer, more rapid, freer, more disciplined than yours, neither you nor I can do anything about it" (*The Art of Poetry*, 179). *Pace* Cioran and Valéry, my hope is to demonstrate that to read aphorisms transhistorically and transculturally, selectively, carefully, with *lento*, as Nietzsche recommends, is to begin to discover something about their infinite horizons and inexhaustible depths.

The power of the aphorism is something we are only beginning to explore. An ancient Chinese saying goes, "The tip of an [animal's] autumn hair [proverbial for the smallest possible thing] can get lost in the unfathomable. This means that what is so small that nothing can be placed inside it is [the same as] something so large that nothing can be placed outside it" (Liu An, *Huainanzi*

16.17). In laying out my argument, I try to look into the small and large, inside and outside. I strive not only to write to the specialist but also for wider readers in the humanities. I hope that the reader of Confucius might find something illuminating in Bacon, and the expert on Pascal might find something interesting in the *Gospel of Thomas*. Needless to say, what I'm proposing is only *a,* not *the,* theory of the aphorism. It imagines one of many possible theories.

# 1

# Confucius

## THE MASTER WISHES TO BE SILENT

Maurice Blanchot once wrote that when philosophy is confronted with the unknown, it has two possible responses:

> One entails the demand for absolute continuity and a language that might be called spherical (as Parmenides first proposed). The other entails the exigency of a discontinuity that is more or less radical, the discontinuity of a literature of fragments (this solution predominates in the Chinese thinkers, as in Heraclitus; Plato's dialogues also refer to it; Pascal, Nietzsche, Georges Bataille, and René Char demonstrate its essential persistence). (*Infinite Conversation*, 6–7)

This passage is found in his *Infinite Conversation*, a dense and elusive book of meditations about the fragments of various European authors, their dialectical ways of thinking, and their encounters with negation. The evocative title alone—*L'entretien infini*—helps us understand what he means by "discontinuity." First, *The Infinite Conversation* refers to two things: the "infinite" for Blanchot signifies the absolute asymmetrical relationship in terms of space, time, and knowledge between teacher and student (5–6). Their "'conversation,' *entretien*, is the endless play of questions and answers, a relationship characterized by openness and free movement" (13–14). Second, the power of the dialogue is marked by the "necessity of interval." This "pause between sentences, pause from one interlocutor to another, and pause of attention" is the "very enigma of language" (75). This mark of the discontinuous is not the failure of the human intellect; rather, it reveals the very "grounds of things" to which we all belong (9). Third, a collection of fragments is a paradox: the attempt to gather the many into the one is a dialectical exercise in which totality can never be realized. This signifies for Blanchot the idea of "the absence of the book" (422–34). Yet while the aphorism is a vector that points at new, unplumbed horizons, it evokes "The Book to Come," the title of a late essay that probes Mallarmé's idea of "Le Livre," the ultimate book that contains all books.

I find all these characterizations enormously suggestive as ways to think about the *Analects* (*Lunyu*, 論語), a record of the purported dialogues between the Master Kongzi and his disciples. These brief exchanges, rarely lasting more than a few lines, can be characterized by Blanchot's sense of an "openness and free movement" that is also marked by deep enigmas and silences. The conversations of Confucius are "infinite" in the sense that they have elicited inexhaustible commentary from the time of their compilation. As one recently excavated bamboo strip has it: "the excellence of a single word is enough for one to outlive a generation" (Cook, *Bamboo Texts of Guodian*, 2:938). At the same time, the conversations of Confucius are "discontinuous" because of their fragmentary nature: the material upon which they were written— bamboo and silk—contains the merest traces of the original scene of instruction; the received arrangement of individual sayings can be said to be only loosely organized at best.

———

Elias Canetti once said that in the *Analects*, what the Master does *not* say is as important as what he does say ("Confucius in His Conversations," 171). The silences of the Master indeed were many. For instance, he never spoke about "prodigies, feats of strength, disorderly conduct, or the supernatural" (7.21), since, as he explains to one disciple: "You are not yet able to serve people—how could you be able to serve ghosts and spirits?" (11.12). He was taciturn: "the good person is hesitant to speak" (12.3); "reticence is close to Goodness" (13.27); "words should convey their point, and leave it at that" (15.41). What you do is more important than what you say: "people in ancient times were not eager to speak, because they would be ashamed if their actions did not measure up to their words" (4.22); "the gentleman wishes to be slow to speak, but quick to act" (4.24). The very last saying warns: "One who does not understand words cannot understand people" (20.3).[1]

## Assembling fragments

From a sinological point of view, it might seem odd, even a bit perverse, to begin our discussion of a revered text of the Chinese tradition with Blanchot and Canetti, but their intuitions hit upon two fundamental matrices in the *Analects*: fragments and collections; words and silence. Let us now turn to slightly firmer historical ground:

> The *Analects* is composed of discussions in which Confucius responded to his disciples and others of his contemporaries, and of his disciples' words when speaking of one another and of speech they heard directly from the Master. At that time, each of the disciples had his own personal records. After the Master died, his disciples gathered them all together to discuss and then compiled them [輯而論篹], and so they were called his "selected speeches" [論語]. (§30 Ban Gu 1717)

These words are from the *History of the Han* (*hanshu*, 漢書) by Ban Gu (班固, 32–92 CE). Already in this early anecdote there is a suggestion that the practice of Confucian exegesis is both hermeneutic ("discuss," *lun,* 論) and textual-critical ("compiled," *ji,* 輯). It would be perhaps too hyperbolic to claim that these two words encapsulate the entire history of debates in Chinese intellectual thought, but Ban Gu's anecdote certainly gives us an incipient sense of the myriad schools and doctrines that would contend for authority in the centuries to come.

In truth, the composition of the *Analects* is more complicated than Ban Gu's idealized etiology would seem to suggest.[2] Like many of the collected aphorisms we will discuss, there is simply no original, no ur-text. Scholars now acknowledge that compositional fluidity marked the earliest stages of *Lunyu.* Early Chinese texts circulated in short, bite-size units that were eventually merged into larger collections. They could be reconfigured in endless ways according to the wishes of an editor.[3] Ban Gu himself is writing some five centuries after Confucius' life (551–479 BCE), so there is a fair amount of mythologizing.

Recent scholarly work on archaeologically excavated manuscripts has shed much light on the production of texts in early China. A huge cache of bamboo strips recovered in 1993 from a fourth-century BCE Warring States Guodian tomb in the Hubei Province demonstrates the fluid and variable formation of the textual corpora. The collection contains the earliest version of the *Daodejing,* ordered differently than the received version; there is a gnomic "thicket of sayings," *yucong,* 語叢; and some sayings of Confucius appear in the section "Black Robes" (*Ziyi,* 緇衣).[4] While he is not explicitly named, his identity is affirmed because the same quotations survive in other testimonia, namely the *Book of Ritual* (*Li ji,* 禮記) and in the Shanghai Museum excavated manuscripts.

By the end of the Western Han, the words of Confucius existed in many other versions besides the *Lunyu,* and all these abundant anthologies attest to his charisma.[5] We simply do not know to what extent changes were made by editors and copyists to the order of the *Analect*'s books (*pian,* 篇) in their transmission. At a certain point (the dating of the collection is fraught with controversy), the *Analects* became the supreme source.[6] This absence of a definite plan, combined with the protagonist's enigmatic reticence, explains in part the text's long exegetical tradition, for much labor was exerted to find some sort of coherence behind its haphazard appearance.

The dynamics of the commentarial tradition thus established the very architectonics of Chinese classical thought, enduring for more than two millennia. In short, the teachings of Confucius "the Uncrowned King" (*suwang,* 素王) began as oral production, were then transcribed by his rag-tag band of disciples into inchoate "fragments," and, after generations and generations of commentaries, were codified into an immense institutional canon, thereby constituting the official "system" of Confucianism (*ru,* 儒).[7] As such, insofar as the commentarial tradition seeks to give coherence to Confucius' scattered sayings, the dichotomy between teacher and follower cannot be maintained—they exist on a continuum.[8]

My hypothesis is that, at least in the *Analects,* the amount of scholarly commentary produced is inversely proportional to the succinctness of the original sayings. In other words, the pithier the teacher, the more voluminous the tradition.[9] The premodern reader would have never read any "clean" text of the *Lunyu.* Printed editions invariably included a raft of paratextual apparatus and propaedeutic aids (see fig. 1). As we will see, sometimes the exegesis served to explain the historical meaning of the text; sometimes it served to explain the text's timeless philosophical import. Though the *Lunyu* as collection is "discontinuous" in Blanchot's sense, the tradition did its best to codify it into a totality of culture. And though Canetti's insight about the master's "silence" is right, the commentators turn out to be very loquacious. That Confucius never wrote anything signifies the Chinese case of the "absence of the book," and the "book to come" is the collection

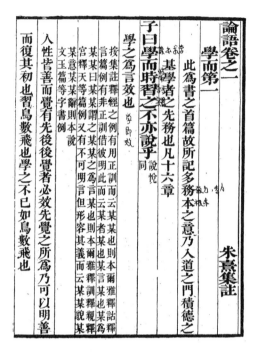

FIGURE 1. Zhu Xi 朱熹, *Lunyu jizhu* 論語集注. In *Sishu jizhu* 四書集注, Sibu beiyao edition. The original text is in the large characters followed by grammatical and interpretive glosses (National University of Singapore Library).

that has been handed down to us today. The "pause" between the two is the pregnant caesura that gives birth to more than two thousand years of commentary.[10]

As such, the nonsequential, seemingly random nature of Confucius' utterances is what makes them conducive to almost infinite modes of interpretation and disputation. We need only turn to Ban Gu again for confirmation, for he had already remarked, "Explanations of five characters from a text would run to twenty or thirty thousand words. Later [this tendency] increased exponentially so that young boys who focused their studies on one Classic had become gray-haired before they could speak about it with authority" (*Hanshu* 30.1723).

## Charisma to bureaucracy

Beginning a book on the Western theory of aphorisms with a Chinese case has several virtues. First, since the Jesuits' translations of the Confucian canon in the seventeenth century, one might argue that Chinese thought constitutes an abiding dialectical "other" to Western thought.[11] Second, when we read the Confucian canon in light of the genre of "wisdom literature," we can point out several common phenomena.[12]

One, the Master (always a male) is an eccentric figure who powerfully critiques the conventions of society. Zoroaster, the Buddha, Jesus—they do not write. The Master speaks and the disciples transcribe. Confucius is an interesting case because while the aversion to writing does certainly seem to be cultivated in the *Analects,* from the late Western Han the Master's name began to be attached to the *Five Classics*, texts that record the daily lives, love songs, sacrificial hymns, ritual conducts, divinatory practices, and annalistic chronicles of early China.[13] Thus we have the construction of Confucius as the philosopher in the *Analects* (one of the *Four Books*) and the philologist in the *Five Classics,* one who compiles and assembles fragments of the past rather than creates *ex nihilo*.

Two, according to Max Weber, a wisdom tradition develops from a charismatic teacher to a group of selected disciples and finally to a sprawling bureaucracy with rigid hierarchies.[14] In wisdom literature, authorship and authenticity is often a false equivalence since so many founding fathers disavowed writing.[15] The main force of authority rests in the hands of the *tradents*, a term used in biblical scholarship for those responsible for the preservation and dissemination of the tradition. One might say that the mystique of the Master is largely a construction of these epigones. Tradition attests that the Buddhist canon—known as the *Tripiṭaka*—was compiled during a series of councils after the Buddha's death. As scriptures were transmitted, often by rival sects, from India to China in the early second century CE and

Tibet in the seventh century CE, monastic communities were confronted with a staggering plethora of commentaries and scholarly apparatuses.[16]

In the late Warring States, a collection of aphoristic texts became canonical (*jing,* 經) if it was accompanied by commentaries (*zhuan,* 傳). A classic, *jing,* had connotations of "boundary" or "demarcation," and when paired with *wei,* "weft," it came to be a guiding principle or constant norm, providing a guide to the proper structure of the world, as in the orderly weaving of fabric.[17] In the Qin-Han encyclopedic compendia of all knowledge such as the *Spring and Autumn Annals of Master Lü (lüshi chunqiu,* 魯氏春秋) and the *Huainanzi* (淮南子), we see an urge to unify fragments into systems. The editors of these massive collections, under political patronage, sought to assemble maxims and precepts from disparate, often competing schools and organize them into a coherent vision of universal authority.

Like the early Christian and Buddhist councils, Confucian scholars held major meetings to address differences in textual interpretation and establish the authorized canon at the Stone Canal Pavilion in 51 BCE and White Tiger Hall in 79 CE. Under the auspices of state sponsorship, the official "Confucian" system endeavored to make the once stateless "Confucius" and his wandering fragments into an ideological whole.

Three, much of this institutionalization is conservative and preservative—exegesis labors to maintain orthodoxy.[18] In the *longue durée,* tradition is attacked by successive waves of heresies but finds its vitality and relevance precisely by combating them. The *Han Feizi*—a Warring States text that establishes the Legalist tradition—already records that after Confucius' and Mozi's deaths, their schools split into eight and three sects, respectively (§50). As we will discuss in chapter 3, a welter of texts about Jesus circulated in the decades and centuries after his death. Successive church councils ultimately reduced these to the canon of the New Testament. All other competing materials were rendered apocryphal. In the development of the Theravāda canon, Steven

Collins surmises that there were four stages of recension for the purposes of "self-definition and self-legitimation by the Mahāvi-hārin monks": the written transcription of the Buddha's oral sayings and their attendant commentaries, the production of a fixed set of writings, the standardization of authorized commentaries, and the establishment of the genre of *vaṃsa,* genealogies and annals that establish the authenticity of transmission ("On the Very Idea of the Pali Canon," 80).

Four, the ordering of topics in a received text is nonsequential (such as the *Lunyu,* the Pali "Numbered Discourses of the Buddha," and the *Gospel of Thomas* in the next chapter). Certainly there are common themes in a work, but they are only loosely connected, lacking a clear architectonic structure. This miscellaneous heterogeneity, I believe, is deliberate. It makes for greater hermeneutic freedom and gives a job for scholars to do—we'll never be out of work.

Fifth, the enunciative moment of an aphorism begins with very little indication of time or place, utterly out of context, as if the reader were hearing the pure voice of the teacher, uncontaminated by the strictures of circumstance. The majority of the fragments in the *Analects* begins with the famous "Master says" (*zi yue* 子曰, the Chinese verb has no temporal marker). In the *Gospel of Thomas,* every *logion* similarly begins with the simple present-tense formula "Jesus says." Pali and Sanskrit Buddhists texts invariably begin with "Thus have I heard."[19] Finally, aphorisms in wisdom literature are usually simple, well-wrought sentences, often in rhythmic parallels, thus making memorization and recitation easy.

In all, we see how the careful selection of aphorisms plays a huge role in the cultivation of the Teacher's charisma.

## Few words

The Master said, "I will not open the door for a mind that is not already striving [*fen,* 憤] to understand, nor will I provide words [*fa,* 發] to a tongue that is not already struggling to speak [*fei,* 悱]. If I hold up one corner of a problem, and the student cannot come back to me with the other three, I will not attempt to instruct him again." (7.8)

This passage presents an exemplary case of "the scene of instruction" between the teacher and his student. Exploding the myth of Confucian learning as only rigid, rote memorization—a stereotype that critics within and outside of China have perpetuated over the centuries—here is a pedagogy that places the burden on the student, requiring a desire and commitment to be a coproducer of knowledge. Like the Socratic method, Confucian learning at its origins is maieutic. In fact, its refusal to give outright answers constitutes a sort of polemic: the primal lesson is not a passive downloading of information but rather an aggressive "hack" from the student. The desire to know must arise inwardly, a stretching forward or reaching outward (*fen, fei*). The teacher only awakens and gives shape to what is already stirring within.

Now, literally speaking, showing the other three vectors on a given coordinate is a simple mathematical equation. Indeed, in the Warring States era (475–221 BCE), which immediately follows Confucius' life (551–479 BCE), the rivals of the Confucian school would attack the Master's seeming simplicity and absence of systematic rigor.[20] The Mohist would develop models of logical argument, standards of proof, and rules for philosophical debate. The references to Confucius in the *Mozi* are extremely polemical (see "Against the Confucians II" 2:39). The Daoist would say the Confucians lack spontaneity. The Legalist would critique them as lacking in a pragmatic theory of statecraft. The *Han Feizi* would reject tradition as the guide for virtuous conduct. The Nominalist would say that the Confucians did not have adequate terminology to engage in rational debates. Even the *Mencius* and the *Xunzi*—both followers of the Confucian sect—favor long, extended essays arranged by topics instead of unconnected aphorisms.

Alternately, others stress the Master's indirection as a sign of his hidden depths. In the fifth century CE, Liu Xie in his extraordinary poetic treatise, *The Literary Mind and the Carving of Drag-*

ons (*Wenxin diaolong,* 文心雕龍), emphasizes the "subtle" or "hidden" speech (*weiyan,* 微言) of the Master.[21] Confucius does not expostulate or demonstrate—his way is only one of the gentle gesture. François Jullien calls this strategy a "detour," one that provides access to multiple perspectives and infinite adaptation.[22] The pedagogy of the opaque, I would add, authorizes, invites, enables, and gives license to the commentarial tradition, a mode of practice that simply would not exist if everything were transparent. We today would call this a metacognitive skill: "If you learn without thinking about what you have learned, you will be lost. If you think without learning, however, you will fall into danger" (2.15). The Master's indirection is what makes learning—and striving— possible.

In the Qing dynasty, the scholar Liu Fenglu (1776–1818) elevates the Master's pedagogical principle into a hermeneutic truth about his language as well as a metaphysical truth about the cosmos. He suggests that boundless depths exist within the circumscribed aphorism: "All the sage's words consist of raising one corner so as to wait for people to come back with the other three corners. *Hence his written words are pithy, but their meaning is without limit*" (my emphasis). This last sentence refers back to Confucius' stated pedagogy in 7.8 and nicely captures the syntactic terseness of the aphorism and its hermeneutic inexhaustibility. Liu goes on cite the Han commentator Master Dong Zhongshu on the *Spring and Autumn Annals*: "It cannot be investigated, silent as if it does not exist. When it is deeply investigated, however, there is nothing which it does not contain." Liu concludes that "This says that the things it does not write about are more numerous than the things it does" (in Makeham, *Transmitters and Creators,* 332).

## The silent heavens

The Master sighed, "Would that I did not have to speak!" [*wuyan,* 無言]. Zigong said, "If the Master did not speak, what will us little ones transmit [*shu,* 述]?" The Master replied,

"What does Heaven ever say? The four seasons are put in motion by it, and the myriad creatures receive their life from it. What does Heaven ever say?" (17.19)

There are many ways to read this passage. First, intertextually, the precedent is 2.1: "One who rules through the power of Virtue is analogous to the Pole Star: it simply remains in its place (*juqisuo,* 居其所) and receives the homage of the myriad lesser stars." The power of a true teacher is silent (*wuyan*) and still (*juqisuo*). In both quotations there is a sense of hierarchy: the "little stars" and Zigong's "little ones." Second, biographically, we know that Confucius spent much time as a wandering scholar seeking to offer counsel to any court that might receive him.[23] Is the Master expressing some frustration in the lack of his advancement? Does he want to be one of those Daoist recluses, so sick of civil corruption that they abandon society once and for all and embrace a mountain life of quietism, as many anecdotes in books 17 and 18 recount? Probably not. This reading would be persuasive if there were no response to Zigong.

A better reading would be the third, analogical one: the silence of heavenly motion is deployed as a pedagogical paradigm. The pivotal word is Zigong's "transmit" (*shu* 述). This word is the same as the "transmit" in the all-important "I transmit rather than innovate" (述而不作, 7.1). It is not the words of the Master that "transmit," but his wordless actions. Moreover, Confucius is saying that the heavens actually *do* speak—only that their language is silent and pervasive, present in the sheer immanence of the myriad creatures. Confucian thought, by analogy, is as expansive as the ways of heaven; the latter manifests its power by animating the changes of the seasons and nourishing all things (*baiwu,* 百物) through its vital principle (*sheng,* 生), the former manifests its power by animating the behavior of individuals, families, institutions, imperia through its principle of humanity (*ren,* 仁).

## How to read

The Kongzi presented in the *Analects* thus embodies a curious paradox: he distrusts speech yet loves to talk to his disciples. Like Socrates in the *Phaedrus,* the Master believes that the best way of learning is the dialectical method, a live encounter between the teacher and the student, in which the teacher intuits the soul of each student and tailors his speech especially for him. Yet now the teacher is no longer here. For those of us who live in his absence, how do we decipher the fragments of his words?

Through a series of lapidary precepts, the Neo-Confucian Zhu Xi (1130–1200), in his treatise "How to Read" (*dushufa*, 讀書法),[24] states:

> In reading a book we must read and reread it, appreciating each and every paragraph, each and every sentence, each and every word. Furthermore, we must consult the various annotations, commentaries, and explanations so that our understanding is complete. In this way moral principle and our own minds will be in perfect accord.
>
> (CHU HSI, *LEARNING TO BE A SAGE*, "ON READING, PART 1, CHAPTER 10," 4.4)

At the heart of Zhu Xi's program is the concept of "comprehending the principle in things" (*gewu*, 格物), the means by which an individual can connect with his or her pure nature. Yet you can't do this on your own. Reading is the first step. You must be guided by "the various annotations, commentaries and explanations." And since "the substance of the Way is infinite," so is the activity of learning. This way of self-cultivation, relentlessly driven by repetition and reflection, is in accordance with the habits of mind that are already established in the *Analects*.[25]

For Zhu Xi, reading is a spiritual and ethical practice. Like Petrarch, he yearns to speak with the worthy ancients: "It's best to take up the books of the sages and read them so that you understand their ideas. It's like speaking with them face to face" (4.6).

The Italian humanist similarly says that he considers Cicero "a friend living in my time with an intimacy that I consider proper because of my deep and immediate acquaintance with his thought" (*Fam* 1.1). Reading in both cases becomes the supplement, the proxy to conversing with the dead. The key for Zhu Xi is endless practice: "Whether we are walking or at a standstill, sitting or lying down, if our minds are always on these texts, we'll naturally come to understand them" (4.41). You must "pass them before your eyes, roll them around and around in your mouth, and turn them over and over in your mind" (4.7).

As in the European Renaissance, the age of print in China brought about a sense of information overload.[26] Zhu Xi expressed exasperation at the overabundance of books: "There are a great many books in the world. If you just read them as you have been, when will you finish them?" (4.19). He urges the student to read not for quantity but quality: "Read little but become intimately familiar with what you read; experience the text over and over again" (4.20).

For Zhu Xi, there is a paradoxical purpose to all this striving: the end of reading is the end of books. "Book learning is secondary," necessary only because we have lost our original nature. But since texts contain the "many manifestations of moral principle," we should study them. Once we comprehend them, we might as well discard them, for what we learn is but what has been hidden within us all along, "from the very beginning, nothing has been added to us from the outside" (4.2). "When we read the Six Classics, it should be just as if there were no Six Classics. We're simply seeking the moral principles in ourselves—this principle is easy to understand" (5.41). As Nietzsche would later say, "What good is a book that does not even carry us beyond all books?" (*Gay Science* §248).

## The silence of textual meditation

Master said, "I once knew a time when scribes would leave the text blank (*que*, 闕), and those who owned horses would lend them to others. Nowadays, there is no one like this." (15.26)

The implied meaning is easy to decipher: Confucius' times lack the modesty and generosity of earlier times. "According to the mode of working in ancient times," Ban Gu explains, "scribes wrote down exactly what was in the documents, and when they were not familiar with a word, they would leave a blank or they would ask senior scholars. But in periods of moral decline, right and wrong could no longer be verified, and so people relied on their own speculations" (Chin, 260). Huang Kan 皇侃 (488–545) writes, "Confucius here laments the fast-paced disorder of his age.... In his later years, it was the case that a scribe who did not know a word would arbitrarily make something up rather than leave the space blank" (Slingerland, 185).

All our interest in lacunae, ellipses, and silence is obliquely condensed in this one saying. Confucius was indeed prescient in choosing the example of the scribe, for this will become the philological principle of understanding in the ages to come. The less Confucius says, the more the commentators have to add (and embellish). For Huang Kan, all patterns of the world (*li,* 理) are contained in the *Analects*—every jot and character must have some deeper meaning. Under the paradigm of "dark learning" (*xuanxue,* 玄學), he elaborated on concepts such as "*weimiao* 微妙 (subtle wonder), *xuantong* 玄通 (mysterious comprehension), *wu* 無 (emptiness), *you* 有 (there is) and *xu* 虛 (vacuity)" of the Master (Henderson and Ng, "The Commentarial Tradition," 48). This *Xuanxue* was a Neo-Daoist movement that resulted in many erstwhile "Confucian" texts being reinterpreted in a way more friendly to the teachings of Laozi and Zhuangzi.[27] Kongzi would probably have been horrified. Nevertheless, *xuanxue* is an important episode in Chinese intellectual history of exegetes doing with the text as they pleased. While the early scribes fondly recalled by Confucius left bamboo strips empty, later commentators after the Master clearly did the opposite. The text did not remain blank for long.

The fragments of the Master from Lu thus became the inexhaustible engine of Chinese thought. As the Confucian tradition coalesced and fragments turned to collections, the millennia of commentarial tradition became a culture industry. Let me point out two exemplary cases, some six hundred years apart. We have already encountered Zhu Xi. He is the prime exponent of the philosophical tendency of the Neo-Confucian movement, or *Dao-xue* (道學), "Learning of the Way."[28] For Zhu Xi, through diligent self-cultivation and textual study, a regular person can learn to become a sage: "There is layer upon layer [of meanings] in the words of the sages. In your reading of them, penetrate deeply. If you simply read what appears on the surface, you will misunderstand. Steep yourself in the words; only then will you grasp their meaning" (*Learning to Be a Sage*, 4.9).

Second, Qing scholars reacted to such subjective feelings by ushering in a more rational methodology that emphasized exacting analysis of ancient artifacts and texts. Aided by an expanding network of bibliophiles, printers, and booksellers, they stress "evidential research" (*kaozheng* 考證) through a mastery of grammar, lexicography, textual criticism, and paleography. No longer is the goal moral perfection but empirical knowledge. Wang Mingsheng 王鳴盛 (1722–1798) criticizes the Neo-Confucians when he writes, "The Classics are employed to understand the Tao. But those who seek the Tao should not cling vacuously to 'meanings and principles' (*yili*, 義理) in order to find it. If only they will correct primary and derived characters, discern their pronunciation, read the explanations and glosses, and master the commentaries and notes, the 'meanings and principles' will appear on their own, and the Tao within them." Similarly, for Dai Zhen 戴震 (1724–1777), "the Classics provide the route to the Tao. What illuminates the Tao is their words. How words are formed can be grasped only through [a knowledge of] philology and paleography. From the study of primary and derived characters we can master the language. Through the language we can penetrate the mind and will of the ancient sages and worthies" (both in Elman, *From Philosophy to Philology*, 28–29). This shift is what Benjamin Elman calls "from philosophy to philology," hence the title of his groundbreaking book.

The hermeneutic mode of self-cultivation versus the more scientific rigors of textual analysis forms a recurring dialectic throughout the tradition. In other words, there is always friction between a universal, all-embracing philosophy of understanding and the local, philological glosses of difficult passages.[29] The former treats received texts as unified, coherent doctrine propounded by an authoritative Master. The latter rejects such totality and points to internal inconsistencies due to textual corruption. This *agon* is never resolved. And this irresolution is imbricated with three related phenomena that we have explored so far: (1) the quandary of whether the Master's thought is occasional or systematic; (2) the asymmetry between the Master's succinctness and the commentaries' voluminosity; (3) the rise of contending schools of thought as a result of interpretive differences. Finite words; infinite meaning.

## Ten out of one

Hegel, when he encountered Confucius, was decidedly unimpressed. He was only a "moral educator" and not a true "philosopher:" "For in his case we do not find theory that occupies itself in thought as such," the German philosopher explains in his 1822 Berlin lectures on world history. Since his purpose is to establish that the spirit of philosophy could only arise from Greece, China by definition had no part to play in his commanding narrative. He excludes Confucius from his canon precisely because he is too aphoristic. He had merely good, competent morality, "nothing more." He summarily declares: "He is not to be compared to Plato, Aristotle, or Socrates. He was about the same as Solon, if we understand by this that he was the lawgiver to his people. His teachings are the foundation for moral instruction, especially that of princes" (*Lectures on the Philosophy of World History,* 1:241).

The German philosopher was probably disappointed because the sayings in the *Lunyu*, at first glance, *do* seem pretty banal.

Admittedly, precepts such as "set your heart sincerely upon Goodness" (4.4) or "Do not disobey" (2.5) appear to be platitudes—their meaning *too* transparent, *too* commonplace for serious philosophical study. Like in much else, Hegel was both right and wrong. He was right that Confucius was no Plato or Aristotle, for he did not engage in long discursive arguments contained in heavy tomes like the *Statesman* or the *Metaphysics*. But he was Socratic in his scene of instruction with his students, as we have seen. His teachings did become the foundation for moral instruction, but that was more because of his followers than because of his own power. Above all, Hegel was wrong about the banality of the sayings. Because of the subtlety (*weiyan*) of the Master's words, their transparency is that of clear, limpid waters that run so deep that you cannot see the bottom.

Yan Hui, the Master's favorite disciple, had the opposite reaction to Hegel:

> The more I look up at it the higher it [the Confucian Way] seems; the more I delve into it, the harder it becomes. Catching a glimpse of it before me, I then find it suddenly at my back. The Master is skilled at gradually leading me on, step by step. He broadens me with culture and restrains me with the rites, so that even if I wanted to give up I could not. Having exhausted all of my strength, it seems as if there is still something left, looming up ahead of me. Though I desire to follow it, there seems to be no way through. (9.11)

Yan Hui here experiences a moment of intellectual seizure at the immensity of it all, illustrating Blanchot's "infinite distance" or "absolute asymmetry" between the master and the student. How do you not disobey? How do you set your heart upon goodness? Easy to say, hard to do. Yet his aporetic moment is unlike that of Socrates' Meno, for whereas the Greek interlocutor can't get beyond his doubts, Yan Hui's realization inspires him to go beyond his horizons. This is the same Yan Hui in 5.9: "The Master said to Zigong, 'Who is better, you or Yan Hui?' Zigong answered, 'How dare I even think of comparing myself to Hui? Hui learns one thing and thereby understands ten. I learn one thing and thereby understand two.'" Yan Hui's exponential intellect has become proverbial, and even *he* has a hard time following the Way.[30]

## The river flows

The sense of the immensity of it all is also captured in this saying:

> Standing on the bank of a river, the master said, "Look at how it flows [*shi* 逝] on like this, never stopping day or night." (9.17)

Commentary on this passage begins with Mencius: "He was asked once, 'Confucius more than once expressed his admiration for water, saying, 'Water, Water,' But what good did Confucius see in water?' ... 'Water from a source rushes forward, never ceasing day and night, filling all the cracks and hollows as it advances, before it drains into the sea. Everything with a source is like that, and this is the good Confucius saw in water'" (Chin, 139). The Jin Dynasty Sun Chuo gives a more melancholic biographical reading: "The river flows on without stopping, like the years ceaselessly passing away; the time is already late, and yet the Way has still not been put into practice. This is the cause of Confucius' lament" (Slingerland, 92). Zhu Xi takes the side of Mencius and reads it as an allegory of the Way: "Confucius used this to bring home the message that all those who wished to learn should be vigilant constantly, not letting their effort slacken even for an instant" (Chin, 139). My point once more is that there are infinite ways of reading a finite saying, especially one that contains an ever-flowing aqueous image.[31] The accumulation of commentaries in the tradition contributes to a cascading effect that becomes as vertiginous as the inundating waters. Exegesis flows, never stopping, day or night. It has irrigated the fields of Chinese culture century after century, bringing sometimes gentle nourishment, sometimes an overwhelming deluge.

It seems appropriate to end this chapter on a river, for this was also a favorite image for Heraclitus. A Heraclitean reading of *Analects* 9.17 would read the image as capturing the world's perpetual flux. Here is "the Obscure One" as reported by Plato:

> Heraclitus says somewhere that "everything gives way and nothing stands fast," and, likening the things that are to the flowing (*rhoē*) of a river, he says that "you cannot step into the same river twice." (*Cratylus* 402a)

Both Confucius and Heraclitus, when confronted with the river, experience a moment of epiphany. What I mean is that, from a European perspective, the "Ultimate Sage" seems to have an experience of the sublime. As the Chinese master ponders the river's ceaseless flow, one imagines him to be filled with a feeling of awe at the inexhaustible phenomena of it all. Nature is immense, human life brief. For Longinus, this ecstatic experience / emotion / concept / aesthetic / rhetorical style is captured in the Greek term *hupsos*, the sublime.[32] Marcus Aurelius writes in his *Meditations*, "Time is a river, the ceaseless flow of all created things. One thing no sooner comes in sight than it is hurried past and another is borne along, only to be swept away in its turn" (4.43). For Kant, the sublime is found in the "formless object as limitlessness," arousing a "feeling of a momentary inhibition of the vital powers" (*Critique of the Power of Judgment,* 5:244–45). It is that which "even to be able to think of demonstrates a faculty of the mind that surpasses every measure of the senses" (5:250). Confucianism has this in common with the sublime: they both generate exhilarating exegesis. In my reading, the recognition of the infinite cosmos is what Confucius encountered at the riverbank. It is a powerful paradox of literary form that the aphorism's concision can capture the inexhaustible. The Chinese commentators explain the unrelenting energy of the water as an allegory of human striving. Struggling to comprehend the Master's sayings is one such example of this striving, a finite tangent to the infinite circle of the Confucian Way.

# 2

# Heraclitus

## WHAT IS HIDDEN

Even in antiquity, Heraclitus was known for his obscurity. In Plato's *Theaetetus*, one of Socrates' interlocutors, Theodorus, complains of those who follow the Heraclitean doctrine:

> If you ask any of them a question, he will pull out some little enigmatic phrase [ῥηματίσκια αἰνιγματώδη] from his quiver and shoot it off at you; and if you try to make him give an account [λόγον] of what he has said, you will only get hit by another, full of strange turns of language [καινῶς μετονομάζω]. You will never reach any conclusion with any of them, ever; indeed they never reach any conclusion with each other, they are so very careful not to allow anything to be stable, either in an argument [λόγῳ] or in their own souls [ψυχαῖς]. (180a–b)

For Theodorus, a mathematician who seeks clarity and certainty, the Heracliteans' stratagem of continual evasion is a problem because they constantly produce new aphorisms in order to subvert closure. Geometry, by contrast, has no "strange turns," only reassuring step-by-step deductions; its operation is to bring "the many powers within a single form." Similarly, as a philosopher Socrates wants to "give one single account of the many branches of knowledge" (148d5). And since the purpose of the dialogue is to establish what knowledge is—knowledge *itself* and not knowledge *of* something—Theodorus, Theaetetus, and Socrates are in search of its definition, to bring the many into the one. While they ultimately end in an impasse, the Heracliteans must be stopped, for their aphorisms bring nothing but needless obfuscation.

The *logos* of Heraclitus is opposed to Plato in at least two fundamental ways: first, his doctrine of flux is contrary to the theory of Forms; and second, the impression one gets (confirmed by tradition) is that his thinking is solitary, monologic, misanthropic, whereas Plato is always social, dialogic, inviting. Theodorus accuses the Heracliteans of having no pedagogy: "There are no pupils and teachers among these people. They just spring up on their own, one here, one there" (180c). In their failure to ask and answer questions, or even to build a community of learning, Heraclitus' dark sayings are contrary to the very idea of Socratic examination. The Heracliteans don't seem to be very good conversationalists—their *gnōmai* are one-way streets that lead nowhere.

The metaphor of the quiver and arrow that Theodorus uses is fitting, for Heraclitus himself has a famous statement on how "the name of the bow [*biós*] is life [*bíos*]; but its work is death" (DK22 B48/LM D53).[1] The philosopher of Ephesus puns on the Greek word for life, *bíos*, which is a near homophone to the word for bow, *biós*, except for its accentuation.[2] By bringing about the coincidence of opposites—life and death—the taut *logoi* of Heraclitus release, and seize, the movement of thought in one swift motion.

I begin this chapter with the Platonic critique of Heraclitus because Plato's repudiation of his predecessor's gnomic style signals an important stage in the development of ancient philosophy: the transition from oracular enunciation to argumentative discourse, obscurity to clarity, and thus the marginalization of the aphoristic style in favor of sustained logical arguments. Of course, Plato had a vested interest in discounting the worth of his predecessors, since his goal was to inaugurate a new program of philosophy by dismantling the old nondialogical ones.[3]

From Socrates onward, there will simply be no philosophy without proof or argument.[4] Socrates says that the ancients "used poetical forms which concealed from the majority of men their real meaning.... In more modern times, the problem is presented to us by men who, being more accomplished in these matters, plainly demonstrate their meaning so that even shoemakers may hear and assimilate their wisdom" (*Theaetetus* 180d1–5). Philosophy henceforth must be clear to all. Plutarch also noticed this when he stated in his dialogue *On the Pythian Oracles* that there was a time when the poetic language of the oracles was clothed in "vagueness and obscurity," but times and customs change, "metaphors, riddles, and ambiguous statements" (407b) fell out of favor. Finally, "philosophy welcomed clearness and teachability in preference to creating amazement (*to ekplètton*), and pursued its investigations through the medium of everyday language (*dia logôn*)" (406e).

Modern scholars have confirmed both Socrates' and the Hellenistic essayist's insight: Glenn W. Most observes that early Greek philosophy seems to have placed more emphasis upon singular pronouncements than extended lines of argument ("The Poetics of Early Greek Philosophy," 349). Abstract thinking emerges when it repudiates epic narrative, where every element is described in loving and painstaking detail. The representation of reality thus enters into a new phase—atomistic rather than encyclopedic. "The *logos,* when it appears," Roberto Calasso writes, "annihilates the particular, the accumulation of detritus typical of every experience, that obligation to repeat every detail" (*The Marriage of Cadmus and Harmony*, 153). Discursive arguments eventually developed, leading to what Jacqueline de Romilly calls "the birth of the human sciences" in the fifth century BCE ("From Aphorisms to Theoretical Analyses").

Thus Heraclitus stands at the elusive edge of discursive philosophy's dawn—his fragments are after and against the poetic surplus of Homer and Hesiod and before and against the prose systems of Plato and Aristotle. His laconic language is drawn from the obscurities of the oracles, yet his sayings are philosophical in the sense that they believe in truth derived from the human intellect rather than divine revelation. Both Greek religion and philosophy, Jean-Pierre Vernant reminds us, agree that there is a world "beyond appearances ... an invisible background ... a truer reality, secret and hidden.... By insisting on this invisible being against the visible, the authentic against the illusory, the permanent against the fleeting, the certain against the uncertain," Vernant continues, "philosophy takes over, in its way, from religious thought" (*Myth and Thought Among the Greeks*, 407).

Here I would like to defend, if possible, Heraclitus against Plato's (or, more precisely, Theodorus') attack. To be sure, perplexity arising from enigmatic sayings need not necessarily lead one to aporetic seizures of thinking. On the contrary, it can catalyze productive inquiry. Socrates famously claims that he is a "midwife," watching over the "labor of souls" (*Theaetetus,* 150c). In my reading, Heraclitus' *logoi* themselves can be considered a sort of midwife, for they can facilitate the birth of philosophical ideas. Indeed, Heraclitus' microform both resists and invites fuller articulations, and so hermeneutics—a conduit between the text and the reader—is demanded from every reader. His fragments are both antithetical to and propaedeutic to argumentative philosophy, antithetical because they are too enigmatic, and propaedeutic because they cannot but prompt one to think about and question the origins and nature of things.

## Signs

It is well known that Heraclitus' paradoxes, antitheses, chiasmus, puns, and repetitions are close to the oracles, ritual incantations, and riddles that were pervasive in the ancient Mediterranean world.⁵ According to Diogenes Laertius' chatty *Lives and Opinions of the Eminent Philosophers* (always to be taken with a grain of salt, to be sure), Heraclitus was descended from the family of Androclus, founder of Ephesus (9.1). Among the duties of the royal family was the office of the priesthood of Demeter Eleusinia.⁶ Heraclitus would have been king had he not renounced the office in favor of his brother. I believe that this biographical tidbit is significant, for it represents, at least in the *testimonia* tradition, an abdication of priestly and political duties in favor of a purely philosophical life.

One revealing fragment might represent a vestige of his abandoned birthright:

> The lord whose oracle is the one in Delphi neither speaks (*legei*) nor hides (*kruptei*), but gives signs (*sēmainei*) (B93/ D41).

> ὁ ἄναξ οὗ τὸ μαντεῖόν ἐστι τὸ ἐν Δελφοῖς οὔτε λέγει οὔτε κρύπτει ἀλλὰ σημαίνει

Each verb in this fragment is deeply resonant. *Legei* is cognate with *logos,* Heraclitus' all-important concept. *Kruptei* is the same as in the famous "Nature loves to hide" (B123/D35). These will be discussed later. The problem for now is *sēmainei.* How does it function as the middle term between the two modes of communication, one that is utterly transparent and the other utterly opaque?

As it happens, this fragment is preserved in the same dialogue in which Plutarch gives his anthropological account of the development of Greek culture from religion to philosophy. After citing Heraclitus, he goes on to say:

> Add to these words, which are so well said, the thought that the god of this place employs the prophetic priestess for men's ears just as the sun employs the moon for men's eyes. For he makes them known through the associated medium of a mortal body and soul that is unable to keep quiet, or, as it yields

itself to the One that moves it, to remain itself unmoved and tranquil, but, as though tossed amid billows and enmeshed in the stirrings and emotions within itself, it makes itself more and more restless. (*Pyth. orac.* 404e)

As we know, divination was a major source of knowledge and belief in ancient Greece.[7] It is by nature obscure and indirect. The entrails of beasts, flight patterns of birds, movement of stars, agitations of dreams, exhalations of earth—these constitute the "signs," *semata*, in which knowledge of the unknown could be made manifest. They mark the beginnings of semiology, as it were.[8] Aristotle in the *Rhetoric* takes a more skeptical stance and states that: "the oracle-mongers use these vague generalities about the matter in hand because their predictions are thus, as a rule, less likely to be falsified" (1407b3–4). At Delphi—where the *omphalos,* the navel of the earth, was located—the inquirer posed the question and waited for the god Apollo to respond through the Pythia.[9] Plutarch, who had actually served as a priest at the sanctuary, records that this virgin would shriek her ecstatic utterances in a hoarse voice (*De Def. Or.* 51). Her gibbering message would then be translated by priests into hexameters so that it would be somewhat intelligible, if not fully comprehensible.[10] The divine voice neither discloses (*legei*) nor encloses (*kruptei*), because there are at least four stages of transmission (*sēmainei*): the god, Pythia, the priests, and the suppliant. If the requester remained at home and sent a messenger, then there is another link.

Plutarch's words on Heraclitus' words on Apollo's words, we may say, also constitute a nested series of signs—wrapped in a written text in the guise of an oral dialogue, they are a signifier of the signifier of the signifier. But even the identity of Apollo in this fragment is indeterminate. In Greek mythology he shifts back and forth between an avenging archer who brought disease and death to the Achaeans in the *Iliad* to the refined patron of medicine and poetry to a solar deity bestriding his gleaming chariot to finally our oracular voice of muffled truth. In the postmythic age, where there is no more face-to-face theophany, only the vestiges of indi-rect, elusive agitations and sympathies remain.

The utterances of the oracles and Heraclitus, then, are both riddles, for they cloak their senses in metaphors, homonyms, and double meanings. Even the subject of this fragment, "The lord whose oracle is in Delphi," is a periphrasis that, while confidently asserting the subject's attributes—his authority and epichoric location—also denies to us what is the most essential—his name. So the subject is already doing the work of all three verbs—not concealing, not declaring, but suggesting. The fragment's mean-ing would have been entirely different had Heraclitus chosen to emphasize the birthplace of Apollo, Delos, since its etymology is "visible," "conspicuous," or "clear to the mind" (s.v. *LSJ*).

In a study on the obscure origins of the name of Apollo, Greg-ory Nagy concludes that he is "the god of authoritative speech, the one who presides over all manner of speech-acts." Moreover, "he is the word waiting to be translated into action" (*Homer's Text and Language*, 139). In this sense, deciphering the signs of the oracle entails precisely their translation into action (say, whether to wage war or not). Even if the desired response was a definite "yes or no," "x or y," it needs to be carefully interpreted. An oracle's answer did not divest suppliants of decision-making; in fact, it is largely their responsibility to make meaning out of it. The famous instance is in the *Histories* of Herodotus when the Lydian king Croesus asked the oracle at Delphi whether to invade Persia; it responded that if he did, a "great empire would fall" (1.267). His tragic mis-take was that he didn't think that the empire would be his.

Oracles and Heraclitean riddles have this in common: they both demand a deep hermeneutics. Cicero in *De divinatione* had already made the comparison between deciphering signs divine and human: "Men capable of correctly interpreting all these signs of the future seem to approach very near to the divine spirit of the gods whose wills they interpret, just as scholars do when they interpret the poets" (1.34). The *logoi* of Heraclitus, however, are no longer hieratic. They can be grasped solely by the operations of the mind, a faculty that all humans possess yet few use: "Thinking (*phroneein*) is in common for all" (B113/D29). This is to say: whereas the enigmatic oracle at Delphi is heavily mediated, the oracular enigmas of Heraclitus place the interpretive burden directly on the reader. Like oracles, the utterances of Heraclitus admit of no simple answer but rather open up a multiplicity of meanings. His sayings are perhaps difficult for the common person, but they invite the uncovering of a truth not by some incantatory medium but by the clarity of human *logos*: "All humans have a share in knowing themselves and in thinking with moderation (*sophronein*)" (B116/D30). The voice of a human, the authority of god—this distinction vanishes when *logos* fully reveals itself.

## First fruits

While the Pythian voice within the caverns of Delphi was perplexing and tailored to individual requests, those chiseled on its temple façade were the maxims that were clear and shining, legible and applicable to all: "Honor the gods," "Praise virtue," "Govern your wife," "Master wedding feasts," "Be yourself." Every educated Greek person would have been familiar with these *dicta*. This is how Socrates puts it:

> At first you will find he [a Spartan, when conducting a debate] can barely hold up his end of the conversation, but at some point he will pick his spot with deadly skill and shoot back a terse remark [λόγου βραχὺ] you'll never forget, something that will make the person he's talking with (in this case you) look like a child.... To be a Spartan is to be a philosopher much more than to be an athlete. They know that to be able to say something like that is the mark of a perfectly educated man. We're talking about men like Thales of Miletus, Pittacus of Mytilene, Bias of Priene, our own Solon, Cleobulus of Lindus, Myson of Chenae, and, the seventh in the list, Chilon of Sparta.[11] You can see that distinctive kind of Spartan wisdom in

their pithy, memorable sayings [ῥήματα βραχέα ἀξιομνημό-νευτα], which they jointly dedicated as the first fruits of their wisdom to Apollo in his temple at Delphi, inscribing there the maxims now on everyone's lips: "Know thyself" [γνῶθι σαυτόν] and "nothing in excess" [μηδὲν ἄγαν].

What's my point? That the characteristic style of ancient philosophy was laconic brevity [βραχυλογία] (*Protagoras* 342e–343c).

While Socrates' description of the Spartan's deft riposte might seem like high praise, in reality it is a polemic. In truth, for Socrates these answers are just dogma, all too easily memorized and accepted without genuine examination.

For Plato, neither the "laconic brevity" of these maxims nor the enigmas of Heraclitus will do. The former too transparent and the latter too opaque, they are deflections that halt rather than invite thinking. True philosophy instead demands the making of arguments through patient, methodical discourse. The dialogues demonstrate time and again that the sayings of the early thinkers are used as *endoxa*, received opinions that are first examined, then appropriated or rejected. Though the maxims of the ancients might have been the "first fruits" plucked from the ancient tree of wisdom, their freshness expires upon arrival, for they cannot compare to the living, breathing vitality of the Socratic dialogues.

Above all, at stake in Socrates' polemic is whether truth is derived from authority or reason. To take the most famous Delphic inscription, "Know thyself," seriously means to interrogate both oneself and the maxim, which is precisely the origin of Socratic inquiry as narrated in the *Apology*.[12] Socrates' investigation begins with a decipherment of the oracle—he does not understand why "no man is wiser than Socrates" (21a). The attempt to understand this statement, it is not an exaggeration to say, instigates the entire enterprise of Western philosophy. Heraclitus' "I searched for myself" (B101/D36), too, is a clear response to the Delphi commandment. By not taking *dicta* as they are, one must examine all

pronouncements, whether they come from the mouth of Apollo
or of mortals. What this means is that once you start interpreting something you don't get at first, you're already on your way
to wisdom.

## Loves to hide

The movement from single utterance to continuous dialogue,
from riddle to solution, is precisely the work of hermeneutics
and the prelude to argumentative philosophy. Philosophical discourse "does not sculpt immobile statues," Plutarch writes in another essay, "but whatever it touches it wants to render active,
efficacious, and alive" (*Max. cum princ.* 776c–d). Rather than
being paralyzed by Heraclitus' arrows, as Theodorus claims, penetrating his thought can render us active, efficacious, and alive, as
Plutarch suggests. This is necessary because, as one of the most
famous aphorisms has it:

> Nature loves to hide. [or]
>
> A nature tends to hide.
>
> φύσις κρύπτεσθαι φιλεῖ. (B123/D35)

These three little Greek words have invited much commentary.
What is "nature"? What is "hiding"? What is "love"? Pierre Hadot
suggests that there are at least five different ways of interpreting
it. "The constitution of each thing tends to hide (i.e., is hard to
know). The constitution of each thing wants to be hidden (i.e.,
does not want to be revealed). The origin tends to hide itself
(i.e., the origin of things is hard to know). What causes things to
appear tends to make them disappear (i.e., what causes birth
tends to cause death). Form (or appearance) tends to disappear
(i.e., what is born wants to die)" (*Veil of Isis*, 10–11).[13] The nature
of Heraclitus himself—and the nature of language in general—
loves to hide. As such, we can claim two corollaries: "aphorisms
too love to hide," and "interpretation loves to illuminate."

The notion that the nature of things likes to hide is in fact already present in Homer's *Odyssey*, the epic of disguises and concealment. The first attested appearance of *phusis* in the Greek language occurs in book 10, as Hermes the messenger god shows Odysseus the true nature of the *moly* plant when he is about to encounter Circe. As the hero narrates:

> [Hermes] gave me the medicine [φάρμακον],
> which he picked out of the ground, and he showed the nature
> of it to me [καί μοι φύσιν αὐτοῦ ἔδειξε]. It was black at the
> root, but with a milky
> flower. The gods call it moly. It is hard for mortal
> men to dig up, but the gods have power to do all things.
>
> (10.302-6, LATTIMORE TRANS.)

At least three things are in disguise in this passage: the plant, the god (Hermes appeared "in the likeness of a young man with beard new grown"), and the identity of Odysseus as he narrates his adventures to the Phaeacians.[14] In the post-Homeric world, Hermes, as his very name suggests, would be known as *the* interpreter: as Socrates explains in the *Cratylus*, he is known as "a messenger, or thief, or liar, or bargainer; all that sort of thing has a great deal to do with language" (408a–b). In Homer, Hermes is dispatched to save Odysseus twice from tricky situations. Odysseus comments that moly "is hard for mortal / men to dig up, but the gods have power to do all things." The Greek hero's words testify to the limitations of human labor and the gift of divine assistance, but taken as a *gnōmē*, his statement is as dark and hard as Heraclitus' "Those who search for gold dig up much earth and find little" (B22/D39).

## Self-showing *logos*

Homer and Heraclitus would agree that one must strive to unveil the hidden nature of reality. How? Unconcealment for Odysseus is a theophany. For Heraclitus, unconcealment has no recourse to divine intervention; it must be achieved through the *logos* alone, to which all humans have access. Since language is composed of signs that are not the things themselves but things that point to other things, its very function is that of discovery. Heidegger points out that Aristotle says *legein*, from which *logos* is derived, is *apophainesthai*, to show itself by itself. The German philosopher then teases out this significance and claims that "the *logos* by itself brings that which appears and comes forward in its lying before us to appearance—to its luminous self-showing" (*Early Greek Thinking*, 64).[15] Logophany, as it were, has now replaced theophany. *Logos* becomes both the method and end of unconcealment:

> And of this account [λόγου] that is—always [or forever, ἀεὶ]—humans are uncomprehending, both before they hear it and once they have first heard it. For, although all things come about according to this account [τὸν λόγον], they resemble people without experience of them, when they have experience both of words [τὸν λόγον] and of things of the sort that I explain when I analyze each in conformity with its nature and indicate how it is. (B1/D1)

> Of all those whose accounts [λόγους] I have heard, no one has arrived at the point of knowing that what is wise is separated from all. (B108/D43)

> After you have listened not to me but to the account [λόγου] it is wise to recognize [ὁμολογεῖν] that all things are one. (B50/D46)

> But although the account [τοῦ λόγου] is in common [ξυνοῦ], most people live as though had their own thought [φρόνησιν]. (B2/D2)

To be sure, *logos* is notoriously difficult to define. Does the *logos* mean the underlying structure of the universe, Heraclitus' argument, or perhaps his own book (*biblion*), which very few will understand? Aristotle cites the first passage and faults him for his bad grammar: "To punctuate Heraclitus is no easy task, because we often cannot tell whether a particular word belongs to what precedes or what follows it. He says: 'And of this account that is— always [or forever]—humans are uncomprehending,'—it is unclear what 'forever' [*aei*] goes with" (*Rhetoric* 1407b14). If the "forever" modifies *logos,* then it would seem to be the underlying structure of the universe; if it modifies men, *logos* could simply be Heraclitus' book.

The Liddell and Scott lexicon alone has five dense columns on *logos* with ten major definitions and many subdefinitions. Some scholars advocate the "simple" view of Heraclitus' *logos*: it means only *legein,* to speak.[16] Others hold a more "metaphysical" view: *logos* is a cosmic principle of "the source of all that is intelligible," an "orderly world," "formula," or "universal pattern of transformation."[17]

I favor the latter reading. In Heraclitus' fragments, the structure of language, the structure of thought, and the structure of the cosmos itself are all underpinned by a hidden *logos.* First, there is spoken *logos,* which humans possess, then there is the *logos* of the cosmos, which is silent. The correct articulation of the former leads to the revelation of the latter. Recognition (*homologein*) itself is the ability to discern like to like—*logos* to *logos.*

How then does one find this silent, pervasive *logos*? By examining the self. "You could not in your going find the ends of the soul, though you travelled every road [*hodos*]—so deep is its *logos* [*bathon logon*]" (B45/D98). The soul that Heraclitus explores is one that is unfathomable, ever expanding, and potentially infinite: "If you do not expect the unexpected you will not find it, since it cannot be searched out nor arrived at" (B18/D37). Heraclitus is not proposing a notion of interiority or inwardness, as later philosophy and religion, particularly Neoplatonism and Christianity, would do.[18] Instead, he posits a model of the psyche in which truth can be discovered by turning to examine oneself.[19] *Logos* is not just an attribute of the soul, it is its very structuring principle: "The soul's *logos* is self-growing" (B115/D99).

From what we have discussed so far, we are confronted with an antinomy: virtually everyone from Plato onward recognizes that Heraclitus was "the obscure," *ho skoteinos*.[20] Yet virtually everyone attempts to reconstruct his thoughts into some sort of coherent argument.[21] I believe there is a way to resolve this paradox. If, as one fragment has it, "all things are one" (B50/D46), then there must be an invisible *logos* that governs the visible universe. Heraclitus establishes a continuum between the structure of the cosmos, the structure of thought, the structure of language, and the structure of his own text. Ultimately, Heraclitus posits that language is the activity of unconcealing the deep structure of the universe. *Logos* is both the method and the subject of inquiry. He creates a *logology*, as it were.

### *Kai*

Thus *logos* is thus self-illuminating and interpenetrating. Unfathomable, trackless, unexplored, it can be articulated only through the language of paradoxes. For example, this fragment preserved in Pseudo-Aristotle's *On the World*:

> conjoinings: wholes and not wholes, converging diverging, harmonious dissonant; and out of all things one, and out of one all things.

> συλλάψιες· ὅλα **καὶ** οὐχ ὅλα, συμφερόμενον διαφερόμενον, συνᾷδον διᾷδον **καὶ** ἐκ πάντων ἓν **καὶ** ἐξ ἑνὸς πάντα. (B10/ D47)

As the Greek demonstrates, the force of this aphorism lies in the repetition of the same words in the first and last colon (*hóla; pánton / pánta*), which encloses the interior juxtaposition of opposite terms sharing the same root (*sumpherómenon / diapherómenon; sunâdon / diâdon*), all tightly constructed with the repetition of the particle *kai*.[22] This most common connective—the copulative "and"—turns out to be the most uncommon of all, for it replicates the unity of opposites that Heraclitus constructs. *Kai* can "imply sameness or likeness" (s.v. *LSJ* def. III), "join an affirmative clause with a negative" (def. IV). That is to say, "and" unites and severs. In Heraclitus' unity of opposites: "The way (*hodos*) upward downward: one and (*kai*) same" (B60/D51); "There is the same thing within, what is living and (*kai*) dead and (*kai*) what is waking and (*kai*) what is sleeping and (*kai*) what is young and (*kai*) old" (B88/D68). In the second quotation, the first, third, and fifth *kai* bring together the binary terms, making differences an identity, whereas the second and fourth *kai* arrange these three opposites. In the syntax of these fragments, *kai* establishes at once a plurality, a duality, and a unity, doing the work announced in the first word of B10/D47—conjoinings.[23] Grammar thus recapitulates dialectic.

Because Heraclitus inquires about the *logos* (the governing principle of the cosmos) through *logoi* (language), his language must be rendered obscure in order to defamiliarize and destabilize fixed meanings (the homonym between *biós* and *bíos*, the polyvalence of *kai*). Such technique loosens the conventional correspondences between the signified and the signifier. It is precisely in this ambiguous zone between "revealing" and "concealing" that thinking dwells.

Through his enigmatic style, then, Heraclitus signals the distance between the surface appearance of the world—a heap of confused phenomena—and its deep structure—governed by a silent *logos* that pervades all things. The interpretation of this deep structure is the task of philosophy—the decipherment of nature's and by extension language's hidden meaning.[24] Linguistic *logos* manifests cosmic *logos*. By attending to silent signs, hermeneutics, like Hermes showing the *moly* plant to Odysseus, manifests what is invisible: "Invisible fitting-together (*harmoniê*), stronger than a visible one" (B54/D50).

This way of hermeneutics works transitively. Heraclitus' gnomic statements make visible the invisible structure of the world. The reader, in turn, has to do the same thing—make visible the invisible structure of his words. As such, Heraclitus invites the reader to construct her own individual thoughts, or to at least reconstruct his hidden argument: "<fire>, when it is mixed together with incense, is named according to the scent of each one" (B67/D48). We don't have a divine Hermes anymore, only human ones, ourselves. The demand upon each reader is that they embark upon this interpretive odyssey, that they make their own perfume and give it its proper name.

## Blessed rage for order

We see how the unity of opposites is a key concept in Heraclitean thought.[25] The scholarship on Heraclitus replays this dialectical opposition: namely, whether his surviving sayings form a coherence or not, whether his "fragments" form a "system." Tradition records that Heraclitus deposited his book in the temple of Artemis of Ephesus. Some say it was in three parts; others read it and judged it to be an incoherent mess (Diog. Laert. 9.7). Whether Heraclitus truly wrote a book has been confounding philosophers and philologists ever since.[26] This problem strikes at the heart of the aphorism as a genre: its order and coherence. The writings of Heraclitus that we possess are scattered, and although we can perceive a constellation of ideas, they might as well be the flotsam and jetsam from his famous ever-changing river.

Philosophers from Aristotle onward have read Heraclitus in the opposite fashion to Theodorus. They attempt to pin him down into coherent, logically sound propositions—even though Aristotle accuses him of disobeying the law of noncontradiction (*Metaphysics* 1062a30–b11).[27] The method of beginning an inquiry—quoting one's predecessors in order to refute them—is why so many of the sayings of Presocratics survive at all.[28] Indeed, the ancient tradition of doxography—from Theophrastus to Philodemus to Clement of Alexandria to Diogenes Laertius to Stobaeus—follows along these lines in presenting summaries of the "doctrine" or *placita* of the early philosophers.[29] In response, much modern philological and philosophical energy has been expended in order to organize the thoughts of Heraclitus into some intelligible sequence.

Yet there is an equal and opposite pull to resist such systematization, mostly from the thinker himself. One cannot so easily disentangle origins and receptions because there is no *fons et origo* of Heraclitus, since according to tradition he purposefully did not want to publish his book. In donating his work to the temple, the philosopher consecrates his work as a treasure, something hidden away for protection. So is its circulation a vulgarization, a profanation? Everything we possess is based on second- and third-hand reports, citations, paraphrases, and testimonies found in later literature. In the last chapter, we saw how the Chinese commentators labored to produce a unified text. Here the Greek ones are happy to let fragments be fragments.

Whereas Confucius sanctions authority, Heraclitus invites dissent. Indeed, many of his sayings are preserved in fervidly polemical Christian texts—Clement of Alexandria's *Stromata* and Hippolytus' *Refutation of All Heresies*—hardly unbiased accounts. By one reckoning, only 89 of the 125 fragments are considered to be verbatim citations.[30] The famous collection by Hermann Diels and Walther Kranz abjures any order in favor of a purely alphabetical one arranged by the author of where the fragment is preserved. Most editions today attempt to group the sayings by themes and wrest them into some sort of narrative sequence.[31] But perhaps whether it is coherent does not matter after all, for "out of all things one, and out of one all things" (B10/D47). What arrangement there is is but a projection of our blessed rage for order.

If this last statement seems too equivocal and does not feel like a very satisfactory way of leaving things, this desire to come to a definitive resolution tells us more about ourselves, about what we want from early philosophy, than what early philosophy wants or its philology is able to give us. The last stage of modern textual criticism—after the work of *recensio* and *examinatio*—is *emendatio*, or aptly also called *divinatio*. "The *divinatory* method is the one in which one, so to speak, transforms oneself into the other person," Schleiermacher writes, "and tries to understand the individual element directly" (*Hermeneutics and Criticism*, 92). It is no accident that the nineteenth-century German philosopher and theologian himself produced a critical edition and commentary on Heraclitus.[32]

So we are back to where we started: divination, making sense of obscure signs.[33] To be sure, whether the Heraclitean fragments comprise a coherent discourse or not is an important question. But it is irresolvable, both philosophically and philologically. The question cannot admit of a singular answer, but a multiplicity. If "God: day night, winter summer, war peace, satiety hunger ..." (B67/D48), then the *logoi* of Heraclitus can be clear and obscure, coherent and scattered, one and many, fragments and systems, foxes and hedgehogs. After all: "The most beautiful order of the world is still a random gathering of things insignificant in themselves" (B124/D60, Davenport trans.).

### Hodos

When given a copy of Heraclitus' book, Socrates replied, "What I understand is splendid; I think that what I did not understand is too—but it needs a Delian diver" (Diog. Laert., "Life of Socrates" 2.22). Socrates' watery abyss bespeaks the danger of perpetual flux, of drowning in discourse. One must be a skilled diver to search deep. Such infinite depths recalls Confucius' surging river at the end of chapter 1. If the world is in perpetual flux, how can language represent such instability without being itself unhinged? How can words be as immense and unfathomable as the sea? "The sea, the purest water and foulest: for fish, it is drinkable and life-giving; for men, not drinkable and deadly" (B61/D78).

Though Heraclitus himself is fond of aqueous metaphors, one of his most powerful is a terrestrial one, that of *hodos*—the road, the path, the clearing: "the way up and down: one and the same" (B60/D51). In the second century CE, Pseudo-Diogenianus says proverbs (*paroimiai*) are "so named from the word *oimos*, which means a way: so they are called roads (*hodoi*). For whatever men discovered that was of common utility, they wrote down to act as 'highways,' on which others (the majority) would find help" (Morgan, *Popular Morality in the Early Roman Empire*, 27). This sense of *oimos* encompasses the Homeric and Pindaric "paths of songs," the dark *hodoi* of Heraclitus as well as the *paroimiai* of Jesus. The title of one of Heidegger's collection of essays, *Holzwege* (translated as "Off the Beaten Track"), means paths through the forest, which the German philosopher insists must be distinguished from *Feldweg*, a path through the field. An admirer of Heraclitus, Heidegger wants to cleave open new pathways through the dense woods of thinking. Though *Holzwege* and *Feldweg* appear to be headed in the same direction, this is not so: "Woodcutters and forest keepers know these paths. They know what it means to be on a *Holzweg*" (v).

*Oimos, hodos, Holzweg*—the literatures and philosophies of the world are constructed out of these pathways, networks, itineraries. A path, of course, means that it has been traversed before and can be traversed after, and that someone once thought it wise to cut tracks into the landscape for later travelers. It suggests a sort of permanence, a marker of human endeavor, an intrusion into nature. Unlike the river, you *can* step into the same path twice. Heraclitus shows us a way. Diogenes Laertius ends his biography with an epigram of Scythinus: "The path is hard to travel. Gloom is there and darkness devoid of light. But if an initiate be your guide, the path shines brighter than sunlight" (Diog. Laert. 9.16). Heraclitus' sayings are often called *gnōmai*, cognate with *gnomon*, the part of a sundial that casts a shadow. Gnomons are the instruments that give us our diurnal orientation. It is within this contour of darkness, a darkness cast by his gnomon, that we find our way through the radiant paths of thinking.

# 3

# *The Gospel of Thomas*

## WHAT IS REVEALED

The prologue of the *Gospel of Thomas* states: "These are the hidden sayings (Coptic, *ᶜnšaje ethēp*; Greek, *hoi logoi hoi* [*apokrupoi*]) that the living Jesus spoke and Judas Thomas the Twin recorded."[1] Immediately after this bold incipit, its first *logion* announces, "Whoever discovers the interpretation (Coptic *ethermeneia*; Greek, *hermēneia*) of these sayings will not taste death."[2] In these opening statements, the text creates a series of binaries: the living Jesus and death; the orality of Jesus and the textuality of *Thomas*; hidden sayings and their revelatory interpretations; the mouth as an organ of production (speech) and consumption (taste). These first lines make a promise as well as a demand—meaning is not given freely to you, you must discover it for yourself. More strongly put, it is not the words of Jesus that give life but their interpretation—the reader's explicit work. Hermeneutics is a matter of life and death: the wages of misreading damnation, the gift of correct interpretation everlasting salvation.

The sayings of Jesus in the *Gospel of Thomas* are, like those of Heraclitus in the previous chapter, difficult, obscure, and mysterious. They challenge the reader to discover the true nature of the world through the discovery of the self, both of which are imbued with the divine. Hermeneutics in this way becomes nothing less than soteriology—the discourse of redemption itself. To achieve this, the *Gospel of Thomas* advocates a radical independence: readers must decipher for themselves the text's meaning rather than rely on any sectarian doctrine or even the authority of Thomas the compiler. This was its promise and peril, and in part explains why the text never made it into the orthodox canon. Not insignificantly, the verb *aphorizō* in the New Testament is frequently used to mean to separate, to cut off, to ostracize and by extension to excommunicate.[3] In the early Christian era, the aphorism unites and divides.

The theory of aphorisms in *Thomas* is that one attains secret knowledge of a hidden God not from a congregation of believers (and there is a great deal of disagreement about which congregation preserved the text) but through the inward meditation on the words of Jesus. In the deepest sense, the enigmatic statements in the *Gospel of Thomas* make not only claims about the nature of the world and the nature of Jesus but also promise transformative change within each reader. One must *seek* oneself to *know* oneself in order to *reveal* the hidden nature of God, because "One who knows everything but lacks in oneself lacks everything" (§67). In this way, the aphorisms of *Thomas* are an invitation to a nonmethodical, nondogmatic way of faith.

## A jar in the desert

The most complete text of the *Gospel of Thomas* that we possess today was unearthed in a large storage jar by an Egyptian peasant in the deserts of Nag Hammadi in 1945. This discovery changed the course of biblical scholarship forever, for the papyri challenged common assumptions about the formation of the early Christian church and its scriptural economy.[4] *Thomas*, from the second tractate in Codex II, is in Coptic and was probably created sometime

FIGURE 2. Folio 32 of Nag Hammadi codex II. Ending of the *Apocryphon of John* and the beginning of the *Gospel of Thomas* (from *The Facsimile Edition of the Nag Hammadi Codices,* 1974).

in the fourth century, but the original is certainly much earlier. Parts of the text appear in three Greek fragments from the *Oxyrhynchus papyri* (1, 654 & 655), all from different periods, as well as in Hippolytus of Rome's *Refutation of All Heresies* (5.6.20; 5.8.32).[5] Yet we know little about the exact compositor, date, place, or even the language of its original composition. Even the title of the text is not clear: the word "Gospel" is not used until the colophon (see fig. 2).

Its transmission, too, is as murky as its genesis. April D. DeConick in *Recovering the Original Gospel of Thomas* hypothesizes that the text began as a small collection of Jesus' sayings, what she calls "the Kernel Thomas," that circulated in the early church in Jerusalem around 30–50 CE. The incipit and the colophon state that the text is written by Judas Thomas Didymus, one of the twelve disciples.[6] Thomas in Syriac Aramaic and Didymus in Greek both mean "twin." Tradition recounts that he was one of the twelve apostles, a missionary to India, and the biological twin of Jesus (which is hard to fathom; others, more sensibly, accept this spiritually).[7] In any case, his gospel gained prominence in Edessa with the Syrian Christians. In the process of transmission, sayings were added or deleted, expanded or contracted in order to accommodate the exigencies of the community, which was expecting an imminent *eschaton*. Eventually, the possibility of Jesus' second coming was growing increasingly unlikely, and so the kingdom of God was reinterpreted to mean a realm within one's inner spirituality, one that is both "encratic and mystical" rather than political or apocalyptic. From this time of crisis, DeConick surmises that the gospel came into its present form around the year 120.

## The mutable Q

Every Christian today knows that the New Testament has four Gospels: Matthew, Mark, Luke, John. But how did the first believers themselves understand the transmission of their scriptures? In his *Histories,* Eusebius, in a role somewhat like Ban Gu, whom we encountered in chapter 1, illuminates the process of assembling the teachings of Jesus by quoting the account of Papias, the bishop of Hierapolis:

> Mark, having become the interpreter of Peter, wrote down accurately, though not in order, whatsoever he remembered of the things said or done by Christ.
>
> For he neither heard the Lord nor followed him, but afterward, as I said, he followed Peter, who adapted his teaching in the form of *chreiai* [anecdotal stories], but with no intention of giving a connected account of the Lord's discourses, so that Mark committed no error while he thus wrote some things as he remembered them. For he was careful of one thing, not to

omit any of the things which he had heard, and not to state any of them falsely. (*His. Eccl.* 3.39.15)

What is important here, as for the Confucians, is the authoritative chain of the transmission from Peter to Mark and the guarantee that there are neither lapses of memory nor additions in his account. As such we can regard this as an example of the orthodox reaction against the hermeneutic freedom afforded by aphorisms.

Despite Eusebius' claims of direct authenticity, scholarship has demonstrated that scriptural compilation in early Christianity was in fact much messier. Since the nineteenth century, scholars acknowledge that Mark was indeed the earliest account. They also hypothesize that a now lost collection of sayings called Q (*Quellen,* "source" in German) was behind the gospels of Matthew and Luke.[8] John appeared much later. They define Q as the material common to both that does not appear in Mark, their primary source. This "two-source hypothesis" postulates that "Q functioned as a kind of algebraic unknown that helped to solve other problems" such as the extent of Matthew's and Luke's editorial interventions (Kloppenborg, *Q, the Earliest Gospel,* viii).

James M. Robinson's seminal article "Logoi Sophon: On the Gattung of Q" establishes definitively that the sayings of Q and *Thomas* are part of a genre of Jewish, Christian, and Gnostic literature that flourished in the Mediterranean world. Indeed, proverbs, *sententiae,* and moral sayings had been the mainstay of didactic literature for millennia, from the Egyptians to the Sumerians to the Hebrews. Robinson conjectures that a "shadowy existence of collections of sayings" such as the Didache and Epistle of Barnabas circulated orally among believers before they were eventually replaced by the written Gospels. John S. Kloppenborg in *The Formation of Q* builds on Robinson's work and reads the collections through Near Eastern didactic instructions, Hellenistic gnomology, and the *chreia* collection.

*Thomas* can therefore be seen as a hybrid of classical rhetorical collections and Near Eastern wisdom literature, both of which afford much compositional freedom. In Greco-Roman pedagogy, students were asked to respond to a given *chreia* by expanding, abbreviating, or modifying it.[9] Similarly, the sayings of Jesus, like any good rhetorical topos, can be adapted, adopted, and reconfigured in myriad ways. In the porous boundaries between oral circulation and textual inscription, *Thomas'* lack of authorial framework is evidence that it represents an early or "primitive" stage of the written sayings of Jesus. Its aphorisms do not so much represent a single coherent theology as much as a hybrid accumulation that reflects different moments of crisis and conflict within a community. The version that we possess represents but the latest written script of communal recitations that were ever mutable.

In the vibrant ecosystem of early Christian texts, the aphorism remained the basic unit of circulation. As found in the Nag Hammadi jar, *Thomas* lives alongside the *Sentences of Sextus*, the *Teachings of Silvanus*, the Gospels of the Egyptians, Philip, Mary, Truth, and Judas. Their capacious natures afford a multitude of interpretations, so that any sect can use it for their own purpose. The Nag Hammadi writings have attracted intense scholarly interest precisely because the fragments raise questions about their own hermeneutic possibilities. Indeed, the *Gospel of Thomas* has been read as anything from the pure and unsullied words of Jesus to a tradition that was independent from the New Testament canon as well as a "fifth gospel," "the invention of heretics," or a Gnostic secret text.[10]

### Jesus says

A great part of *Thomas'* enigma, and the chief characteristic that separates it from the canonical Gospels, is that the speeches of Jesus are devoid of any indication of time and place. Each of its 114 aphoristic remarks begins simply with "Jesus says," similar to "The Master says" in the *Analects*.[11] Far from supplying a firm authorial voice, Thomas is a silent editor who refuses to give any coherence to the Lord's discourses. Each *logion* starts with the purity of the present tense, "Jesus says." Unattached to any specific event, above any historical boundedness, the savior's sheer presence is allowed to shine forth. By stripping away all contexts, the *logia* collectively present the "living" Jesus as opposed to only a "historical" one.[12]

For a cross-cultural comparandum, almost all Buddhist texts in Pali and Sanskrit begin with the formula "Thus have I heard." Whereas *Thomas* foregrounds the moment of oral production, for the sutras it is the moment of aural reception.[13] The implied meaning is that the Buddha's teachings would be fruitless without their remembrance and propagation. Even though we know that Buddha lived some two thousand five hundred years ago, and his teachings were not committed to writing until some four centuries later, the construction of "Thus have I heard" in one stroke guarantees the authenticity of a firsthand testimony, binding together the moment of utterance, the process of transmission, and each subsequent reiteration, expanding and multiplying eons upon eons.

In contrast to the coherent narratives of the canonical Gospels—beautifully arranged with genealogies, parables, sermons, miracles, and dialogues—the sayings in *Thomas* are nonsequential and defy any internal order. Eusebius is correct by at least one count: the Lord's discourses are "not in order," and some of his disciples had "no intention of giving a connected account." *Thomas* demands that each reader piece together for themselves an image of the ever present, ever "living" Jesus in the here and now. One might say that this rhetorical technique is a sort of phenomenological *epoché*, a suspension or "bracketing." This becomes the very work of unconcealing, the hermeneutic process of revealing the hidden yet ever present Jesus.

In the first century of the Common Era, scriptural interpretation, Guy Stroumsa argues in *The End of Sacrifice*, replaced blood sacrifice as the central element of religious life. In this sense, the new self of the believer is formed through individual reading as much as it is from communal rituals. The truth derived from a believer's private meditation became as important as any ecclesiastical authority. *Ekklesia* at that time simply meant an "assembly." In my reading, the main advantage of *Thomas* is that it doesn't challenge the reader with miracles ranging from the Virgin birth to the Resurrection, or with the horrors of the Passion narrative. It also does not appeal to any written authority, in contrast to the canonical Gospels. Even the institution of a church as a corporation of like-minded believers might not be necessary, since salvation is found from turning inward. *Thomas'* cryptic aphorisms therefore become a gentle alternative to the canonical Gospels: all the uplift and none of the epistemic or social risk. It had something for everyone, especially those with a mystical or philosophical bent.

## Invention of heretics

Except the heresiologists. Around 180, Irenaeus of Lyon vociferously denounces those of the "gnostic" sect as "evil interpreters of the good word of revelation" (*Against Heresies* 1, pref. 1), "endeavoring like slippery serpents to escape at all points" (3.2.3). They "abuse the Scriptures by trying to support their own invention from them" (1.9.1), and "each one of them comes up with something new every day" (1.18.1). This sort of polemic persists for many generations.[14] In 367 the archbishop of Alexandria, Athanasius, writes an influential Easter letter to the monasteries in Egypt in which he definitively establishes the canonical scriptures, calling all others apocryphal, an "invention of heretics" that must be mercilessly suppressed (*Ep.* 39.7). The Nag Hammadi codices were probably among those to be eliminated. Hence they were buried for safekeeping in sealed jars, perhaps by the Pachomian monks who defied the archbishop's decree.[15]

Whether the *Gospel of Thomas* was Gnostic (a controversial designation), it is clear that it assiduously avoids any discussions on church governance or theories of the sacraments such as baptism or the Eucharist. All this made *Thomas* simply unacceptable to the early church fathers. Due to its obscurity, interpretation can become too idiosyncratic, too free-for-all. This lack of clear doctrine poses a dangerous liability. Its fragments, then, precede and resist the systematization of the synoptic Gospels and the institution of the early churches.

This movement roughly corresponds to Max Weber's theory of the "routinization" of religion from the charismatic authority of an individual leader to a complex bureaucracy of strict dogma and hierarchical structures.[16] The selection and deselection of Jesus' aphorisms played an operative role in this process. As his sayings circulated freely through different communities of faith, each would produce a collection that suited their particular needs. Written texts eventually intermixed or replaced the oral versions, and a collection of sayings such as the Nag Hammadi corpus could be rearranged infinitely. In truth, given the vast amount of energy the leading church fathers devoted to combatting the "heretics"—a full two centuries from Clement of Rome to Clement of Alexandria—*Thomas* and other apocrypha might be said to constitute an ever present, dark "other" that ironically sharpens the main contours of official doctrine. That is to say, orthodoxy *needs* heresies in order for it to become more brightly powerful.[17] The official "system" of the church had to wrestle mightily with these wayward "fragments."

### Absconditus

As scholars have established, the *Gospel of Thomas* is a descendant of the genre of wisdom literature that flourished in the ancient Near East. Advice manuals such as the Egyptian *Instruction of Amenemope* or the book of Proverbs offered instruction to the young by elders, and they were mostly pragmatic, preoccupied with *oikonomia,* or the management of the household: how to acquire and maintain wealth and status, how to govern women, servants, and children.[18] In their exhortatory function, these collections aim to establish a set of normative behaviors, affirming tradition, orthodoxy, and the establishment—all values that *Thomas* rejects.

Though the didactic import in wisdom literature seems to be relatively transparent, that is only part of the story. Hiddenness is also a pervasive topos.[19] The Egyptian *Sayings of Ptah-hotep* (circa 2450 BCE) states that "Good speech is hidden more than the emerald, but it may be found with maidservants at the grindstones" (Pritchard, *Ancient Near Eastern Texts*, 342). In Proverbs, wisdom is God's gift to Israel:

> My child, if you accept my words
> And treasure up my commands within you ...
> If you seek it like silver
> And search for it as for hidden treasure,
> Then you will understand the fear of the Lord
> And find the knowledge of God. (2:1–5)

With its analogies of "silver" and "hidden treasure," Proverbs claims that the difficulty in attaining wisdom is only because of her great price and its scarcity—there is nothing mystical or esoteric about her. *Ptah-hotep* even claims that wisdom transcends class boundaries. Proverbs notes that "I love those who love me, and those who seek me diligently find me" (8:17). Similarly, the Book of Ecclesiasticus (or Wisdom of Sirach) records, "Wisdom exalts her sons and gives help to those who seek her. Whoever loves her loves life, and those who seek her in early morning will be filled with joy" (4:11).[20]

In other passages of the Hebrew Bible, the idea of God as hidden (Heb. *histîr pānîm;* Lat. *deus absconditus*) is also prominent. The Psalmist in his lamentation expresses his despair over God abandoning him: "Do not hide your face from your servant, / for I am in distress—make haste to answer me" (69:17). Isaiah states, "Truly, you are a God who hides himself, O God of Israel, the Savior" (45:15). God withholds himself because of Israel's sin and disobedience. Yet divine concealment does not mean absence, for silence after all *does* indicate a presence.

To atone for the sin of Israel, the prophetic books promise that a new savior must be born, a Messiah who will manifest himself in the world. This thus stages the epochal arrival of Jesus: whereas the God of the Hebrew Bible hides, the God of the Christians manifests himself fully. The contrast between the hidden and the revealed forms the typological interpretation of Christianity, a mode of reading that would underwrite the late classical and medieval understanding of providential history as revelation.[21] The totality of Jesus' mission, in fact, is based on the fulfillment of a promise that is prefigured in the writings of the prophets. What was once shadowy is now clothed in radiance (Col. 2:17–19). And whereas the Hebrew scriptures show wisdom *personified*, Christian writings celebrate Jesus as wisdom *incarnate*. This movement from hiddenness to revelation—figuration to reality—is a movement from a transcendental deity to a man in flesh and blood. Jesus proclaims that "I will proclaim what has been hidden from the foundation of the world" (Matt. 13:35); "There is nothing hidden, except to be disclosed, nor is anything secret, except to come to light" (Mark 4:22). This verse is almost exactly the same as *Thomas* 6: "All things are disclosed before heaven. For there is nothing hidden that will not be revealed, and there is nothing covered that will remain undisclosed."

## Ivy without a wall

If everything hidden is revealed, then why does Jesus speak in riddles? Both Mark and Matthew claim that Jesus never spoke to the crowd "without a parable":

> To you has been given the secret of the kingdom of God, but for those outside, everything comes in parables; in order that [ἵνα] they may indeed look, but not perceive, and may indeed listen, but not understand; so that they may not turn again and be forgiven. (Mark 4:11–12)

To you it has been given to know the secrets of the kingdom of heaven, but to them it has not been given. For to those who have, more will be given, and they shall have abundance, but from those who have nothing, even what they have will be taken away. This is why [διὰ τοῦτο] I speak to them in parables, because [ὅτι] seeing they do not see, and hearing they do not hear, nor do they understand. (Matt. 13:11–15)

Oceans of exegetical ink have been spilled on the difference between Mark's *hina*, "in order that," and Matthew's *hoti*, "because."[22] The former suggests that Jesus is speaking obscurely by intention, that the parables are by design a stumbling block; the latter suggests that the listeners had a preexisting disability, meaning the parables are by design a test of vision and understanding.

Matthew's account here occurs in chapter 13, when Jesus goes out in the sea and gives a series of parables to a crowd gathered on the beach—the sower, the mustard seed, the weeds, and yeast. He proclaims at the end: "So it will be at the end of the age; the angels will go out and separate [*aphoriousin*] the wicked from the righteous" (Matt. 13:49). In other words, the divine will render his judgment by means of *aphorizein* based on the believer's judicious interpretation of *aphorismoi*.

Though Jesus is the agent of divine revelation, it is the duty of each believer to seek out his message. Pascal writes in a *pensée*, "Instead of complaining that God has hidden himself, you will give him thanks for revealing himself as much as he has, and you will thank him too for not revealing himself to wise men full of pride and unworthy of knowing so holy a God" (Sellier §13). Most Christians today understand that their Savior's words are enigmatic so that they must be pondered rather than taken blindly.[23] But as the Gospels record, the difficulty of this hermeneutic task was highly perplexing to the early believers. The task must have been shocking to the disciples themselves.

For this reason, parables and aphorisms become the perfect vehicles to express hiddenness, for both share a literal surface meaning and a figural meaning that lies behind or beyond it. They both admit an infinitude of possible readings. In the famous parable of the sower (Matt. 13:1–23; Mark 4:1–20; Luke 1:1–15), in which seeds are compared to words, the solution to the riddle is a simple *x* for *y* substitution: seeds are the words of Jesus. In the *Gospel of Thomas*, although there are at least nine parables, such a simple formula will not work, for the mystery lies in the difficult words themselves, not in their symbolic signification: that is, the potency of a *logion* rests not in its narrative framing but in its enunciative singularity. Walter Benjamin once said, "A proverb, one might say, is a ruin which stands on the site of an old story and in which a moral twines about a happening like ivy around a wall" (*Illuminations,* 108).[24] In early Christian writings, parables are stories with a moral; aphorisms are morals without a story, ivy without a wall.

The aphorisms of Jesus are invitations to eternal life. This eternal life is open to all, yet only a few seek it because this seeking is so confounding: "In the past, however, I did not tell you the things about which you asked me then. Now I am willing to tell them, but you are not seeking them" (§92). The key to unlock these hidden things is hermeneutics. The second *logion* of *Thomas* captures this journey:

> Let the one who seeks not stop seeking until one finds. When one finds, one will become troubled. When one becomes troubled, one will marvel and will reign over all.

Compressed within these three sentences is the entire epic of the spiritual self, a voyage from poverty to perplexity to power everlasting. Through its syntactic and lexical repetition, this *logion* mirrors the progressive unfolding of Jesus' promise. The activities of ceaselessly seeking and finding lead to two affective states— "troubled" and "marveling"—and finally to victory "reign[ing] over all." It is difficult to gloss what this "all" is, except to say that it ranges from the anticipation of Jesus' imminent return to rule heaven on earth to the more interior sense of "all" that is the control of the self and its response to the slings and arrows of outrageous fortune.

"Seek and you will find" (Matt. 7:7, Luke 11:9) is perhaps the simplest and most encouraging good news of all. The clean binary of this dictum—imperative and promise—maps out the two halves of the salvation story: first the believer must do the work of searching, and then Jesus will do the rest. And seeking is certainly the basic activity of biological life, a mechanism of survival. All motion, after all, is a type of striving, a craving for something. Jesus' rhetorical gift transforms this primal agitation into a spiritual yearning. Time and again, "seek and you will find" is not just a commandment but also a covenant of hope: "Know what is in front of your face, and what is hidden from you will be disclosed to you. For there is nothing hidden that will not be revealed" (§5); "There will be days when you will seek me and you will not find me" (§38); "One who seeks will find, for [one who knocks] it will be opened" (§94).

## ΓΝΩΘΙ ΣΑΥΤΟΝ

In comparison to the revelation of the hidden God in the Hebrew Bible or the canonical evangelists, the *Gospel of Thomas* promises something more radical. In the Hebrew Bible, Yahweh is an almighty cultic deity beyond the comprehension or reach of any human. In the Gospels, Jesus insists that the written tradition verifies the truth of what he says (John 5:46; 10:34). In *Thomas*, Jesus' sayings are verified by the inward truth of every individual. *Logion* 3 reads:

> Jesus said, "If your leaders say to you, 'Look, the kingdom is in heaven,' then the birds of heaven will precede you. If they say to you, 'It is in the sea,' then the fish will precede you. Rather, the kingdom is inside you and it is outside you.
>
> "When you know yourselves, then you will be known, and you will understand that you are children of the living Father.

But if you do not know yourselves, then you dwell in poverty, and you are poverty."

The vision of the kingdom here, instead of being metaphysical or unattainable, is immanent and immediate. Jesus invests authority not in any institution but rather in one's own inner light. By contrasting a "kingdom" that is residing in the celestial firmament beyond or the oceanic depths below with one that "is inside you and ... outside you," *Thomas* promises a God who is both omnipresent and intimate.

An astute scholar has pointed out that *logion* 3 is actually a midrash on Deuteronomy:[25]

> Surely, this commandment that I am commanding you today is not too hard for you, nor is it too far away. It is not in heaven, that you should say, "Who will go up to heaven for us, and get it for us so that we may hear it and observe it?" Neither is it beyond the sea, that you should say, "Who will cross to the other side of the sea for us, and get it for us so that we may hear it and observe it?" No, the word is very near to you; it is in your mouth and in your heart for you to observe. (30:10–15)

Speaking in the finale to a long recitation of rules and restrictions, the Lord here implicitly denies the need for any specialist priest to explain his words. His revelation is so close and clear that anyone can get it. Yet the crucial difference between Jesus in *Thomas* and in the Torah is that God's commandment is not God himself but his "words." But Jesus is the "word" embodied, made flesh, *incarnate*. He rewrites and transforms the laws of the commandment into the *logos* of his living presence.

While the first part of *logion* 3 is Hebraic, the second part is Hellenic: with its insistence on knowing oneself, the *Gospel of Thomas* incontrovertibly taps into the ancient Delphic maxim "Know thyself," γνωθι σαυτον. The idea of knowing oneself is repeated in the rest of the discourse: "One who knows everything but lacks in oneself lacks everything" (§67); "If you bring forth what is within you, what you bring forth will save you. If you do not have that within you, what you do not have within you [will] kill you" (§70); "when you make the inner like the outer and the outer like the inner … then you will enter [the kingdom]" (§22).

What does it mean to know yourself? What does it mean to make the inner and the outer the same? As any student of philosophy would know, "Know thyself" is the greatest of all Greek precepts. According to Pierre Courcelle, its interpretation throughout the tradition can be divided into two types: a restrictive one—know your limitations as a mortal—and an expansive one— know that you have an element of the divine within yourself.[26] Ancient philosophy emphasizes the latter. Socrates says in *Alcibiades major*: "If the soul, Alcibiades, is to know itself it must look at a soul, and especially at that region in which what makes a soul good…. That region in it resembles the divine, and someone who looked at that and grasped everything divine—vision and understanding—would have the best grasp of himself as well" (133b4–c4). Cicero in *De legibus* likewise celebrates our potential to attain wisdom: "For he who knows himself will realize, in the first place, that he has a divine element within him, and will think of his own inner nature as a kind of consecrated image of God" (1.22.59). Seneca says you need not go to temples to find the divine; you need only turn inward: "God is near you, he is with you, he is within you … a holy spirit indwells within us" (*Ep*. 41.1–2).

Philo of Alexandria urges, "Know thyself, and the parts of which you consist, what each is, and for what it was made, and how it is meant to work, and who it is that, all invisible, invisibly sets the puppets in motion and pulls their strings, whether it be the Mind that is in you or the Mind of the Universe" (46–47). These lines are from *On Flight and Finding*, a commentary on the latter chapters of Genesis, and are indicative of his remarkable synthesis of Jewish thought and Middle Platonism. In particular, he fuses the Hellenic idea of the divine within the self and the concept of humans made in the image of God drawn from the first chapter of Genesis.

With early Christianity, these ideas from the Hellenic and Hebraic traditions—the hidden God, knowing oneself, and the divine within—intermingle into the deepest mysteries of faith: the union between humans and God through the mediation of Jesus. "Whoever drinks from my mouth will become like me," *logion* 108 reads, "I myself shall become that person, and the hidden things will be revealed to that person." The metaphor of drink harkens back to the first saying about avoiding the "taste" of death by understanding Jesus' word.[27] This *logion* actually goes further to claim the merging of Jesus with the reader: "Know thyself" means nothing less than "Become one with God."

The idea that God resides within each one of us is common to many religions.[28] In early Christianity, the Greek and Jewish senses of the godhead within each person coalesce, and in turn Christianity will articulate a sense of interiority as a journey to the divine that will culminate centuries later with Augustine: "Do not go outside yourself. Return within yourself. In the inward man dwells truth" ("Of True Religion," 29.72).

## Invention of heretics

By the accidents of cultural transmission, the fragments of both the *Gospel of Thomas* and Heraclitus are preserved in the early church fathers, namely, Clement of Alexandria's *Stromata* and Hippolytus' *Refutation of All Heresies*.[29] For example, Clement quotes from the second *logion* of *Thomas*:

> He who seeks shall not cease until he finds, and finding he will be astonished, and having been astonished he will rule, and having ruled, he will rest. (5.14.96)

This sense of searching is also present when the bishop justifies the bric-a-brac nature of his second-century *Stromata* (meaning "patchwork;" its full title, according to Eusebius, is *The Miscella-neous Collections of Gnostic Notes Bearing upon the True Philoso-phy of Titus Flavius Clement*):

> Let these notes of ours, as we have often said for the sake of those that consult them carelessly and unskillfully, be of varied character—and as the name itself indicates, patched together—passing constantly from one thing to another, and in the series of discussions hinting at one thing and demon-strating another. "For those who seek for gold," says Heracli-tus, "dig much earth and find little gold." But those who are of the truly golden race, in mining for what is allied to them, will find the much in little. For the word will find one to under-stand it. The *Miscellanies* of notes [στρομάτα] contribute, then, to the recollection and expression of truth in the case of him who is able to investigate with reason [λογοζ]. (4.2.1–3)

Clement uses Heraclitus' fragment as a metaphor for the herme-neutic process. Heraclitus' saying, itself deeply ambiguous, con-cerns, on one hand, inquiry and discovery (searching, digging, finding) and, on the other hand, the disproportion between what is worthless (earth) and valuable (gold).[30] Clement audaciously reverses the metaphor, claiming that "the word will find one who understands it" (gold will reveal itself to those who understand it, i.e., the "golden race").

A century later, Hippolytus' *Refutation of All Heresies* is also a veritable thesaurus for Gnostic and Greek doctrines.[31] Little is known about the author—he might have been the bishop of Porto near Rome or the head of a schism. But eight of the ten books were rediscovered in 1841 in which he painstakingly and vociferously catalogs the "incoherent tenets" of Middle Platonism, Aristotelianism, Neopythagoreanism, mystery cults on one hand and the "excessive madness" of the Gnostic schools—the Naas-senes, Peratae, Sethians, Basilides, Valentinus, "Simon Magus," Marcion, Tatian, and many others—on the other (*Proemium*). Hippolytus yokes these two worlds together, for he holds that the false thoughts of Gnostics are derived from nowhere else but the Greek philosophers.

For Heraclitus, "the Demiurge and creator of itself" is demonstrated "in the following passage: God is day, night; winter, summer; war, peace; surfeit, famine. All things are contraries—this appears to be his meaning—but an alteration takes place, just as if incense were mixed with other sorts of incense, but denominated according to the pleasurable sensation produced by each sort" (DK B67). The heretic Noetus, too, maintains that "one and the same God is the Creator and Father of all things; and that when it pleased Him, He nevertheless appeared (though invisible) to just men of old." Therefore, "Did not Heraclitus the Obscure anticipate Noetus in framing a system of philosophy, according to identical modes of expression?" (9.5).

Elsewhere he cites an aphorism from *Thomas*:

> The Naassene says "the kingdom of heaven is within you" [Luke 17:21]. And concerning this nature they hand down an explicit passage, occurring in the Gospel inscribed according to *Thomas*, expressing themselves thus: "He who seeks me, will find me in children from seven years old; for there concealed, I shall in the fourteenth age be made manifest" [§4]. This, however, is not the teaching of Christ, but of Hippocrates, who uses these words: "A child of seven years is half of a father." And so it is that these heretics, placing the originative nature of the universe in causative seed, and having ascertained the aphorism of Hippocrates, that a child of seven years old is half of a father, say that in fourteen years, according to *Thomas*, he is manifested. This, with them, is the ineffable and mystical Logos. (5.2)

In both Clement and Hippolytus, Greek and Gnostic texts have been zealously atomized, wrested out of context, and taxonomized into a sprawling catalog. We do not have to be persuaded by the heresiologists' heavy-handed rhetoric to recognize that in late antiquity there were free exchanges and syntheses of ideas, images, parables, and apothegms from all parts of the Mediterranean. Any text or system of thought can be broken down into portable units for expedient and pell-mell citation. We see again how aphorisms are elements that can be reconfigured to fit any ideological matrix. Hippolytus claims that Greek philosophy did that; Gnosticism did that with Greek philosophy. In turn, Hippolytus and Clement do the same.

As a result, the Ante-Nicene fathers' condemnations managed to preserve dozens of Presocratic fragments and several from the *Gospel of Thomas*. What they tried to destroy they ironically saved. These catalogs of heresies are now an important source for both scholars of the classical world and early Christianity. Hermann Diels based most of his doxography on Hippolytus (for which he was later criticized).[32] And with the recovery of both the Nag Hammadi writings and Hippolytus' tract we can rewrite the history of Gnosticism from within and without. By means of such polemics, the construction of paganism and Christianity galvanized, and the chasm between orthodoxy and heterodoxy became irreparable.

The mixing of Heraclitus and the *Gospel of Thomas* by Clement and Hippolytus thus represents one of the great encounters between Hellenism and Christianity in the late antique world. This encounter was possible because of the primacy of *logos* in both their discourses. Clement writes in the *Pedagogue*:

> That man in whom the *Logos* is indwelling does not transform himself, he does not put on appearances, he possesses the form of the *Logos*, he is assimilated to God.... That man becomes God because he wants what God wants. So Heraclitus was right to say, "Immortals mortals, mortal immortal": for the *Logos* is the same. A manifest mystery: God in a man, and the man in God, and the mediator accomplishes the will of the father. (3.1.5–3.2.1; Laks and Most R84)

Heraclitus, Thomas, and the apologists all grapple with the same problems—how to seek and discover truth, the nature of things, the nature of the soul. In Heraclitus, truth is found within *logos*, a possession of all (that few use). In the *Gospel of Thomas*, truth is found in oneself, for Jesus dwells within. Clement summons the famous beginning of the Johannine Gospel, which announces that Jesus is the *logos* incarnate. Hippolytus triumphantly proclaims that he has "burst through the labyrinth of heresies," "unraveling their intricacies" and "by the force of truth, we approach the demonstration of the truth itself" (10.1). Whereas Christians believed the Greek philosophers possessed only one portion of the many *logoi* of the world, they thought themselves to be in possession of the entire *logos*, incarnate in Jesus Christ.

## Hupomnêmata

Philosophies come and go, theologies rise and fall, but the aphorism abides. In the last three chapters, we have seen how in the ancient cultures of China and the Mediterranean, the aphorism functions as the basic unit in the propagation and circulation of ideas. The sayings of Confucius competed with those of the Daoist sect and later with the Buddhists. Besides Heraclitus there were many other wise men vying for authority. (Plutarch somewhere calls the Mediterranean "a well-mixed bowl of myths.") The early Christians' project of collecting the sayings of their spiritual master partakes in a larger tradition in which sects as disparate as the Stoics, Epicureans, Essenes, and Manicheans meditated ceaselessly on the *apophthegmata* of their teachers. Pierre Hadot has devoted his entire career exploring ancient philosophies of life and their affinities with Christian spirituality.[33] An admirer of Hadot was none other than Foucault, who toward the end of his life reflected much on the care of the self. He wrote, "In this period there was a culture of what could be called personal writing: taking notes on the reading, conversations, and reflections that one hears or engages in oneself; keeping kinds of notes on important subjects (what the Greeks call '*hupomnêmata*'), which must

be reread from time to time so as to reactualize their contents"
("Self Writing," 210).

To be sure, the cultivation of the self is the ultimate purpose
of the Master's aphorisms. Foucault suggests that the individual
reader eventually composes their own aphorisms after reflecting
on those of others. But what we have discovered so far is that
there are some important preconditions before that can happen:
(1) Because of the instability of the textual materials, it is impossible to decipher the aphorist's philosophy or theology without
philology. Thus the question of how the collected fragments become authoritative (or not) is a burning one. (2) The ideological
agenda of a community is always imbricated with the aphorisms'
transmission. (3) The disconnected nature of the collected sayings turns out to be an advantage as well as a liability: it affords
greater hermeneutic fluidity. (4) From the multiplicity of clash-
ing voices the singular voice of the Teacher, as constructed by the
Tradition (both in capital T's) eventually emerges. The Teacher
becomes the Tradition *and* the Tradition becomes the Teacher,
though the anti-Tradition (like the "Gnostics") always lurks in
the shadows. The self is indeed formed and transformed by the
aphorism, but we have to first determine whose aphorisms they
are and whether or not we really want to read them.

# 4

# Erasmus and Bacon

## ANTIQUITY AND THE NEW SCIENCE

In the classical tradition of the European Renaissance, no humanist inhabited, cultivated, and chased after ancient proverbs with as much passion as Desiderius Erasmus (1466–1536). The verbal fragments of antiquity are gathered in his lifelong project known as the *Adages*. It began modestly when the Dutch humanist was in Paris. In desperate need of money, he hastily published a quick-turnaround quarto of 838 sayings entitled *Adagiorum collectanea* (1500). Eight years later, during a prolonged stay in Venice, consulting with Greek scholars from Byzantium, he annotated and amassed even more texts. Nourished by these voracious readings, the collection matured into the *Chiliades*, containing 3,260 items, published by the Aldine Press. As he wrote in an epigram, "Proverbs are easy to collect and string, / But thousands? That's a very different thing" (Phillips, *Adages,* 147). The collection would not stop growing, morphing and metastasizing for three decades, up to the year of his death in 1536. The final tabulation was a heavy folio volume crammed with over 4,215 proverbs.[1] It took him exactly half his life to do it.

Midway through the introduction to this last edition lies an arresting passage:

> Aristotle, according to Synesius, thinks that proverbs were simply the vestiges of that earliest philosophy which were destroyed by the calamities of human history [*nihil aliud esse paroemias quam reliquias priscae illius philosophiae maximis rerum humanarum cladibus extinctae*]. (31:14; vi.8–10)[2]

In this citation the form of the philosopher's remark mimics its contents: in a work dedicated to fragments, it is a fragment about fragments, a fragment that praises the power of fragments.

And this fragment is preserved in the Greek "In praise of baldness" (*Calvitiae encomium*), a mock eulogy by the fourth-century bishop of Ptolemais, Synesius:

> A wise saying is a proverb [ει δέ καί ἡ παροιμία σοφον]. According to Aristotle, they are the remains [ἐγκαταλείμματα] of ancient philosophy strewn among the great ruins of mankind; these monuments were preserved on account of their brevity and elegance. Therefore a proverb is this: a saying whose dignity comes from the same antiquity where philosophy originated. (*Patrologia Graeca* 66.1204b)[3]

With this statement we get a glimpse into the mechanism of the classical tradition at work: Erasmus in the sixteenth century is quoting a fourth-century CE Egyptian bishop quoting a fourth-century BCE Athenian philosopher. The specific Greek term— *egkataleimmata*—would have simply meant "remnant, residue or trace" (s.v. *LSJ*, citing this very passage), but the Latin word that Erasmus uses—*reliquias*—is charged, for it also denotes Christian relics, the bones and dust of saints that carry some thaumaturgical power. In the course of their millennial survival, the Christian humanist reimbues these pagan vestiges with some measure of numinous potency.

Broadly speaking, for European thinkers from Petrarch to the Romantics, the fragments of antiquity summon nostalgia and melancholy.[4] Erasmus is more optimistic: a fragment gives us a key to open the vast archives of the past. "Underlying the [proverbs] there are what one might call sparks [*igniculos*] of that ancient philosophy which was much clearer-sighted in its investigation of truth than were the philosophers who came after" (33:14; vi.15). Some of these tiny *igniculi* include: "Friends have all things common." "War is sweet to those who have never tried it." "Make haste slowly." "The blind leading the blind." "One swallow does not make a summer." "He who gives quickly gives twice." "So many men, so many opinions." "To judge the lion from its claw." "You write in water." "Time reveals all things." Of course, "Know thyself" and "Nothing in excess." And yes, "The fox knows many things, but the hedgehog one great truth."[5] Taken together, these adages sparkle as points of light that guide the voyage of philosophical and philological inquiry over the ocean of antiquity.

The Renaissance was called a rebirth because for the first time in European history, antiquity was seen *as* antiquity.[6] Out of this desire to reach the past, humanists forged the tools of the philological method. As Erasmus laments, "The works of the ancients, which are as it were the springs from which proverbs are drawn, are in great part lost. Greek comedy, for instance, in both its forms has perished entirely except for Aristophanes, and so has tragedy in Latin, with the sole exception of Seneca" (34:170; III.i.1). His multiple editions of the *Adages* are perhaps the period's most exemplary attempts to recover these forgotten texts. Proverb by proverb, phrase by phrase, the bits and pieces of ancient authors are slowly assembled into a rhetorical cornucopia. Its visual counterpart is Bruegel's *Netherlandish Proverbs,* for both share the same *homo ludens* spirit of play, wit, and generosity (see fig. 3).[7] From within its digressive, expansive folds, accumulations of scholarly conjectures, and shaggy-dog anecdotes, what emerges from these pages is an ever-growing and inexhaustible catalog. All these, we shall see, Francis Bacon would later critique.

FIGURE 3. Pieter Bruegel the Elder, *Netherlandish Proverbs*, 1559, Gemäldegalerie, Berlin (Wikimedia Commons).

## Bouquet of flowers

The microform permeated the culture of the Renaissance. It encapsulates a set of humanist oppositions: brevity and expansion, timelessness and timeliness, revelation and concealment, vulgarity and rarity, truth and persuasion, fragments and collections. Readers, like bees, plucked out sweet bits of texts into commonplace *florilegia* or *anthologia* (Latin and Greek for "collections of flowers") and arranged them topically, alphabetically, or by author.[8] These are then condensed, reinfused, and rearranged as rhetorical bouquets.[9] Erasmus' *De Copia* (1512) teaches you how to do that. Turn to any page in Tasso, Marlowe, Rabelais, or de Vega—sixteenth-century literature would simply not exist without commonplaces. A well-placed sententia arrests the welter of narrative and provides a moment of moral clarity. Considered as distillations of experience and authority, maxims were frequently summoned and explicated in law courts.[10] Calvin ends his thousand-page *Institutes of Christian Religion* (1536) with one hundred aphorisms that epitomize "a Narrow Compass, the Substance and Order of the Four Books." John Dee entitles his astrological treatise *Propaedeumata aphoristica* (1558). The editions of Hippocrates' *Aphorisms* went through many editions, translations, and commentaries.[11] Robert Dallington has a collection called *Aphorismes Civill and Militaire* (1613). Greek and Latin inscriptions from scripture and classical authors adorned the ceiling beams of Montaigne's library tower.[12]

The foundation of all this cultural production was the schoolroom, in which the aphorism was the basic unit of rhetorical instruction. In ancient textbooks called *progymnasmata*, students learn how to explicate a proverb (*gnōmē*) as part of a sequence of oration that moves progressively from fable to *chreia* (an anonymous maxim) to ekphrasis to finally a law case.[13] Erasmus' "On the Method of Study" (*De ratione studii*, 1511) teaches you how to do that.

The adage thus addressees a number of issues raised in this book. First, Erasmus' thirty-page introduction to the 1536 *Adages* stands as "one of the most thorough discussions of the proverb up to that time in Western literature, even including those surviving from the ancients" (Barker, *The Adages of Erasmus*, 3). Second, coming after the monuments of ancient philosophy, his adages also come before the creation of new texts, as humanist authors crushed and reconstituted them as raw materials for their own works. Third, in this way the compilation of ancient "fragments" forms the basic building blocks to the humanist "system" of learning. Finally, they embody the hedgehog-versus-the-fox nature of aphorisms that is at the heart of my study.

## What is an adage?

The 1536 introduction presents a complete anatomy and theory of the microform: its definition, value, origins, development, difficulty, hermeneutic and rhetorical uses. Etymologically, the Latin *adagium* is from *circumagium*, "something passed around," and the Greek *paroimia*, from *oimos*, "road" (33:4; "Introduction," ii.4–6). Erasmus admits that there is no one definition that can cover a short saying's "character and force." All the same, his own definition is: "a proverb is a saying in popular use, remarkable for some shrewd and novel turn" (*Paroemia est celebre dictum, scita quapiam novitate insigne*; 33:4; i.44). Though he cautions, "There are however some near neighbors to the proverb, for instance *gnōmai,* which are called by us *sententiae* or aphorisms, and *ainoi,* which among us are called fables; with the addition of *apophthegmata,* which may be translated as quick witty sayings, as well as *skômmata* of facetious remarks, and in a word anything which shelters behind a kind of mark of allegory or any other figure of speech associated with proverbs" (33:7; iv.3–8).[14] For Erasmus the difference between proverbs, maxims, and aphorisms that I established in the introduction is not so strict, although his requirement that an adage be "shrewd and novel" means that there must be a figurative meaning or problematic turn to be deciphered.

How do you use an adage? Rudolph Agricola in his landmark treatise *De inventione dialectica* (1479) heralded a new humanist method that synthesizes the rhetorical art of persuasion with the dialectical art of logic.[15] By organizing proverbs as discrete topics in the arrangement of commonplaces, the first step in writing becomes simply choosing appropriate quotes from the authority of ancients. Erasmus follows in his footsteps—various editions of the *Adages* have indexes by topic or author in the back pages, and readers even made their own. The Dutch humanist is, however, much more playful, eclectic, and even subversive (think *Praise of Folly*). Whereas for Agricola composition mainly involves looking to the genus and species of a particular topic, a discussion about causes and attendant circumstances, the proper organization of questions, examples, refutations, and proofs, for Erasmus the highest achievement of rhetoric is *copia*, a qualitative and quantitative "copiousness," an exuberant, rhapsodic display of rhetorical fireworks. But this does not mean we overload our writing with an excess of proverbs: as Aristotle "elegantly recommended ... we should treat them not as food but condiments, not for sufficiency but for delight.... In letters to one's friends, it will be permissible to amuse oneself in this way a little more freely; in serious writing they should be used both more sparingly and with more thought" (31:19–20; 24–26).

## Prismatic gems

Erasmus employs various images to describe the adage's potency: they are gems, mustard seeds, Silenus boxes. Underlying these topoi is a semantic expansion from the infinitesimally small to the boundless, the granular to the global, for an infinitude of possibilities resides within one monad of a *paroimia*. Proverbs

in their concision and brilliance should be as clear-cut as gems
(*gemmae*):[16]

> for adages, like gems, are small things, and sometimes escape
> your eye as you hunt for them, unless you keep a very sharp
> lookout. Besides which they do not lie on the surface, but
> as a rule are buried, so that you have to dig them out before
> you can collect them.... And who can make an adequate es-
> timate of the infinite labor required to seek out such small
> things everywhere, one might say, by sea and land? (34:170–
> 72; III.i.1)

A gem is a polished, precious adornment. Erasmus knows very
well the medieval tradition of lapidaries, or *mineralia*.[17] A material manifestation of divine glory and household wealth, precious
gems adorned royal crowns, bishops' rings, reliquaries of saints,
marriage dowries, and even Bible covers. As the abbot in Umberto Eco's *The Name of the Rose* explains, his ring "is not an orna-
ment: it is a splendid syllogy of the divine word whose guardian I
am" (447).

We must also remember that Erasmus is from the Netherlands. Already, in the early modern period, Antwerp was a center
of the gem trade. Then as now, the beauty of a gem is determined
not only by its intrinsic natural qualities—brightness, color, and
clarity—but also by the craftsmanship of the jeweler—the cut.
After cutting and polishing a choice piece of rock comes its careful setting: "the jewel does not shine in manure but in a ring,"
he says (*Adagiorum Collectanea,* in *Opera omnia* 2:9, 46). Later
writers picked up on the same exquisite metaphor. The *Athenaeum Fragments* would say: "The ancients, it seems, loved eternity in miniatures as well: the gem-carver's art is the miniature
of the sculptor's" (§191). Nietzsche warns: "Caution in quoting:
... an excellent quotation can annihilate entire pages, indeed an
entire book, in that it warns the reader and seems to cry out to
him: 'Beware, I am the jewel and around me there is lead, pallid,

ignominious lead'" (*Human, All Too Human II*, "The Wanderer and His Shadow" §111).[18]

In the early modern period, gems moved from precious ornaments of religious devotion to secular objects of commodity to scientific instruments. Prisms were made of gemlike glass; it was believed that white light was colorless, and that the prism itself produced the color.[19] A prism is "a transparent object . . . used for refracting light that passes through the sides" (*OED*), and in doing so the "spectrum as produced by refraction" reveals the nature of light. As the prism is to light, so is an adage to a philological reading. A prismatic aphorism's form and nature remain the same, but the richness of its spectrum—its polychromatic meanings—depends on the reader's hermeneutic angle of approach—the reflection, refraction, and deflection of the light source as it travels through the transparency of the verbal prism. After Erasmus, Newton's experiments demonstrated that a white light shone through a prism disperses into the spectrum of the rainbow. Under the right conditions, what an aphorism finally reveals is not only its own crystalline color but also the luminous, variegated power of the reader's hermeneutics. My point is that deciphering the meaning of the aphorism requires that both the aphorism and the reader be brilliant.

## Mustard seeds

From the gem's opalescence Erasmus turns to the organic metaphor of seeds. In the "Sileni of Alcibiades" entry, he remarks on how a seed is "in appearance tiny and negligible, [but] in power immense," and thus "it differs utterly and diametrically from the system of this world" (34:262; III.iii.1). Seeds are hidden in the depths of the earth, like precious stones and metals, and yet are the originators of all life:

> Look at the trees: their flowers and leaves appeal to every eye, and their great bulk is inescapable, whereas the seed which

contains the vital force of the world—what a tiny thing it is, how well-concealed, how far from appealing to the eye, how little given to self-advertisement. (34:266)

The topos of the human mind as a garden is an old one, and it began with the Stoics. For Cicero and Seneca, under proper pedagogical cultivation, the intellect may nourish noetic and moral seeds—*semina virtutum et scientiarum*—that will eventually flourish into the flower of human wisdom.[20]

Indeed, seeds of the mind form the kernel of the Christian faith. The parable of the sower is one of the most memorable, found in all three synoptic gospels (Mark 4:1–9; Luke 8:4–15; Matt. 13:1–9). In Matthew's version, the parable of the mustard seed follows right after it:

The kingdom of heaven is like a mustard seed [κόκκῳ σινάπεως] that someone took and sowed in his field; it is the smallest of all the seeds [μικρότερον ... σπερμάτων], but when it has grown it is the greatest of shrubs and becomes a tree, so that the birds of the air come and make nests in its branches. (13:31–33)

Here, the genre and its message converge in meaning, for "parable" is from the Greek *para* + *ballein*, "to throw." Are seeds not disseminated by their scattering? The mustard seed, in particular, measures only one or two millimeters in diameter; but under the right conditions, it flourishes into a plant taller than a person, with bright yellow flowers and large verdant leaves. For Erasmus, if the kingdom of heaven is "like a grain of mustard seed," so then are the words of scripture, in appearance plain but immense in their hidden power:

The parables of the Gospel, if you judge them by their outward shell, would be thought, surely, by everyone to be the work of an ignoramus. Crack the nutshell and of course you will find that hidden wisdom which is truly divine, something in truth very like Christ Himself. . . .

It is the same with knowledge: the real truth of things is always most profoundly concealed, and cannot be detected easily or by many people. (34:264)

Already in his *Enchiridion,* Erasmus remarks that both secular and sacred texts "are made up of a literal sense and a mysterious sense, body and soul, as it were, in which you are to ignore the letter and look rather to the mystery" (66:67; v28D). Erasmus calls proverbs *paroimia,* the same word Jesus uses to describe his own way of preaching: "I have said these things to you in figures of speech [*paroimiais*]. The hour is coming when I will no longer speak to you in figures [*paroimiais*], but will tell you plainly [*parrēsia*] of the Father" (John 16:25, also 10:6).

Erasmus' analogy between a proverb and a seed is apt, for at the time he was compiling the *Adages* he was engaged in what he considered his more important enterprise—the Latin and Greek critical editions of the New Testament. Erasmus saw a continuity between his works on pagan wisdom and holy writ.[21] With his 1516 *Novum Instrumentum omne* (later changed to *Novum Testamentum omne*), he attempted to revise the text of the Vulgate by comparing it to the surviving Greek manuscripts.[22] And for the purposes of ecclesiastical reform, Erasmus regarded his *Paraphrases* as equally as important as the original text of the scripture. In other words, there is a constant interplay between interpretation and textual criticism. As such, the genealogical discourses in the *Adages* are as valuable as the original sayings themselves—the *fontes* exist hand-in-hand with the *magisterium.*

Interestingly, in the Jewish tradition, the medieval rabbi Nachmanides says that in the beginning the universe was as tiny as a grain of mustard. And the Buddhist tradition also uses the commonplace of the mustard seed. A story goes that once a grief-stricken mother took the corpse of her only son to seek consolation from the Buddha. The Buddha asks her to bring a handful of mustard grains from a family who has never lost a child, husband, wife, father, or mother. Unable to do so, she realizes that death is common to all. The Buddha explains, "If an individual were to pick a single mustard seed every hundred years from a seven-mile cube worth of mustard seeds, then by the time the last seed is picked, the age of the world cycle would still continue" ("Story of Kisā Gotamī," in Burlingame, *Buddhist Parables*, 93). This of course is intended to demonstrate the interminable span of this world's *seculum*. But whether Christian, Jewish, or Buddhist—they all recognize that the mustard seed's tiny size harbors within a mighty potential. It is the humble catalyst in the vast ecosystem of divine providence.

In whatever culture they are found, seeds must be planted under the right conditions for them to flourish. The Neo-Confucian Zhu Xi, whom we encountered in chapter 1, also has a striking analogy between gardening and reading: he says that a good gardener knows exactly how much water each plant needs. You can't water too much or too little (*Learning to Be a Sage*, "On Reading," part 1, 4.31). Reading, he says, has the same principle. "In reading, don't strive for quantity. Instead become intimately familiar with what you do read" (4.24). Though Erasmus himself does not exactly follow the first half of this precept, he would wholeheartedly agree with the second half.

Understanding the words of Jesus, as we saw in the last chapter, certainly requires much effort. That is why he uses agricultural images so often in his parables. Seeds vividly illustrate the full gamut of faith: they signify not only the promise of growth, abundance, and harvest but also the inevitability of droughts, floods, and calamity and thus the necessity for labor, patience, and endurance. The reader needs to cultivate these habits if they are to interpret Jesus' words. While the seed is the gift of the teacher, its survival and flourishing depend on the reader.

For Erasmus, truth in language, like the mustard seed in the parable, needs hermeneutic engagement. In other words, parables and aphorisms present an ecology of thought, a georgics of the mind. Textual seeds sown upon the good soil of the mind are those that will bear fruit. As Novalis would write in *Grains of Pollen,* "Fragments of this kind are literary seeds: certainly, there may be many sterile grains among them, but this is unimportant if only a few of them take root!" (*Blüthenstaub* 2:463).

## Sileni Alcibiadis

Along with the images of the gem and the seed, another image Erasmus deploys for the adage is the Silenus figure (III.iii.1) from Plato's *Symposium.* This is how the drunken Alcibiades describes Socrates in the dialogue: "Isn't he just like a statue of Silenus? You know the kind of statue I mean; you'll find them in any shop in town. It's a Silenus sitting, his flute or his pipes in his hands, and its hollow. It's split right down the middle, and inside it's full of tiny statues of the gods" (215b). This figure appears again in *Praise of Folly*: "It's well known that all human affairs are like the figures of Silenus described by Alcibiades and have two completely opposite faces ... the same applies to beauty and ugliness, riches and poverty, obscurity and fame ... you'll find everything suddenly reversed if you open the Silenus" (27:102–3).

With this Platonic imagery, Erasmus yokes together Greek thought and Christian faith. Erasmus calls Plato the *paroimiōdesteros* —the master of proverbs. That is why he begins his collection "friends have all things in common," since this phrase is from the end of the *Phaedrus* (279c). "Scripture too has its own Sileni," Erasmus says. "Pause at the surface, and what you see is sometimes ridiculous, were you to pierce to the heart of the allegory, you would venerate the divine wisdom" (34:267; III.iii.1). The adages of Erasmus themselves are verbal Silenus boxes, rough-hewn and misshapen from the outside, but once penetrated, they glow with marvelous riches. So even the seemingly obscene ones— "giving one the finger" or "to look into a dog's anus"—contain some worth.[23]

## Flood of my language

The adage arrives to us as a time capsule, shorn of its historical locus and cut off from the nourishing culture that gave birth to it. But it has a powerful passport, traveling far and wide across time and geography, "everywhere on the lips of men" (31:4; "Introduction," ii.6). The goal of Erasmus' commentary is to chart its genealogy or etiology, exposing its rhizomes, networks, and correspondences through the variegated itineraries of the classical tradition. Although the deep hermeneutics afforded by the gem, mustard seed, and Silenus figure might seem to evoke the spiritual tradition of *lectio divina* in which the Christian believer focuses on only a phrase or word for silent meditation and prayer, Erasmus is instead much more voluble—much more philological, pedagogical, and polemical.[24] He usually starts with an adage's citations in ancient texts, variants, variations through later authors, amusing anecdotes, and advice on how we might use it today. After his initial gloss, he might use the adage as a jumping-off point to talk about something more pertinent to his times. "Man is a bubble" (*Homo bulla*, II.iii.48), for instance, provides an occasion for him to mourn for the death of Prince Philip, the archduke of Austria. Erasmus' capacious erudition cuts open the anatomy of the aphoristic hedgehog (the medical practice of dissection was a Renaissance invention), revealing a Silenian congeries of associations, spilling into a cornucopia of sharp-tongued foxes.

In general, commentaries on the adages vary from a couple of sentences to long discursive essays spanning dozens of pages. They are like accordions: capable of synopsis and digression, compression and dilation, melody and harmony. Here is an example of the former:

*In canis podicem inspicere* / To look into a dog's anus (II.ii.36)

Aristophanes in the *Ecclesiazusae*: "I told him to go and look into a dog's anus." The scholiast informs us that this was commonly applied to near-slighted people, and he adds a trochaic line about peering up the breech of a bitch and three vixens. He alludes to it again in the *Acharnians:* "Blow up the dog's arse on your pipes of bone." The line is too obscene to give much pleasure to the translator. In fact, I could hardly bring myself to write out such rubbish, were I not determined to perform my allotted task at all points and, having received this Sparta as my portion, to do my best for her. (33:92)

The best response to an aphorism, especially a crude one, is of course another aphorism, especially a recondite one. The basic meaning of *Spartam nactus es, hanc orna* is that you put your country above yourself. This adage also turns out to be one of the long entries: "Sparta is your portion, do your best for her" (II.v.1), a pretext for a diatribe on bishops who act like "oriental princes," "fraudulent magistrates," and rulers who encroach on the territories of others (33:239–42). Others include "Make haste slowly" (II.i.1), an encomium about how *Festina lente* "arose in the ancient heart of philosophy," and no other proverb "so richly deserves to be inscribed on every pillar, written up over the gate of every church (yes, and in letters of gold!) ... be brought before the eye on all public buildings everywhere and become widespread and familiar, as something which ought ideally to be always in every man's mind and never very far from men's eyes" (33:3). It goes on to explain the hieroglyphic enigmas of adages, narrate an autobiography of their adventures in print, and praise the Aldine press, whose emblem of the dolphin twisted around an anchor exemplifies the oxymoron of the fast and slow (see fig. 4). The longest entry in the 1515 *Adages*, "War is sweet to those who have not tried it" (IV.i.1), is a fervent antiwar tract (35:399–440). These essays are Erasmus in his full glory: erudite, charming, judicious, polemical, garrulous, seamlessly synthesizing classical philology, biblical scholarship, theological disputation, passionate rhetoric, and ecclesiastical censure.

FIGURE 4. Aldus Manutius, printer's device, from
the title page of *Adagiorum Chiliades*, Venice, 1508.

Let us return to "*Sileni Alcibiadis*" (III.iii.1) and follow upon
its tracks. The commentary begins in a sober fashion, dutifully
laying out the ancient sources: the figure appears in the *Symposia*
of Xenophon and Plato as well as Athenaeus' *Deipnosophistae*.
Erasmus then gives examples from antiquity of those who are ugly
on the outside but beautiful within: Antisthenes, Diogenes, and
Epictetus. After this short three-page prelude, Erasmus pivots
from the classics to Christianity, calling Christ himself "a marvelous Silenus (if one may be allowed to use such language of Him)"
(34:264). He then talks about Christ's humanity and humility.
Above all, the simplicity and rudeness of his "philosophy" makes
him "worlds away from the principles laid down by philosophers
and from the reasoning of the world." The prophets, sacraments,
the Old Testament, knowledge: all these are Sileni figures.

Erasmus then sharply pivots and launches a full assault on the
hypocrisies of his contemporary church. The commentary turns
out to be less an exercise in unpacking Socratic Chinese boxes
than a cunning Trojan horse: a pretext for him to inveigh against

the simony, pride, lust, ambition, anger, impiety that he thinks is poisoning the clerics of the church. When the pontiffs are given wealth, "you give him at the same time all the troubles of accumulating wealth, a tyrant's bodyguard, troops in full armour, scouts, horses, mules, trumpets, warfare and carnage, triumph and tumult, treaties and battles." In the last paragraph, he writes:

> But whither has the flood of my language carried me away, so that I, who profess myself a mere compiler of proverbs, begin to be a preacher? Of course it was Alcibiades in his cups and his Sileni, that drew me into this very sober disputation. But I shall not be over-penitent for this error if what does not belong to an exposition of proverbs does belong to the amendment of life, if what does not contribute to learning contributes to religion, and if what in the light of the task I have undertaken may seem a sideline and "nothing to do with Dionysus" may prove not ill-adapted in the light of the life we have to live. (34:281–82)

This entry brilliantly demonstrates how for Erasmus classical erudition serves as an instrument of church reform. The purpose of studying an adage is not only to recover its historical genealogy, the frequency of its citation, or the cultural conditions from which it sprung; more importantly, studying an adage must be for the "amendment of life," "in the light of the life we have to live." Erasmus moves beyond the classroom and into the fraught stage of ecclesiastical politics. As a religious reformer he strives to renew the church and theology on the paradigm of the early church of the first centuries. ("Erasmus laid the egg that Luther hatched," according to one tag.) And his many controversies and correspondences amply show that he did not suffer fools gladly. It is no surprise that many conservative Catholic theologians opposed his humanism, and Erasmus was given a formal doctrinal censure by the University of Paris in 1531. Recall that one of the meanings of *aphorizō* in koine Greek is to excommunicate. Erasmus was never excommunicated, but the *Adages* were placed in the *Index of Prohibited Books* in 1559.[25]

## Infinite labor

A jewel, a seed, a Silenus figure—taken together, these form an iridescent, geminating, cryptic kaleidoscope that represents the adages' myriad possibilities. If their interpretation is infinite, so is collecting them. As Erasmus admits, "the enterprise was such as in itself would have no limits and therefore I felt it essential to measure the scale of it not by the logic of the task but by my own commitments." He complains of "the infinite labour required to seek out such small things everywhere ... they do not lie on the surface, but as a rule are buried, so that you have to dig them out before you can collect them" (34:171; III.i.1).

So the work of the *Adages* can never truly end. Erasmus praises Aldus Manutius for "building up a library which knows no walls than the world itself" (33:10; II.i.1). Erasmus' compilation and Aldus' publications are coextensive in the sense that both have an ambition for the infinite expansion of texts to be circulated in the republic of letters. Thus the genre of anthologies and florilegia creates a jagged continuum between the poverty and plentitude of antiquity, between the minimal aphorism and the maximal collection. And beginning with a single humble adage, there emerges in the myriad editions and translations of the early modern printing houses the dream of a total archive, a Borgesian infinite library.

## "Alexandrian culture"

This obsessive ethos of collecting can lapse into what Nietzsche would call an "Alexandrian" culture: an unhealthy, secondary, antiquarian mode of trying to preserve the old rather than create anew.[26] There is an unmistakable strand in the classical tradition of the know-it-all. We see this in the sprawling compilations of Pliny's *Natural Histories*, Zenobius' *Epitome*, Aulus Gellius' *Attic Nights*, Diogenes Laertius' *Lives of the Philosophers*, Athenaeus' *Deipnosophistae*, Plutarch's *Moralia*, Clement of Alexandria's *Stromata*, Macrobius' *Saturnalia*, Stobaeus' *Florilegium* and *Anthologium*, and the massive tenth-century Byzantine encyclopedia *Sudas*. Erasmus draws from most of these sources, but even he criticizes their heterogeneous nature: "There is so little agreement among these compilers that their work is often contradictory, with the result that a further weight is added to your labours" (34:173; III.i.1).

At the same time, there is within the classical tradition an equally strong stance against such bibliomania. This impulse was criticized as early as Heraclitus: "Much learning does not teach one to have intelligence; for it would have taught Hesiod and Pythagoras, and again, Xenophanes and Hecataeus" (DK B22 40). Didymus of Alexandria in the late first century BCE has a thirteen-volume collection, *Against the Authors of Proverb Collections* (now lost), in apparent criticism of earlier *paroimiographoi*. Callimachus contends, "big book, big evil" (*mega biblion, mega kakon*). Seneca writes that "a florilegium is fine for teaching children to memorize famous sayings, but adults should not rely on such means of knowledge" (*Ep.* 33.25). Petrarch's *De librorum copia* cautions that having too many books is a distraction (*Remedies for Fortune Fair and Foul* 1.43). Erasmus frequently admits to fatigue in amassing his text; he says it takes a labor of Hercules to inspect and analyze "all those poets in both languages, those grammarians, those orators, those dialecticians, those sophists, those historians, those mathematicians, those philosophers, those theologians, when the mere listing of their titles would exhaust a man" (34:173; III.i.1). Montaigne in "Of Pedantry" challenges the authority of the ancients and wonders why we can't speak for ourselves: "We know how to say 'Cicero says thus; such are the morals of Plato; these are the very words of Aristotle.' But what do we say ourselves? What do we judge? What do we do? A parrot could well say as much" (I:25; *The Complete Essays*, 100).[27]

As I mentioned in the introduction, there is a paradox regarding the individual and collective identity of aphorisms. By nature they are creatures that crave solitude. "The maxim is a hard, shiny—and fragile—object, like an insect's thorax," Roland Barthes remarks, "like an insect, too, the maxim possesses a sting, that hook of sharp-pointed words which conclude and crown it— which close it even as they arm it (the maxim is armed *because* it is closed)" ("La Rochefoucauld," 5). Allergic to any prolixity, its ambition is to silence every other utterance so that its singularity would shine all the more supreme.[28]

Yet aphorisms are also intensely social creatures. Indeed, they flourish not in spite but because of their residence in the cramped quarters of the anthology. From antiquity to the Middle Ages to the Renaissance, collections of proverbs were manifold. They all illustrate Umberto Eco's observation in *Infinity of Lists* about how the practice of inventory aims at the encyclopedic, at the self-contained, complete archive that summons the boundless, infinite nature of the universe. John Heywood, of the *Four PPs* fame, even composed a verse treatise on marriage with the satirical title, *A Dialogue Containing in Effect the Number of All the Proverbs in the English Tongue* (1546).

This brings us back to the one-versus-the-many problem at the heart of the hedgehog and fox aphorism. In short, aphorisms by their nature are supposed to condense, distill, purify; but in their composition and compilation they explode into a proliferation of verbal excesses. By the late sixteenth century, this reaches a cultural crisis: there is just too much to know.[29] So out of this welter of discourses, how do you cut through all this learned heap?

## A fresh start

Enter Francis Bacon (1561–1626). He too was a strident critic of this everything-but-the-kitchen-sink mentality. In the *Novum organum* (1620), he vividly writes that "when the barbarian flood burst into the Roman Empire and human learning suffered shipwreck, the philosophies of *Aristotle* and *Plato* were, like timbers of lighter and less solid matter, saved from time's breakers" (1.77).[30] A favorite metaphor in Western thought is the shipwreck with spectator.[31] Described in a famous passage of Lucretius, the spectator from an elevated vantage looks calmly at the shipwreck and feels relieved that he is not part of the catastrophe (2.1–19). In the early modern period, this is allegorized as the calamity of history perceived as a mere speck from the privileged perspective of the modern individual. But Bacon audaciously overturns the commonplace of tradition as a shipwreck: "time (like a river) carrying down to us matter lighter and full of wind, while letting the heavier and solid stuff sink" (1.71). He playfully—and unkindly—reduces all of ancient learning to nothing but flotsam and jetsam, saved only by virtue of its density relative to the waters of history.

The obsessive "Alexandrian" need to collect everything is critiqued in the *Advancement of Learning* (1605):

> ANTIQVITIES, or Remnants of History, are, as was saide, *tanquam Tabula Naufragij*, when industrious persons by an exact and scrupulous diligence and obseruation, out of Monuments, Names, Wordes, Prouerbes, Traditions, Priuate Recordes, and Euidences, Fragments of stories, Passages of Bookes, that concerne not storie, and the like, doe saue and recouer somewhat from the deluge of time. (*OFB* 4:66)

Bacon is mostly likely referring to antiquarians such as William Camden, John Speed, and John Stow.[32] But the aqueous images of the "deluge of time" and *naufragium* connect back to the metaphor of Aristotle and Plato as nothing but the floating wreckage in the sea of history as well as to Aristotle's remark, via Synesius and Erasmus, on the strewn ruins of humanity with which we began this chapter. Here Bacon's famously suspicious view of antiquity is plain to see: what holds scholars back from progress in the sciences has been the veneration, "the almost spell-bound reverence for antiquity." Bacon regards most learning as nothing but "endless repetitions ... men keep doing and saying the same things." His instructions to the budding scientist in *Parasceve* reads like an explicit rejection of the Erasmian model: "all that concerns ornaments of speech, similitudes, treasury of eloquence and such like emptinesses," he declares, "let it be utterly dismissed" (Spedding 8:359).

"To speak the truth," he says, "antiquity, as we call it, is the young state of the world; for those times are ancient when the world is ancient; and not those we vulgarly account ancient by computing backwards; so that the present time is the real antiquity" (*De augmentis scientiarum,* Spedding 6:lv). But underneath Bacon's sonorous rejection lies a hidden debt to ancient wisdom. Scholarship in the last generation has amply demonstrated that Bacon's enterprise—and early modern scientific culture at large—would have been impossible without the humanist revival of classical learning.[33] And Reformation interpretations of scripture had a profound influence on the scientific interpretation of nature.[34] Be that as it may, acknowledging the way in which Bacon was indebted to the earlier Renaissance tradition only underscores his radical departure from it.

Bacon's concept of the hidden nature of the things is drawn from the Presocratic and biblical traditions. He agrees with Heraclitus that nature loves to hide: "nature's recesses still conceal many secrets [*recondita*] of excellent use" (*N.O.* 1.109). In the same way that we must scrutinize and seek for meaning in the Bible, we must also do the same for the meaning in nature. Bacon rewrites Proverbs 24:2 when he declares, "The glorie of God is to conceale a thing, But the glorie of the King is to find it out" (*OFB* 4:36).

Like Erasmus, Bacon too believed that the aphorism would stir readers to contemplate and inquire further. But unlike Erasmus, Bacon maintains that this process of discovery is accomplished not through endlessly combing through the library of the ancients but rather by interrogating the book of the world. Therefore there can be no doubt that Bacon and Erasmus were engaged in fundamentally opposite enterprises: one wanted to transmit old knowledge, the other wanted to create new ones. And whereas

Erasmus celebrates the *copia* of rhetoric, Bacon celebrates the *copia* of nature. But this abundance is not always apparent: "Nature's secrets [*occulta Naturæ*] betray themselves more through the vexations of art than they do in their usual course" (*N.O.* 1.98). The aphorism—this sharpest of the rhetorical forms—becomes the best prying instrument to extract nature's innards.

Bacon seeks to bypass the epistemological crisis brought on by the humanist accumulation of commonplaces. First, we have seen how the obsessive search for ancient fragments can lead to a musty sort of antiquarianism. Second, Bacon warns that when men became excessively concerned with eloquence, then they "began to hunt more after wordes, than matter, and more after the choisenesse of the Phrase, and the round and cleane composition of the sentence, and the sweet falling of the clauses" (*OFB* 4:22). Third, the aphorism can become too fixed and reductive. He accuses both humanist and scholastic authorities of preaching from the pulpit "for the most part Magistrall and peremptorie"; the knowledge they peddle is only to be "soonest beleeued" but "not easilest examined" (4:31). These aphorisms are nothing but dogmatic soundbites that the student merely regurgitates.

Bacon's great task is to transport the capacious form of the aphorism from the kingdom of the *trivium* to the empire of the *quadrivium*. In other words, whereas for Erasmus the aphorism is the object of theological, philological and philosophical study, for Bacon the aphorism is the instrument of empirical, inductive, and scientific study. By evacuating the aphorism from its rhetorical inheritance and recasting it as the "pyth and heart of Sciences" (4:124), Bacon frames the aphorism as an invitation to participate in the enterprise of modern inquiry: "The instauration must be built up from the deepest foundations, unless we want to go round in circles forever, with progress little or pitiable" (*N.O.* 1.31). Though Bacon boldly announces such new beginnings, many of his ambitious projects were unfinished. We shall see how he too had trouble reconciling "fragments" and "systems."

## Heap of particulars

The lord chancellor is an avid theoretician and practitioner of the genre.[35] When we survey his polymathic oeuvre—which encompassed everything from ethics, statecraft, history, biography, law, religion, medicine, myth, and religion—the microform is everywhere. His practice and theory began in his humanist education, developed in his political career, and became fully realized in his scientific work. As a student at Cambridge, he kept a commonplace book called *Promus of Formularies and Elegancies* (ca. 1594). His early *Essayes* (1597), like those of Montaigne, abound in sententiae. The *Maxims of the Law* (ca. 1597, published 1630) attempted to derive legal principles from the axioms of natural philosophy. In the *Advancement of Learning* (1605), he devotes the latter pages to glossing the "sentences politic" of Solomon.

In the great *Novum organum* (1620), the aphorism becomes nothing less than the structuring principle of the text. Its first book is composed of "aphorisms concerning the interpretation of nature and the kingdom of man," and the second book of "aphorisms on the composition of the primary history." In the *Parasceve* (1623, tellingly "the day of preparation before the Jewish Sabbath"), there are aphorisms on how to lay the groundwork for natural and experimental histories. Similar to the end of *Advancement*, book 8 of the *De augmentis* (1623) contains explications of thirty-four "excellent civil precepts and cautions," mostly from Proverbs and Ecclesiastes. The year before his death, Bacon published *Apophthegms New and Old* (1625). Thus he never abandoned rhetoric; it is rather reappropriated, radically and completely, in the service of science. His posthumous *Sylva Sylvarum* (1627), dubbed "an Indigested Heap of Particulars" by his chaplain and editor William Rawley (Spedding 4:156), is a scientific miscellany organized into ten "centuries" and subdivided into one hundred fragmentary paragraphs or "experiments."

### Against method

So much of Bacon's writings are metawritings: he writes on why he writes, what he has written, what he is going to write (like Pascal in the next chapter). In these meditations he invariably turns again and again to the power of the aphorism. In *Filum labyrinthi*, he states, "Antiquity used to deliver the knowledge which the mind of man had gathered, in observations, aphorisms, or short and dispersed sentences, or small tractates of some parts that they had diligently meditated and labored; which did invite men, both to ponder that which was invented, and to add and supply *further*" (Spedding 6:418–19). In the *Maxims of the Law*, he states: "This delivery of knowledge in distinct and disjoined aphorisms doth leave the wit of man more free to turn and toss, and to make use of that which is so delivered to more several purposes and applications" (Spedding 7:321). The goal of Bacon's aphorisms is to stimulate the "wit of man" to "turn and toss" more freely, so that he can "add and supply further" to the sum of knowledge.

Whereas an Erasmian aphorism spurs a philologist to discover the truths of *human* history, the Baconian aphorism catalyzes a scientist to discover the truths of *natural* history.[36] His new conception of aphorisms provides an open horizon of investigations rather than a closed system of accumulated knowledge. To this end Bacon consistently contrasts aphorisms with methods:

> Another diuersitie of METHODE, whereof the consequence is great, is the deliuerie of knowledge in APHORISMES, or in METHODES; wherein wee may obserue, that it hath beene too much taken into Custome, out of a fewe *Axiomes* or Obseruations, vppon any Subiecte, to make a solemne, and formall Art; filling it with some Discourses, and illustrating it with Examples; and digesting it into a sensible *Methode*: But the writing in APHORISMES, hath manye excellent vertues, whereto the writing in *Methode* doth not approach.

> For first, it tryeth the Writer, whether hee be superficiall
> or solide: For *Aphorismes*, except they should bee ridiculous,
> canot bee made but of the pyth and heart of Sciences....
>
> And lastlye *Aphorismes,* representing a knowledge broken,
> doe invite men to enquire further; whereas *Methods* carrying
> the show of a Total, do secure men; as if they were at furthest.
> (*Advancement of Learning, OFB* 4:124)

What does "method" mean here? One might legitimately ask, doesn't Bacon himself have a method? We must be careful to consider the pre-Cartesian sense of "method," for questions of order and discourse were much debated before the French philosopher.[37] The "method" here refers to the two reigning discourses of the period: first, the logical method—derived from the Scholastics in their reception of Aristotle's *Organon*; second, the dialectical method, as developed by Petrus Ramus' *Dialecticae institutiones*. Ramus' innovation was, among many other things, the reduction of entire systems of thought to a simple order and easily memorized epitome.[38]

In short, the aphorisms of Bacon come *after and against* these two great "systems." He sought to debunk both the immense medieval inheritance of the *Organon* and the newfangled, one-size-fits-all pedagogy of Ramus. Ramus is that "pestilent bookworm, that begetter of handy manuals. Any facts he gets hold of and begins to squeeze in the rack of summary method soon lose their truth, which oozes or skips away, leaving him to garner only dry and barren trifles" ("The Masculine Birth of Time," in Farrington, *Philosophy of Francis Bacon,* 64). The Aristotelians fared no better in Bacon's eyes. The Greek philosopher is but a "mere bondservant to his logic," his followers "crafty triflers who ... spun out for us the countless quibbles of the Schools." Dialectic is but a degenerate and corrupt" mode of sophistical "juggling" (63). Citing by name Anaxagoras, Leucippus, Democritus, Parmenides, Empedocles, and Heraclitus, Bacon claims that these early Greek thinkers are far superior to the flimsy dialectics of Aristotle because they are guided by observations and have "something of the natural philosopher about them and smack of the nature of things, experience and bodies" (*N.O.* 1.63). Hippocrates too is elsewhere praised: "He was a man of wisdom as well as learning, much given to experiments and observation, not striving after words or methods, but picking out the very nerves of science and so setting them forth" (Spedding 10:63).

## Between aphorisms and axioms

Indeed, the very title of the *Novum organum* throws down an unambiguous gauntlet in its ambition to replace the old Aristotelian *Organon*. For Bacon, the problem is that the Ramian and Aristotelian methods presuppose that knowledge is already complete and thus can be nicely packaged and dispensed like a vending machine. In contrast, Bacon wants his readers' minds to "toss and turn" in order to create new scientific inquiries that open uncharted domains of knowledge:

> There are and can only be two ways of investigating and discovering truth. The one rushes up from the sense and particulars to axioms of the highest generality and, from these principles and their indubitable truth, goes on to infer and discover middle axioms; and this is the way in current use. The other way draws axioms from the sense and particulars by climbing steadily and by degrees so that it reaches the ones of highest generality last of all; and this is the true but still untrodden way. (*N.O.* 1:19)

In other words, the first way is that of Aristotle's syllogisms, the second way his principle of induction. Bacon's "true" way of science moves in "gradual and unbroken ascent" from observations to experiments to axioms back to the things themselves. Yet as we will see, Bacon does not often follow his own advice, as his experimental "histories" are not systematic and exhaustive but rather proceed by leaps and jumps, guided by instinct and intuition and inspiration.

As such the presentation of one's research in the "knowledge broken" of aphorisms is the best way to provoke other minds to embark on further experimentation. Aphorisms destabilize the reigning epistemologies so that the scientist can directly interrogate the particulars or *specialia* of Nature itself without the interference of superannuated authorities. Aphorisms and axioms come to constitute an ever-expanding network that captures the feedback loop of knowledge creation.[39] This is precisely why the architectonics of the *Novum organum* is aphoristic. This is how he announces the unfinished second book:

PARTUS SECVNDAE

SVMMA,

DIGESTA

IN

APHORISMOS

[Summary of the

second part

digested

in

aphorisms]

Yet when we read the aphorisms in the text, they do not appear to be aphorisms in the conventional sense of scattered statements or unconnected thoughts. They are not very "pithy" either. If one were to remove the numbers, they would be read as typical early modern English prose, since they are ordered by virtue of discursive paragraphs. My sense is that what makes Bacon's writing aphoristic is not so much its formal properties as much as its function to "invite men to enquire further."

For example, in book 2, he launches into an investigation of heat. He presents a table of twenty-eight "instances" marked by "the existence and presence" of heat (2.11), then thirty-one instances "where the nature of heat is absent" (2.12), and finally forty-one instances when heat increases or decreases (2.13). Here is one from the third grouping:

> The anvil is heated a great deal by the hammer, so much so that if the anvil were made of thin plate, I suppose that it would grow red like red-hot iron from heavy and repeated hammer blows; but let this be tested by experiment. [*sed de hoc fiat Experimentum*] (2.13.31)

In this compressed form we see an observation, a hypothesis, and then an invitation for further study. When confronted with these examples, the best thing to do, he repeats in the next paragraph, is *"Perform an Experiment or Investigate further" (Fiat Experimentum, vel Inquiratur vlteriús; 2.14)*. In comparison to the many other aphorisms we've seen, there is certainly nothing very heroic, enigmatic, or mystical about this. But that is precisely the point— its interpretation is practical rather than contemplative.

In the *Novum organum,* each aphoristic paragraph thus contributes to the overarching plan, forethought, and trajectory of Bacon's architectonic thinking. By casting his discursive prose as aphorisms, Bacon pins together all that is crucial to his enterprise: the relationship between particulars and generalities; the principles of observation and induction; the order of discovery and the order of presentation. Instead of giving the appearance of an encyclopedic *summa*, impressive and magisterial as a definitive monument, the "fragmentary" aphorisms provide only a provisional blueprint, an invitation for the reader to participate in the construction of an entirely new "system" of science. If Erasmus is a hedgehog who ended up as a fox, Bacon is fox who wants to be a hedgehog.

## The open sea

We are now in a position to give a new interpretation of the *Novum organum*'s famous frontispiece (see fig. 5).[40] As we have seen, the aphorism is an epistemological vector that points to the horizon of thinking, and Bacon is fond of using shipwreck imageries. Within the text he explicitly draws the connection between geographic and epistemic discoveries: "Nor should this fact count for nothing: that by prolonged voyages and journeys (which have become prevalent in our times) many things in nature have been disclosed and found out which could shed new light on philosophy. And surely it would be a disgrace to mankind if, while the expanses of the material globe, i.e. of lands, seas, and stars, have in our times been opened up and illuminated, the limits of the intellectual globe were not pushed beyond the narrow confines of the ancients' discoveries" (1.84). In the engraving, the most prominent element is the ship between the Pillars of Hercules. Its direction is curious: the hull is pointed toward the columns, signifying a return to society, but the sails are being blown *backward*. One might read it as the continuous voyage of arrivals and departures, or perhaps its suspension. But then there is also a smaller ship that usually escapes attention. It is approaching the horizon that spreads across the middle of the engraving, close to the left column. For me, this *navicella* is laden with aphorisms and axioms. Cutting through the choppy waters, she signifies the voyage of the new science, burdened with risk and contingency.

It too may suffer the same shipwreck as the ancients. Yet the horizon toward which the ship sails seems calm and promising. As its etymology suggests, *aphorizein* means to mark the earthly boundary, the *horos,* between the known and the unknown. A horizon has no beginning or end, no departures or arrivals. Wherever you sail, there is always a new one. It is both transcendent and immanent.[41] Nietzsche would write centuries later, "*In the horizon of the infinite.*—We have left the land and have embarked. We have burned our bridges behind us—indeed, we have gone farther and destroyed the land behind us. Now, little ship, look out!" (*Gay Science* §124). In the Baconian enterprise, aphorisms are no longer the flotsam and jetsam of antiquity but the navigational vectors that point toward the infinite horizon of natural philosophy.

FIGURE 5. Francis Bacon, *Novum Organon*, frontispiece, London, 1620.

## Romance of the system

The problem for us remains how to reconcile the nonmethodical aphorisms with the ambitious six-part architectonics of the *Instauratio magna*. It is announced in the "Plan of the Work," in the beginning of *Novum organum*:

> The first: The Partitions of the Sciences.
> The second: *Novum Organum,*
>     or Directions concerning the Interpretation of Nature.
> The third: The Phenomena of the Universe,
>     or Natural and Experimental History for the building
>       up of Philosophy.
> The fourth: The Ladder of the Intellect.
> The fifth: Precursors, or Anticipations of the Philosophy
>       to Come.
> The sixth: The Philosophy to Come, or The Active
>       Science.
>
> (*OFB* 11:27)

The Oxford editors call the *Instauratio magna* a "massive, unfinished meta-work" (11:xix).[42] Part 1 is realized in *De augmentis scientiarum* (1623), an autopsy of the deficiencies of current knowledge and the ways to ameliorate them. We have explored how part 2, *Novum organum* (1620), is a comprehensive program for the rebuilding of philosophy. Yet Bacon did not finish its conclusion. The rest are in fragments or nonexistent. Part 3 would have been collections of natural-historical data for the reconstruction of scientific knowledge. *History of winds* (1622), *History of life and death* (1623), and *History of density and rarity* (post-1658) are three of the six planned histories. Of the remaining three parts, part 4 would have been a practical demonstration of the hypothetical precepts of part 2. Sketches exist in manuscript but were not discovered until the 1980s. Part 5 was to be a repository of provisional theories and hypotheses. Only a short preface exists. There is no surviving work at all that testifies to the contents of part 6.

As such, the *Instauratio magna* appears to us as a monumental ruin, a halted prologue to experiments never completed, interminable inquiries never embarked upon. Northrop Frye once wrote of Edmund Spenser that he "is not a poet of fragments, like Coleridge. He thinks inside regular frameworks—the twelve months, the nine muses, the seven deadly sins—and he goes on filling up his frame even when his scheme is mistaken from the beginning" ("The Structure of Imagery in *The Faerie Queene*," 153–54). Spenser's exuberant synthesis is bound to collapse because its ability is incommensurate to its ambition. In his desire to construct an encyclopedic system of allegories, the poet frustratingly fails to achieve any sense of finality: he only finished six of the twelve envisioned books (and a fragment of the seventh) of his epic romance. Twenty-four years after Spenser's 1596 poem, the *Novum organum* appears. Its title page boldly declares: "It is not yet set out as a finished treatise" (*tamen in Corpore tractatùs iusti, OFB* 11:48–49). At the end of the book's first part, the author already admits: "I have nevertheless no universal or systematic theory" (*Theoriam nullam vniuersalem, aut integram; N.O.* 1.116). Bacon's *Instauratio magna* is the *Faerie Queene* of natural philosophy.

## The unfinishable

One way to interpret Bacon's multitude of aphorisms within his visionary system is through the category of the *desiderata*. Vera Keller argues that early modern "wish lists"—for flexible glass, diving bells, burning mirrors, longitude, solutions for squaring the cube, the philosopher's stone, the Alkahest (a universal solvent), perpetual motion—link the desire for social improvement to the advancement of knowledge (*Knowledge and the Public Interest, 1575–1725*). Bacon's wish lists appear frequently, in the 1623 *De augmentis* as "The New World of Sciences, or Desiderata," the end of *Novum organum*, *History of winds*, *History of life and death*, and most spectacularly in the "centuries" of the *Sylva Sylvarum*.

He is fascinated by the velocity of air: "Let all kinds of prognostics of winds be collected with satisfactory diligence" (*OFB* 12:29). He wants to know the "precise calculation of the quantity of matter and how it is distributed through bodies" (13:37). He seeks to uncover the causes of the longevity and brevity of life: "In Bedlam Hospital on the outskirts of London, which was set up for the care and custody of the insane, we find from time to time many long-lived mad people" (12:219). Why are apples red, leaves green, lilies white (Spedding 4:393–96)? Why do cucumbers become "more tender and dainty" if their seeds are dipped in milk (4:461)? Collectively, the late works sketch out an *abecedarium* of "particular histories," catalogs or epitomes of natural inquiries—arranged aphoristically—that expand the realm of human knowledge.

In the brief preface to part 5, "Precursors *or* Anticipations of the Philosophy to Come," Bacon writes that "I have decided to scatter [*spargere*] the thoughts themselves and not connect them by rhetorical method." Indeed, the inquiries in *History of Density and Rarity* are entitled "Scattered History," *Historia sparsa* (*OFB* 13:74–75). Rather than impose an artificial order on things under investigation, he seeks to present a "free inquiry" (*inquisitionem liberam*) of natural philosophy that respects the particularity of things (13:264–65). Knowledge does not advance through the clean linearity of a codified "method"; rather, experience must be "broken and grinded" (Spedding 2:336). And since scientific explanations are fallible and undergo revision, aphorisms are the best way to express the contingencies of experiential truth.

Recognizing that the establishment of a new science cannot be borne by one person, Bacon is happy to "sow seeds of a purer truth [*semina veritatis sincerioris*] for the generations to come" (*N.O.* 1.116). In the utopian *New Atlantis*, the culmination of his vision is "Salomon's House"—an enormous, well-endowed research institute dedicated to ever-advancing knowledge: "the merchants of light" crisscross the globe to gather data; "the mystery men" conduct experiments in the liberal and mechanical arts; "the depredators" look into the archives of the past; "the pioneers or miners" try out new experiments. Higher up are the "lamps" who evaluate the data collected from below in order to generate more advanced experiments. At the summit is a supercommittee—"the interpreters of nature"—that turns these empirical facts into "greater observations, axioms, and aphorisms," the crown jewels of his inductive philosophy (Spedding 5:409–11).

One imagines the scientists in Salomon's House conducting the experiments that are proposed in the *Sylva*. These include everything from "turning air into water," "exercise of the body, and the benefits or evils thereof," to "causes of putrefaction" (4:480, 482, 483; 5:167).[43] Here is an amusing one:

*Experiment in solitary touching yawning.*

685. It hath been noted by the ancients, that it is dangerous to pick one's ear whilst he yawneth. The cause is, for that in yawning the inner parchment of the ear is extended, by the drawing in of the spirit and breath; for in yawning and sighing both, the spirit is first strongly drawn in, and then strongly expelled. (4:464)

This gives us a glimpse into the aphoristic operations of natural history. The classical source is from Aristotle (*Problems* 32.13). Bacon then provides an explanation that has to do with human physiognomy—and this is just one of the one thousand medical, botanic, chemical, meteorological, and geological curiosities to be investigated.[44]

As such, aphorisms are thereby infinite because the end of science—to comprehend and conquer all natural phenomena—is an endless task. Bacon's work is finally, and always, unfinished and unfinishable. Incompleteness constitutes its very DNA. The title page of *The New Atlantis*, published posthumously in 1627 as an appendage to the *Sylva Sylvarum*, announces that it is "A Worke unfinished" (5:357). Likewise, the headnote of the *Faerie Queene*'s last canto reads "vnperfite." Rawley in the preface writes that "Certainly the model is more vast and high than can possibly be imitated in all things" (5:358). The paths—*Holzwege*—through the "forest of forests" are long and dark.[45]

Explaining the apparently random nature of the *Sylva Sylvarum*, also incomplete, Rawley writes:

> I have heard his lordship say also, that one great reason why he would not put these particulars into any exact method (though he that looketh attentively into them shall find that they have a secret order) was because he conceived that other men would now think that they could do the like, and so go on with a further collection; which, if the method had been exact, many would have despaired to attain by imitation. (4:157–58)

If Erasmus' *Adagia* is a multidecade project whose *telos* is infinite, so much more so is Bacon's *Instauratio magna*. Both men were engaged in "infinite labors."

## End of knowledge

As with Erasmus, the continual publications of Bacon's works form a fundamental part of his project. The Dutch humanist wanted to construct the total library of antiquity through adages, whereas the English lord chancellor's project was to construct the laboratory of modernity, its progress presented in the propagation of research projects. Walter Benjamin writes that the baroque aesthetic is "to pile up fragments ceaselessly, without any strict idea of a goal, and in the unremitting expectation of a miracle, to take the repetition of stereotypes for a process of intensification" (*Origin of German Tragic Drama*, 178).

In contrast to Aristotle, whose natural philosophy is ultimately theoretical, for Bacon, natural philosophy is ultimately practical. He is not content only in trying to understand nature but instead seeks to transform it—his memorable image is that we must wrestle and pin down nature like Proteus.[46] More pointedly, Baconian science intervenes in the operations of nature in order to help human beings: "The true ends of knowledge" presuppose "that we seek it not for personal gratification, or for contention, or to look down on others, or for convenience, reputation, or power, or any such inferior motive, but for the benefit and use of life, and that it be perfected and regulated in charity" (*N.O.* preface, *OFB* 11:23). Here, too, the aphorism reveals its ethical dimension. Bacon's natural philosophy in many ways is based on his moral philosophy, for both must combine practice and theory. Aphorism cleaves to both realms, for its purpose, after all, is its application after reading. Science as a collective enterprise must ultimately be beneficial to society. If Galileo's Book of Nature is written by God in numbers, Bacon's Book of Nature is an open-source program, a wiki for all users who know how to code in endless aphorisms.

# 5

# Pascal

## THE FRAGMENTS OF INFINITY

"Many of the works of the ancients have become fragments. Many modern works are fragments as soon as they are written," Schlegel states in the *Athenaeum Fragments* (§24). By this definition, the *Pensées* of Pascal would be fragments at their birth. During the last ten years of the French thinker's short life (1623–62), by which time he had abandoned his earlier scientific studies and turned his attention exclusively to religious matters, his first biographer records that "he would grab the first piece of paper that he could find in his hand, on which he noted his thought in a few words, often in even half a word, because he was only writing for himself, he did this so as to not tire his spirit, and so he only put what was necessary to remind him of the ideas and opinions that he had" (Lafuma 24–25; Ariew xii). Later, he would cut and sew these sheets into different bundles (*liasses*). In either 1658 or 1660, Pascal organized his writings into a core set of twenty-seven bundles, and seven were set aside as extraneous.[1]

When Pascal died in 1662, the fact that these writings still remained in heaps—more than eight hundred notes—caused much

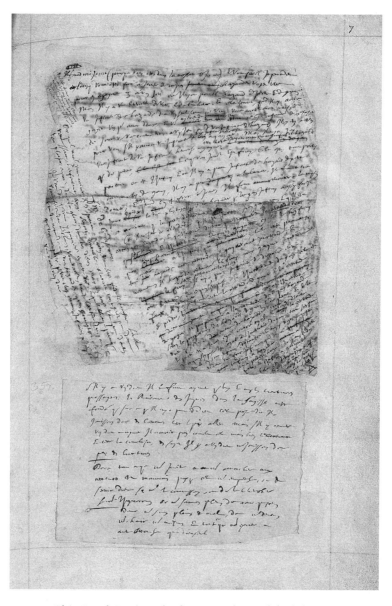

FIGURE 6. Blaise Pascal, *Pensées sur la religion,* recueil original, fonds français 9202, Bibliothèque Nationale, Paris.

perturbation for his survivors (see fig. 6). His *Nachlass* was an assault on the classical sensibilities of the late seventeenth century, a world that sought order in all things—decorum in behavior, neatness in arrangement, and, above all, clarity in thinking.[2]

In other words, the philology of the Pascalian *Nachlass* has its epistemological roots in Cartesian philosophy. The textual editors' insistence on a systematic order and a "clear and coherent" presentation is founded on the authority of none other than the one who so famously advocated for "clear and certain" thinking in all matters of inquiry. From the time of Descartes, clarity and order became the *sine qua non* of French thinking: "concerning objects proposed for study, we ought to investigate what we can clearly and evidently intuit or deduce with certainty," the philosopher asserts in his *Rules for the Direction of Our Native Intelligence* (Rule 3). In the posthumous 1670 edition of the *Pensées*, Étienne Périer, Pascal's nephew and editor, confesses almost apologetically, "the most perfect thoughts, those most ordered, clear, and developed [*les pensées plus parfaites, plus suivies, plus claires et plus étendues*], were mixed in and, as it were, lost among so many other imperfect, obscured, and half-digested ones [*imparfaites, obscures, à demi digérées*]—some almost unintelligible to anyone other than the person who wrote them" (Lafuma 25; Ariew xii). For more than 350 years—from Pascal's first editors to a host of modern-day ones—no one has disagreed that his writings are hopelessly disorganized and deeply enigmatic.

Périer's preface illuminates the *Pensées*' inchoate genesis and subsequent reconstitutions. He recounts the massive labor with which the editorial team was faced:

> The first thing we did was to have them copied such as they were and in the same confusion in which we had found them. But when we saw them in this state, with greater facility to read them and to examine them than when they were in their original state, they seemed at first so infirm, so badly thought

out, and most of them so ill-explained that for a long time we did not think at all to publish them. (Lafuma 24; Ariew xii)

This long time would last eight years. The *Pensées de Monsieur Pascal sur la religion et sur quelques autres sujets, qui ont esté trouvées après sa mort parmy ses papiers* was eventually published in 1670 in what is known as the Port-Royal edition. The editors had considerable difficulty in deciding what to do:

> The first [way] that came to mind, and the one that was no doubt the easiest, was to have the fragments published immediately in the state in which we found them. But soon we judged that to do it that way would be to lose almost the whole fruit for which we could hope....
>
> There was another way to give these writings to the public, which was to work on them beforehand: to illuminate the obscure thoughts, to complete the incomplete ones, and, taking into account Pascal's aim in all these fragments, to supplement in some way the work he intended to accomplish. This way was assuredly the most perfect, but also the most difficult to execute well. We decided on that path and began, in fact, to work on it. But in the end we rejected it as we did the first path, because we thought that it was almost impossible to enter very well into the thought and aim of an author, especially that of a dead author; and that we would not be giving the work of Pascal, but a completely different work.
>
> Thus, to avoid the disadvantages in these two ways of producing these writings, we have chosen a middle path, which we have followed in this collection. Among the great numbers of thoughts, we have taken only the ones that seemed clearest and most complete [*les plus claires et les plus achevées*], and have given them such as we have found them without adding anything to them; except that, instead of their being without sequence, without linkage, and dispersed confusedly [*sans suite, sans liaison, et dispersés confusément*] at various places,

we have put them in some sort of an order and placed under the same title those that were about the same subjects, and we have suppressed all the others that were either too obscure or too imperfect. (Lafuma 24–25; Ariew xii–xiii)

At least in their self-presentation, Périer's team was nothing if not conscientious. Their three strategies indicate three different methods of textual criticism: the minimalist, the maximalist, and the middle path. They ask the questions fundamental to the task of any editor: how do you "enter into the thought and aim of an author"? What should be the level of intervention? What are the ethics of "suppressing" writing that is "too obscure or too imperfect"?

In truth, as recent scholarship has demonstrated, the Port-Royal editors were heavy-handed interventionists.[3] They sought to make Pascal's thoughts into an apologetics for Jansenism, a heretical movement that emphasized the depravity of human nature, grace for only the elect, and the denial of free will in the course of salvation. An influential member of the *comité* was Pierre Nicole, who had co-authored with Antoine Arnauld the textbook *Port-Royal Logic* (1662), a Cartesian application of Aristotelian logic.[4] He also did a Cartesian application of Pascal: the rough edges of the *pensées* were polished to be clear-cut, bite-sized maxims; the discontinuous made continuous; various *liasses* suppressed; the passages critiquing the Jesuits censored; rational demonstrations of faith preferred over the mysterious revelations of belief.

Like the Confucian commentators, the followers of Pascal did with the text as they pleased (we shall examine other editions later). The master's words are so opaque, vast, and profound that they can be made to fit any discourse. Pascal's writings thus present us with a test case for most of this book's preoccupations: the nature of aphorisms, the methodology of organizing fragments, the relationship between parts and wholes. His focus on the hidden and the revealed God brings us back to the *Gospel of*

*Thomas*. Moreover, what is the relationship between the presentation of inquiry and its order? What is a work in progress? What is a finished piece of writing?

## Against Cartesian certitude

While textual criticism of the *Pensées* is grounded in the criterion of Cartesian decorum, my argument is that Pascal's *Pensées* is a repudiation of Cartesian philosophy. There are a number of excellent studies that document the encounter between the two thinkers.[5] For my purposes, I'm interested in how the Pascalian practice of the fragment is, in large part, a direct consequence of his rejection of the Cartesian insistence on order and clarity.

Descartes, like many other philosophers, begins his inquiry by way of "considerations and maxims" (*Discourse on the Method* §1.3). His purpose is to give "precepts," not so much to "teach the method which everyone must follow in order to direct his reasons correctly, but only to reveal how I have tried to direct my own" (§1.4). In his initial thought experiment, he binds himself to a "provisional moral code" expressed in "three of four maxims" (§3.23). His early *Rules for the Direction of the Mind* is written as a set of short instructions. Many of the chapters in the *Discourse on the Method* and the *Meditations* are about the same length as the fragments of Pascal. So one could make the case that Descartes is a *maximist*. I say *maximist* and not *aphorist* because there is something indubitably didactic about Descartes' approach—he loves definitions, rules, instructions, whereas an aphorist like Pascal is much more enigmatic and indirect. Descartes arrives at an architectonic structure, whereas Pascal's execution is much more wobbly, given to hesitations and ruptures.

Pascal's principal criticism of Descartes is that he reduces philosophy to a rational, all-too-rational system. For Pascal, the proposition "I think, therefore I am" rests on shaky grounds, for this self that Descartes posits to be the foundation of all reasoning is but an impoverished thing: "what a novelty [*nouveauté*], what a monster, what chaos ... weak [*imbécile*] earthworm; repository of truth, and sewer of uncertainty and error; the glory and garbage of the universe!" (s164/L131). The glorious heap that makes up the *Pensées* might then be conceived of as a monumental rejection of Cartesian reason's supreme confidence in itself. Pascal believes, on one hand, in the finitude of the self and, on the other, in the infinities of space, time, number, and God, so that the human is suspended between the "two abysses of the infinite and nothingness" (s230/L199).[6] He eagerly embraces the swarming multiplicities of the self rather than reduce them to the fallacy of a single, fixed axiom.

The famous fragment—"The heart has its reasons of which reason does not know" (*Le cœur a ses raisons, que la raison ne connaît point;* s680/L423)—is precisely the opposite of the Cartesian insistence on having clear and distinct ideas. Descartes' last philosophical work, *The Passions of the Soul* (1649), reduced the origins of the motions of the soul to a "little gland in the brain" and rejected the scholastic claim that the seat of the passions is in the heart. The problem for Pascal is that this scientific reductionism "speaks of corporeal things in spiritual terms, and of spiritual things in corporeal terms." He writes that "We know truth, not only through reason, but also through the heart" (s142/L110). This *cœur* is not to be taken in the Romantic sense of a spontaneous outpouring of emotion but rather in the sense of intuition, the faculty that allows us to have direct apprehension of the "first principles"—space, time, motion, number (thus anticipating the Kantian categories).[7] These first principles cannot be derived through reason, only intuited by the heart. And since all demonstrative or analytical knowledge rests upon these first principles, the heart in truth precedes reason in the order of inquiry.

Yet as Pascal insists time and again, space and time and number and God are infinite. The fragment "Disproportion of Man" is a probing meditation on how the human is but an "imperceptible trace" in relation to the immensity of the cosmos. To the things of the very small (a mite, an atom), however, he can be considered a "colossus, a world, or rather a whole, with respect to the nothingness beyond our reach" (s230/L199). Contrary to Descartes' confidence in human reason, Pascal's belief is that the intellect can never comprehend everything, for what is finite can never approach the infinite: "The infinite number of things is so hidden from us that what is expressible in speech or thoughts is only an invisible trace of it" (s230/L199). Here, then, at the dawn of philosophical modernity, the quavering Pascalian aphorism is poised after and against the confidence of Cartesian certitude.

## The salon and the sacred

Besides its quarrel with Descartes' method, the *Pensées* of Pascal can also be viewed from the legacy of the *mondanité* of social observation and religious critique. The great moralists of the day—La Rochefoucauld, La Fontaine, and La Bruyère—are all about sociability, etiquette, and wit in the frothy ambience of elite social networks. The glittering salons of the Marquise de Rambouillet, Madame de la Sablière, and Marquise de Sablé provide us with untranslatable words such as *honnêté, politesse, amour-propre,* and *mondain*.[8] Though he did at times frequent these societies, one cannot but imagine Pascal in his immense solitude rejecting all this: "Man's unhappiness arises from one thing alone: that he cannot remain quietly in his room" (s168/L136).

On the religious side, the succinct style was also in wide circulation. One can point to such examples as the novelist Charles Sorel's *Pensées chrétiennes* (1634), St. François de Sales' *Sentiments et maximes du Bienheureux* (1653), the Jesuit François Guilloré's *Maximes spirituelles* (1670), the mystic Jean de Bernières' *Œuvres spirituelles* (1670), and Abbé de Villiers' *Pensées et réflexions sur les égarements des hommes dans la voie du salut* (1693). The Archbishop Fénelon, famous for his *Les aventures de Télémaque* (1699), also composed *Explication des maximes des saints sur la vie intérieure* (1697).[9]

But the one religious movement that had the greatest influence on Pascal was without doubt Jansenism. This deeply Augustinian movement, emerging from Holland and eventually condemned by Rome, emphasized the entire dependence of fallen humans on divine grace for salvation.[10] Its moral instruction took the form of aphorisms too: its leader, Abbé de Saint-Cyran, published *Maximes saintes et chrestiennes* in 1648: "This is not the time for great knowledge, but of good works and suffering" (§24); "Faults, according to St. Augustine, make the elect and the true lovers of God stronger: they are humbled by them and they make them more vigilant for the time to come" (§27).

Yet the cosmopolitan and contemplative worlds were not so far apart. Both La Rochefoucauld and Pascal visited the salon of Madame de Sablé. Saint-Cyran, Pascal, and La Rochefoucauld all saw the immense capacity of humans for self-deception. They all point to the fundamental weakness and hypocrisy of human beings. Moral precepts floated between the two worlds seamlessly. Here is one from Saint-Cyran: "One knows how to acquire virtues only by exercising them, because virtues without practice are only illusions" (*Maximes saintes et chrestiennes* §237); another from Madame de Sablé: "It is quite a common fault never to be happy with one's fortune and never unhappy with one's soul" (*Maximes* §67). And finally the greatest of them all, La Rochefoucauld: "We never denounce vice or praise virtue except out of self-interest" (*Collected Maxims* §I:151). Are not all three continuations of each other's thoughts, increasing only by degrees of cynicism?

Under the pressures of the Cartesians, the social and spiritual moralists, Pascal finally says with some measure of exasperation, "All the good maxims already exist in the world: we just fail to apply them" (s458/L540). How, then, can we read the *Pensées* against the grain of these aristocratic, lapidary epigrams, polished from the choicest diction, ricocheting through the witty conversations of the rarified salons, or those severe penitential maxims that warn of the utter worthlessness of human beings, damned to perdition? If elegance and wit are the hallmarks of La Rochefoucauld, and stern opprobrium the tone of the Jansenist, fragmentation and silence are surely the very grounds of the *Pensées'* being.

## The hazards of order

Pascal's lifelong task was an exercise of endlessly reducing words to their essence, in order to probe a pure nothingness and bring us to its edge. For Pascal, all finite things are fragments for they are nothing but pieces torn from infinity. All the same, the nature of finitude is such that not even a vast quantity of fragments could ever approach wholeness, "a unit added to infinity does not increase infinity at all, any more than a foot added to an infinite length" (s680/L418). The Pascalian lack of order is an acknowledgment of the failure of the human intellect to understand such infinity. As such the *Pensées* must operate within a poetics of the fragment. And this fragmentation is symptomatic of a pervasive existential, epistemological, and rhetorical crisis.

The crisis, simply stated, is *ordre*. It is the first in the list of topics announced in the project of June 1658, and the word is used some seventy times in his oeuvre.[11] All of Pascalian philosophy and philology is haunted by this failed ideal. In a passage anticipating the Heideggerian condition of "thrownness," Pascal laments, "I do not know who put me into the world, nor what the world is, nor what I myself am. I am in terrible ignorance of everything" (s681/L427). Insofar as the human condition is disoriented, so is the text that strives to represent it: "I would be honoring my subject too much if I treated it with order, since I want to show that it is incapable of it" (s457/L532).

Pascal, deeply influenced by Port-Royal theory of language (itself deeply influenced by Augustine), regards language to be as contingent and fallible as the creatures that claim to have mastery over it.[12] As a result he chafed against the logic of orderly arrangement:

> Order. I could have well composed this discourse in an order like this, to show the vanity of all sorts of conditions: to show the vanity of ordinary lives, and then the vanity of philosophical lives, skeptic or stoic. But the order would not have been

kept. I know a bit about it, and how few people understand it.
No human science can keep it. Saint Thomas did not keep it.
Mathematics keeps it, but is useless in its depth. (s573/L694)

In this manner Pascalian composition is a rejection of the ways of
both Cartesian inquiry ("mathematics") as well as rhetoric es-
poused in ancient ethics ("skeptic or stoic"). In both, *inventio*—
the first step of investigation—proceeds *dispositio*—the arrangement of matter for presentation. Modern science and ancient
rhetoric both hide the messy process of thought underneath the
polished façade of the presentation. Not so Pascal. He is suspicious of the artificial imposition of orderliness: "I will write my
thoughts here without order, but not perhaps in unplanned con-
fusion. This is true order, and it will always indicate my aim by its
very disorder" (s457/L532).[13]

In this sense Pascal's fragments are seventeenth-century versions of *hupomnêmata*, what Foucault, late in his life, calls a "material record of things read, heard, or thought, thus offering them
up as a kind of accumulated treasure for subsequent rereading
and meditation" ("Self Writing," 209). Pascal continues the rich
tradition of spiritual self-cultivation found in Seneca, Marcus Aurelius, the Desert Fathers, Augustine, all the way to his immediate predecessors Jansenius and Saint-Cyran. While Pascal rejects
Cartesian order, he retrieves the style of another French master—
Montaigne—for both believe in the impossibility of fixity in writing, thought, or emotions.[14] The author of the *Essais* seeks a di-
vagating prose that captures the "day to day, minute to minute"
experience of life: "The world is but perennial movement. All
things in it are in constant motion.... Stability itself is nothing
but a more languid motion" ("Of Repentance," III.2).

Even La Rochefoucauld, whom we usually deem to be so ur-
bane and self-assured, had difficulties arranging his maxims. He
issued no fewer than five editions in his lifetime, all with significant alterations, deletions, and addenda. In the fifth edition of
1678, his publisher apologetically notes, "As for the order of these

reflections, you will easily appreciate that it was difficult to arrange them in any order, because all of them deal with different subjects" ("To the Reader," *Collected Maxims,* 3). La Rochefoucauld and Pascal struggled with order from opposite directions—the former proceeds from the glitter of the social world, the latter from the despair of the spiritual self—they meet at the recognition point of the weakness (*faiblesse*) of the human condition.

Interruption, digression, repetition—these become the rhetorical modes that best represent the human condition. Louis Marin notes that "the *Pensées* constitute a sort of text-laboratory that permits the production of a text to be tested against its form which is the fragment, against its discursive mode which is interruption, and against its own logic which is digression" ("'Pascal': Text, Author, Discourse," 133). For what other suitable modes of expression are there if you are wrestling with the paradoxes of absence and presence, the hidden and the revealed, silence and language? Pascal describes a common phenomenon: "A thought has escaped, I wanted to write it down: I write instead that it has escaped me" (s460/L544). This has a Montaignian (and even a Proustian) sensibility. A later fragment goes down the same path but descends into a more existential despair: "When writing down my thought, it sometimes escapes me, but this makes me remember my weakness, which I am constantly forgetting. This is as instructive to me as much as my forgotten thought, for I care only about knowing my nothingness [*mon néant*]" (s540/L656). It is this last phrase—*mon néant*—that marks him as distinctly Pascalian.

### Opera interrupta

Pascal's death at the age of thirty-nine prohibited him from finishing his *Apology.* The scholarly debate ever since has focused on whether he would have arranged his fragments in some systematic form.[15] Clearly he envisioned some sort of order, as the plan of June 1658 with its tentative list of twenty-seven topics suggests (see fig. 7). But then again, "The last thing we discover in

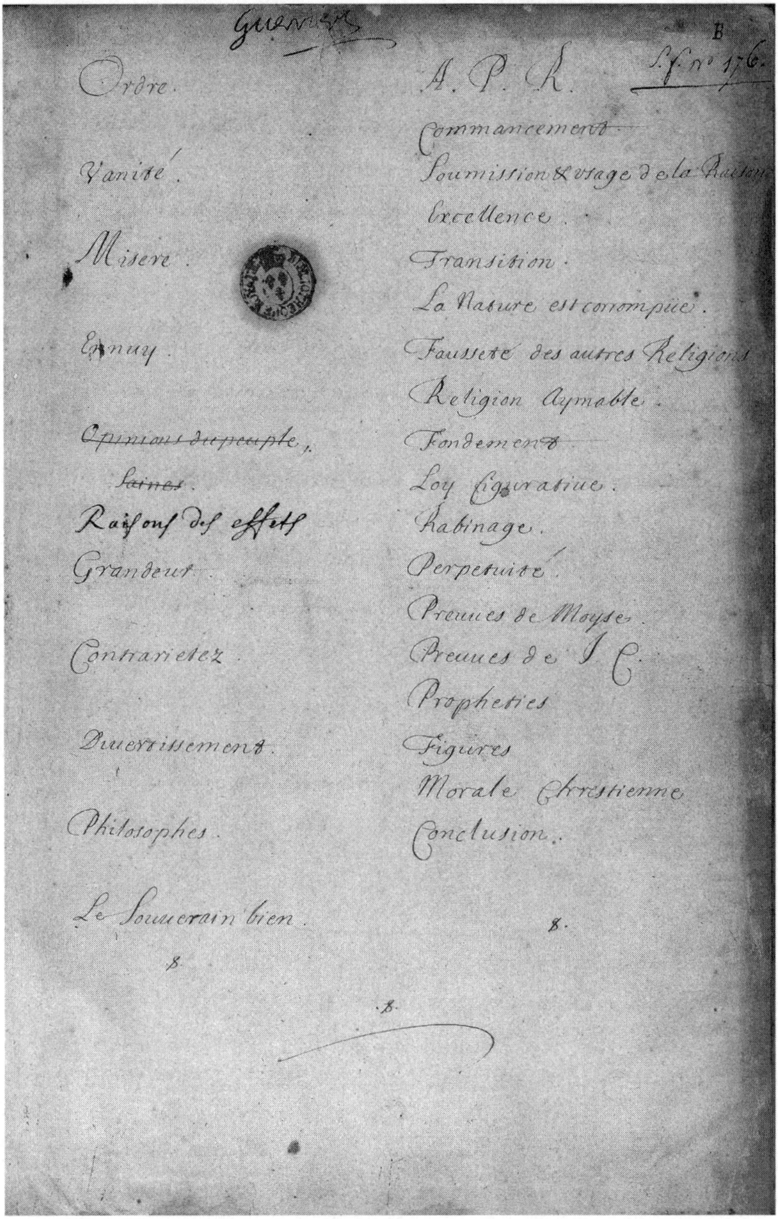

Guerrier

B
A. P. R.  L. f n° 176.

Ordre.

Vanité.

Misère.

Ennuy.

Opinions du peuple,
 saines.
Raisons des effets
Grandeur.

Contrarietez.

Divertissement.

Philosophes.

Le Souverain bien.

8.

   8.

Commencement
Soumission & usage de la Raison
Excellence.
Transition.
La Nature est corrompue.
Fausseté des autres Religions
Religion Aymable.
Fondement
Loy figurative.
Rabinage.
Perpetuité.
Preuves de Moyse
Preuves de J. C.
Propheties
Figures
Morale Chrestienne
Conclusion.

8.

FIGURE 7. Pascal, list of topics for his projected *Apology*, *Pensées sur la religion*, Copie B, fonds français 12449, Bibliothèque Nationale, Paris.

writing a book is what to put first" (s740/L976). Pascal stopped before reaching the end. Thus the discontinuity of his fragments is what gives the work both the impasse and possibility of meaning. In the spaces between each *pensée,* the reader's voice comes in to fill the void left by the author's silence.

In endeavoring to find some harmony out of the dissonant fragments, editors end up making Pascal fit into their ideological mold.[16] In the 1670 Port-Royal pocket-sized volume (perfect for individual contemplation), the head engraving to the first page of the *Pensées* is telling. Under the banner of a Virgilian tag *pendent opera interrupta* ("interrupted works hang," *Aen.* 4.88), a magnificent neoclassical building, much like the Institut de France, is flanked by rubble on the right and a construction site on the left (see fig. 8). No doubt this is the editors' vision of their task—to bring architectonic order to the author's disorder. In the eighteenth century, Nicolas de Condorcet (1776) and Voltaire's editions (1778) make Pascal seem like a misanthropic skeptic, even an atheist of the Enlightenment. In the nineteenth century, Prosper Faugère (1844) and Ernest Havet (1852) made considerable advances in objective textual criticism. In 1897 and 1904, Léon Brunschvicg, a secular Jewish philosopher at the Sorbonne, schoolmate of Proust and later advisor of Bachelard and Bourdieu, produced editions that stressed his mathematical demonstrations and made the ordering highly readable to the general reader. In 1941 Zacherie Tourneur gave a paleographic reproduction of the manuscript preserving all the erasures, additions, hesitations, and marginalia. In recent decades, Louis Lafuma and Philippe Sellier rely on the two "copies" of the lost original *Copie.* Lafuma prefers the first copy (fonds français 9203 at the Bibliothèque Nationale) and labeled the *liasses* as "papiers classés" and "papiers non classés." By scholarly consensus, it is now believed that the second copy (fonds français 12449), edited by Sellier, is more trustworthy because it is continuous, without blank leaves between each *liasse* (see figs. 9 and 10).

FIGURE 8. Pascal, *Pensées,* Port-Royal edition, 1670, *"pendent opera interrupta."*

All these permutations are made possible because of the open-ended nature of the fragments. "Words differently arranged have different meanings. And meanings differently arranged produce different effects" (s645/l784): this is an apt motto for the conflicting editions. The multiplicity of interpretive meanings is reflected in the manifold ways of arranging a text. Every generation produces its own fragments. And the following generation produces its own critical edition according to its own needs. I am surely not the only reader to think that the *Pensées* are infinitely richer, infinitely more interesting because they *are* in fragments. My wager is that Pascal had no definitive ordering when he died. All reconstructions are hypothetical at best. This does not occlude the valuable work on the *Pensées* through the centuries. Rather, the enigmatic instability of the text generates such productive multiplicity.

Ordre.

1. Les Pseaumes chantez par toute la terre.
2. Qui rend tesmoignage de Mahomet ? luy mesme.
3. J. C. veut que son témoignage ne soit rien.
   La qualité des tesmoins fait qu'il faut qu'ils soyent tousjours
   & par tout & miserable il est seul.

Ordre
par Dialogues.

Que dois-je faire, je ne vois partout qu'obscuritez, croiray-je
que je ne suis rien, croiray-je que je suis Dieu ?

Toutes choses changent & se succedent.
Vous vous trompez il y a

Et quoy ne dites vous pas vous mesme que le ciel & les
Oyseaux prouvent Dieu ? non, & nostre Religion ne le dit elle
pas ? non. car encore que cela est vray en un sens pour quelques
ames a qui Dieu donne cette lumiere, neanmoins cela est faux
à l'esgard de la plus part.

Lettre pour porter à rechercher Dieu.
Et puis le faire chercher chez les Philosophes Pyrroniens
& dogmatistes qui travailleront luy qui les recherche.

Ordre.

6. Une Lettre d'exhortation a un amy pour le porter à chercher
   & il respondra mais a quoy me servira de chercher, rien ne
   paroist, & luy respondre ne desesperez pas, & il respondra
   qu'il seroit heureux de trouver quelque lumiere, mais que selon
   cette Religion mesme quand il croiroit ainsy cela ne luy serviroit de
   rien, & qu'ainsy il ayme autant ne point chercher & cela luy
   respondre. la machine.

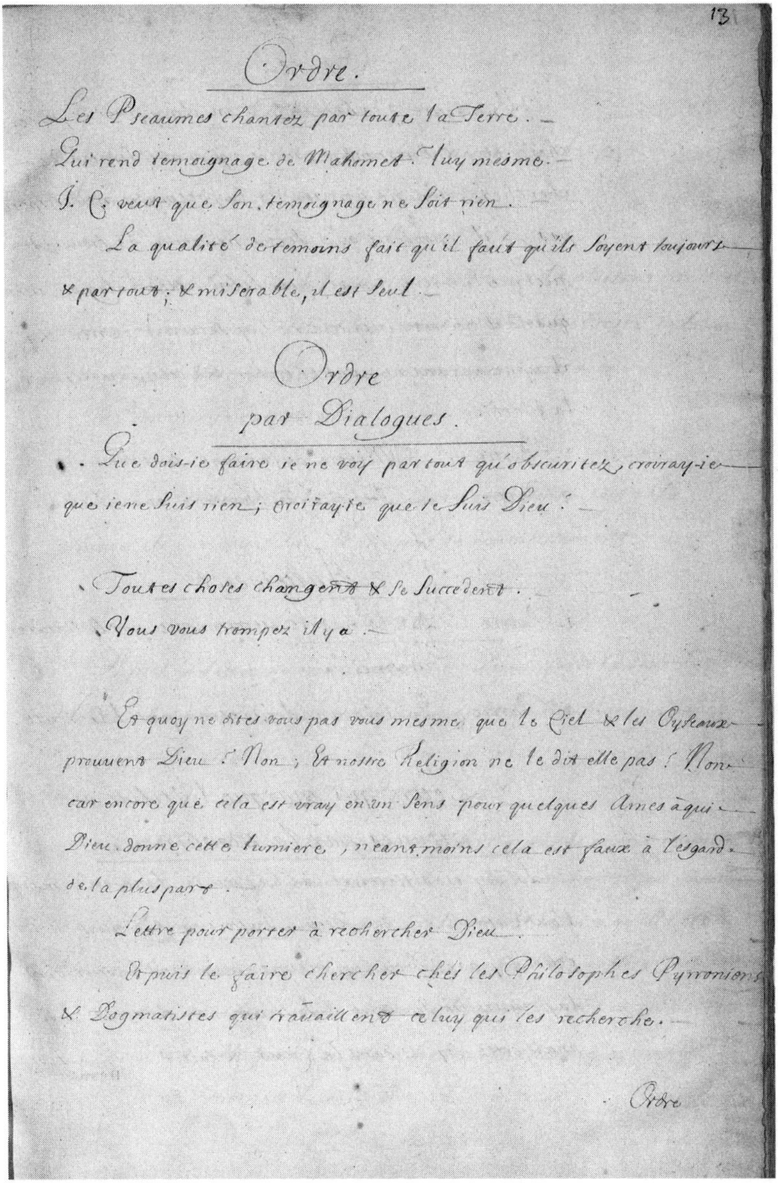

13

Ordre.

Les Pseaumes chantez par toute la Terre. —

Qui rend temoignage de Mahomet, luy mesme. —

J. C. veut que Son temoignage ne Soit rien.

La qualité de temoins fait qu'il faut qu'ils Soyent toujours —
& par tout; & miserable, il est Seul —

Ordre

par Dialogues.

Que dois-ie faire ie ne voy par tout qu'obscuritez, croiray-ie —
que ie ne Suis rien; croiray-ie que le Suis Dieu? —

Toutes choses changent & Se Succedent.

Vous vous trompez il y a —

Et quoy ne dites vous pas vous mesme que le Ciel & les Oyseaux —
prouvent Dieu? Non; Et nostre Religion ne le dit elle pas? Non —
car encore que cela est vray en un Sens pour quelques Ames à qui —
Dieu donne cette lumiere, neantmoins cela est faux à l'egard —
de la plus part.

Lettre pour porter à rechercher Dieu.

Et puis le faire chercher chés les Philosophes Pyrroniens —
& Dogmatistes qui travaillent celuy qui les recherche. —

Ordre

FIGURE 10. Pascal, *Pensées sur la religion*, copie B, fonds français 12449, Bibliothèque
Nationale, Paris.

## M'effraie

It is common knowledge that Pascal's mathematics and his apologetics share an abiding interest in infinity.[17] He takes the most pressing problems of pure science—infinity in geometry, the void in physics, chance in mathematics—and elevates them to metaphysical problems. For example, Girard Desargues, one of the founders of projective geometry, creates a "geometry of infinity" in which he applies the idea of infinity to pure geometry. In Desargues' framework, the two extremities of a line infinitely extended meet each other.[18] Pascal appropriates this to a theological paradigm in the *Pensées*: "These extremes touch and join by force of distance, meeting in God and God alone" (S230/L199). Whereas infinite distance in projective geometry allows a generalization in the study of conic sections, infinite distance in the *Pensées* is an incommensurable figure for humanity's disproportion.

For this reason, infinity for Pascal becomes an inexhaustible figure for probing the capacity—and limitations—of the mind in understanding the world. The infinite is existential: "For, after all, what is man in nature? A nothing compared to the infinite, a whole compared to the nothing, a midpoint between nothing and everything, infinitely removed from understanding the extremes; the end of things and their principle are hopelessly hidden from him in an impenetrable secret" (S230/L199). It is mathematical: "We know that there is an infinite, but we do not know its nature; as we know that it is false that numbers are finite, so therefore it is true that there is an infinite number, but we do not know what it is: it is false that it is even and false that it is odd, for by adding a unit it does not change its nature" (S680/L418). It is epistemological: "*Incomprehensible:* Everything that is incomprehensible does not cease to exist. Infinite number, an infinite space equal to the finite" (S128/L149). It is hermeneutic: "*Two infinities. Mean.* When we read too quickly or too slowly, we understand nothing" (S601/L723).[19] It is philosophical: "The infinite distance between bodies and minds [*esprit*] is a figure of the infinitely more infinite distance between minds and charity, for charity is supernatural" (S339/L308). Finally, it is a metaphysics of onto-theology: "The finite is annihilated in the presence of the infinite and becomes pure nothingness. So it is with our mind before God" (S680/L418).

Thinking about the infinite, we see, leads one to reiteration. But this is not a redundant practice, rather what Deleuze would call expression "by excess in the Idea" (*Difference and Repetition*, 24). If according to Deleuze "the greatest effort of philosophy was perhaps directed at rendering representation infinite" (262), Pascal's greatest effort, I think, is to represent infinity through the finite figurations of the fragmentary. And because the *pensées* are discontinuous, the repetitions that abound in the collected and uncollected *liasses* can be understood by an intensified coexistence rather than a succession of discursive arguments.

Now armed with these diverse senses of infinity in Pascal's work, we are finally well equipped to read the most haunting dictum of them all:

> *Le silence éternel de ces espaces infinis m'effraie.*

> The eternal silence of these infinite spaces terrifies me. (S233/L201)

The syntax is simple: it is composed of a binominal subject, a transitive verb, and a first-person pronoun as the direct object. By itself, the subject is classically balanced, resting in equipoise. (In a strained reading, one can even say that the subject *almost* forms that *sine qua non* of French classical verse—the *alexandrine*—with its twelve-syllable line divided into two halves. But here we have thirteen syllables.) The orders of time and space are separated by the lexical caesura, *de*. But this august symmetry of the two hemistichs is destabilized by intrusion of the verb—*effraie*—with its prefix "m." It is as if the grandeur of the seven-word subject overwhelms the puny, singular letter of the first-person pronoun, whose fullness is reduced by an elision of the vowel.

My reading is that "eternal silence" is an attribute of the "God of Abraham, Isaac, Jacob"—and "infinite space" is an attribute of the "God of the philosophers." That is to say, "eternal silence" resides in the realm of revealed theology, and "infinite space" resides in the realm of rational philosophy.[20] As God exists outside of time, the problem for any Christian is how to approach him from and in the *seculum*. The believer's fear is that God remains hidden in the "eternal silence" without revealing himself through the incarnate word. "Silence is the greatest persecution," Pascal writes in an uncollected fragment (s746/L916).

As Alexandre Koyré demonstrated in his classic *From the Closed World to the Infinite Universe*, early modern natural philosophy brought about a fundamental revolution in the scientific understanding of our place in the universe. Not only was the human dethroned from a geocentric model of the universe to a heliocentric one, but through the ideas of Bruno, Copernicus, Galileo, Descartes, and Henry More, the structure of the cosmos was also reconceived from a finite world to an endless expanse of space.

In Cartesian terms, this world, the "entirety of the corporal substance," has no limits in its extension. There cannot exist a finite space separate from a body; space and body and voice are actualities that can be comprehended by the rational intellect. Eternity and the infinite, on the contrary, are potentials that can be comprehended only by intuition. For a Cartesian who believes in the "God of the philosophers," the existence of an infinite being is axiomatic, "utterly clear and distinct." It causes no predicament whatsoever for the intellect: "It does not matter that I do not grasp the infinite, or that there are countless additional attributes of God which I cannot in any way grasp, and perhaps cannot even reach in my thought; for it is in the nature of the infinite not to be grasped by a finite being like myself" (*Meditations on First Philosophy* 3.46). And because it is not possible for a body to have no extension, likewise for space. As such, whereas God is infinite, the world is an *indefinite extension of space*.

Once the world became an uncircumscribed extension, the fabled "harmony of the world"—the ancient idea of a *musica universalis* that governs the harmonic, mathematical movements of celestial bodies—would no longer be possible. Silence now pervades the universe. This is what terrifies Pascal. Although the music of the spheres had always been inaudible to human organs, this Pythagorean principle nestled the comforting notion that the universe was well ordered, proportional, and intelligible. But the Copernican model (against the protestations of Kepler) had decisively shattered this harmonious cosmos of "fixed stars" and replaced it with a model of a boundless universe.[21]

As a consequence, the early modern dimensionless extension of space—*ces espaces infinis*—fills the finite self with vertigo: "I see nothing but infinites on all sides, surrounding me like an atom and like a shadow that lasts only for an instant and returns no more" (s681/L427). For the Pascalian who embraces the "God of Abraham, Isaac, Jacob," this incommensurability between the finite and the infinite brings immeasurable dread to the heart, causing an existential frisson: "What is a man in the infinite? ... He is equally incapable of seeing the nothingness from which he derives and the infinite in which he is engulfed" (s680/L418). Descartes, in contrast, bears no such fear: "The mere fact that God created me is a very strong basis for believing that I am somehow made in his image and likeness, and that I perceive that likeness, which includes the idea of God, by the same faculty which enables me to perceive myself" (*Meditations* §3.51).

To be sure, there is probably no doubt in European early modernity more famous than Descartes' in the second *Meditation*, but this is finally resolved for good. Pascal, too, has moments of clarity and faith, as the *Mémorial* of 1654 attests. But this spiritual epiphany occurs before the composition of the *Pensées*, and he is subsequently wracked by many more deluges of despair. I think that these ruptures, repetitions, and resistance make our interpretive struggle more akin to Pascal's own struggle for faith and understanding. That is, we go through the same experience as he does when we read his long, repetitive (and, yes, at times convoluted) passages. If Descartes' philosophical quest begins with *cogito ergo sum*, we may say that Pascal's begins with *timeo ergo sum*, "I fear, therefore I am."

## Horizon of the infinite

For Blanchot, the fragment is "a noun, but possessing the force of a verb that is nonetheless absent: brisure, a breaking without debris, interruption as speech when the pause of intermittence does not arrest becoming but, on the contrary, provokes it in the rupture that belongs to it" (*The Infinite Conversation,* 307). Fragmentation, in this sense, becomes both a formal necessity of Pascal's work and a philosophical exigency. It is the only viable form of expression for a philosophy that insists on the "disproportion of man" and the paradox of totality and the particular: "I hold it to be equally impossible to know the parts without knowing the whole, and to know the whole without having a particular knowledge of each part" (s230/L199). Therefore: *whole : part :: infinity : fragment.*

To be sure, not everything Pascal wrote was in aphorisms. Entries like "The Wager" and "Disproportion of Man" carefully develop arguments with abundant folds of periphrasis and amplification, piling on clauses upon clauses, topoi upon topoi, tropes upon tropes. Nevertheless, Pascal struggled to put these mini-treatises into some orderly form, and they read like shards torn from a larger nonexistent textual fabric. His poetics of the fragment thus becomes not so much an expression of brevity as much as an expression of the impossibility of wholeness in the human condition: "If man were to begin by studying himself, he would see how incapable he is of going beyond himself [*passer outre*]. How could it be possible for a part to know the whole?" (s230/L199).

Pascal's fragmentary style, then, is nothing other than the textual aftermath of his metaphysical speculation about "the eternal silence of infinite spaces." It respects the silence that dwells in the finite spaces between words. In this sense his poetics expresses the antinomy of pure reason, for it acknowledges the possibility of rational order and partakes in its operations but is nevertheless painfully aware of its limitations. Clarity is but a dissimulation that masks the reality of humanity's sorry condition. Only the brevity of the aphorism can capture Pascal's silence. Only fragments can express the universe's infinite spaces.

Another philosopher who pondered deeply on infinity was Nietzsche. In the last chapter we saw how an aphorism in *The Gay Science* resonated with the frontispiece of the *Novum organum* and, more distantly, with the flow of Confucius' and Heraclitus' rivers. Here is the lofty proclamation again:

> *In the horizon of the infinite.* – We have left the land and have embarked. [*Im Horizont des Unendlichen. – Wir haben das Land verlassen und sind zu Schiff gegangen!*] We have burned our bridges behind us indeed, we have gone farther and destroyed the land behind us. Now, little ship, look out! Beside you is the ocean: to be sure. It does not always roar, and at times it lies spread out like silk and gold and reveries of graciousness. Hours will come when you will realize that it is infinite and that there is nothing more awesome than infinity. (§124)

Hans Blumenberg reads this as a reference to Pascal: "But you must wager. There is no choice. You are already embarked [*vous êtes embarqué*]" (s680/L418).[22] For me, this is closer to another fragment: "We float over a vast ocean, ever uncertain and adrift, blown this way or that.... Let us therefore not seek certainty and stability. Our reason is always deceived by inconstant appearances, nothing can affix the finite between the two infinites that both enclose and escape it" (s230/L199). It is significant that Nietzsche's passage occurs immediately before the famous "madman" episode in which he declares that "God is dead.... And we have killed him" (3.125). For Nietzsche the death of God is liberating and exhilarating. For Pascal existence itself brings drift and despair. But as we will see in the next chapter, the German philosopher too had to resort to the aphoristic form. Nietzsche embarks. Pascal floats.

## Ciphers of the hidden God

"Languages are ciphers in which letters are not changed into letters, but words into words. So an unknown language can be deciphered" (s465/L575). This fragment might very well serve as Pascal's theory of interpretation. Again and again in the *Pensées* he labored to reconcile the literal and the figural in the scriptures, so much so that this massive heap of texts itself also assumes the status of a cipher. The reader in turn must work to decipher the "unknown language" of the *Pensées*. In Pascal's hermeneutics, one seeks meaning in a text in the same way one seeks God, for meaning in language and meaning in God are both hidden.

Pascal reflects on the hidden nature of God in a number of passages: "God begins thus hidden, any religion that does not say God is hidden is not true, and any religion that does not explain it is not instructive. Our religion does all this. *Truly you are a hidden God*" (s275/L242, quoting Isaiah 45:15). Pascal writes in a letter to Mademoiselle de Roannez, "Having concealed himself in all things for others, he has uncovered himself in all things and in so many ways for us" (ed. Sellier, 709); "God is hidden. But he lets himself be found by those who seek him. Visible signs of him have always existed throughout the ages" (s785/L992). Three hundred years later, Simone Weil would write in her luminous, aphoristic *Gravity and Grace*: "The absence of God is the most marvelous testimony of perfect love, and that is why pure necessity, necessity which is manifestly different from the good, is so beautiful" (106).

Faced with the dual nature of divine presence and absence, Pascal's poetics is suspended between kataphasis and apophasis, the theology that uses respectively "positive" or "negative" terminology to describe God.[23] At its extreme, Pascal's apophatic poetics is recorded in his famous "night of fire" (*nuit de feu*) of November 23, 1654, the mystical experience of rapture that marked his definitive conversion to Jansenism. The vestige of this experience is inscribed on a parchment sewn into the lining of his coat, found after he died:

FEU.

« DIEU d'Abraham, DIEU d'Isaac, DIEU de Jacob »
non des philosophes et des savants.
Certitude. Certitude. Sentiment. Joie. Paix.
DIEU de Jésus-Christ.
*Deum meum et Deum vestrum.*

Fire. God of Abraham, God of Isaac, God of Jacob. Not of philosophers and scholars. Certainty, certainty, feelings, joy, peace. God of Jesus Christ. My God and your God.

Here, language is stripped of all predicates. Only bare subjects remain, a broken litany of praise and thanksgiving. This is the so-called *Mémorial*, which functions as an abiding talisman, unreadable (since it was fastened inside his coat) but ever present on his person (see fig. 11).[24] At the other extreme, Pascal's kataphatic poetics is expressed in the incandescent "Disproportion of Man" and "The Wager." They stand as two of European literature's most intense explorations of the existential relationship between the human and the divine.

Lucien Goldmann's *Hidden God* (*Dieu caché*, 1959), a ground-breaking if flawed Marxist sociological study of Pascal and Racine, explores the seventeenth-century revival of the idea of God as pervasive in all things but utterly incomprehensible to human beings.[25] Goldmann's contribution to the history of early modern ideas lies in his account of how Pascal's recuperation of the hidden God topos is imbricated in the pivotal transition from the rationalism of Descartes to the dialectic idealism of Kant and Hegel, and their eventual overturning by Marx and Lukács. For a

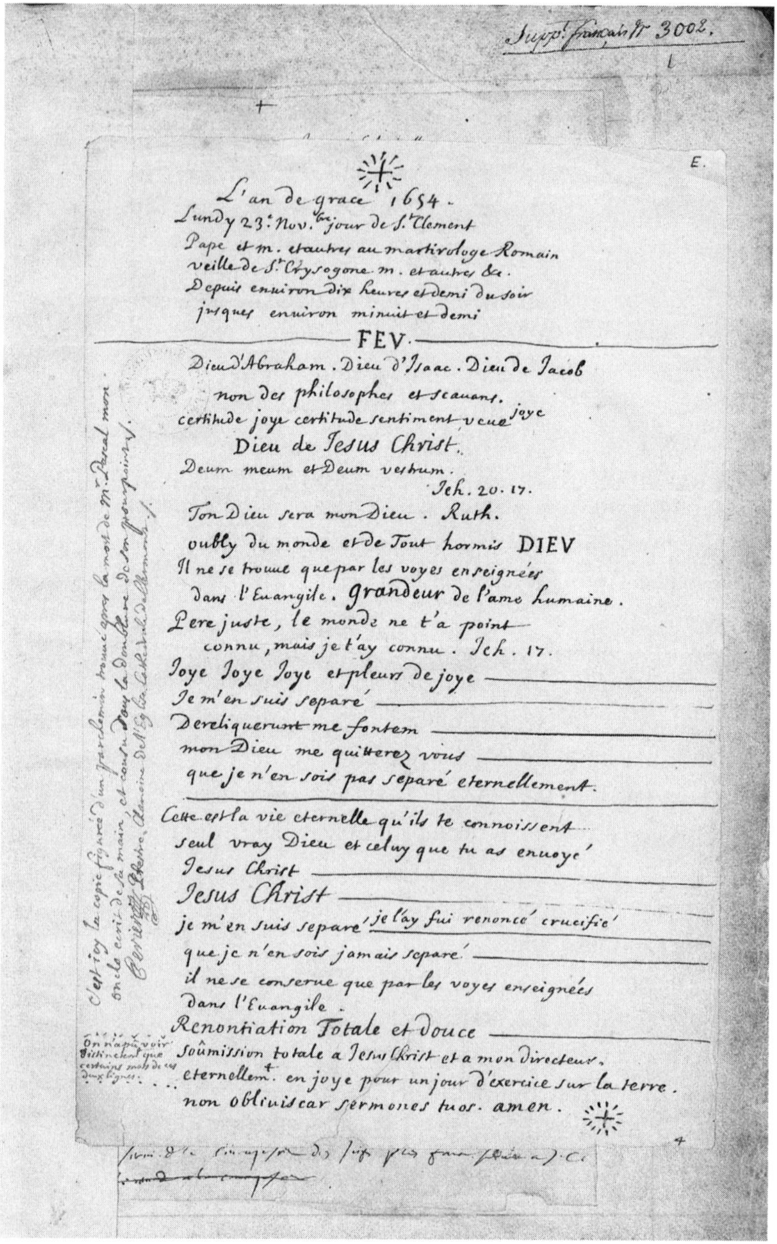

FIGURE 11. Pascal, *Memorial,* recueil original, fonds français 9202, Bibliothêque Nationale, Paris.

deist, God is hidden, the transcendent deity who establishes the rules of reason, creates the world and the laws of nature with a mere "flick of the fingers" (Krailsheimer, 330). As soon as that's done, he withdraws. For the Pascalian, God is hidden to humans because of our wretched, sinful condition.

In the Hebrew Bible, Yahweh hides his face because he is so sickened by the depravities of the human heart (Is. 45:15). Nicholas of Cusa saw God as ultimately unknowable through the faculty of human reason; hence he is a *deus absconditus*. These notions of the hidden God bring us back to the discussion of the *Gospel of Thomas* in chapter 3: "Know what is in front of your face, and what is hidden from you will be disclosed to you. For there is nothing hidden that will not be revealed" (§5); "There will be days when you will seek me and you will not find me" (§38).

What Goldmann ignored, and what many scholars have subsequently recuperated, is that Pascal is deeply engaged in negative theology.[26] Pseudo-Dionysius, one of its foremost proponents, explains in *The Divine Names* that the "supra-essential being of God" means that "it is at a total remove from every condition, movement, life, imagination, conjecture, name, discourse, thought, conception, being, rest, dwelling, unity, limit, infinity, the totality of existence" (57). Pascal continues this line of thinking by stating, "If there is a God, he is infinitely incomprehensible, since, having neither parts nor limits, he bears no relation to us. We are therefore incapable of knowing either what he is or whether he is. This being so, who will dare undertake to resolve this question? Not we, who bear no relation to him [*n'avons aucun rapport à lui*]" (s680/L418).

From the God who hides and reveals, Pascal makes a connection to the hidden and revealed language of Scripture:

The Old Testament is a cipher [*un chiffre*] (s307/L276).

*Figures.* To know whether the law and the sacrifices are reality or figurative, we must see whether the prophets, in speaking of these things, thought and looked no further, so that they saw only the old covenant. Or whether they saw in them something else of which they were the representation. For in a portrait we see the thing figured [*la chose figurée*]. (S291/L260)

Pascal here and elsewhere taps into the exegetical method of typology. In short, Christian commentators for millennia understood scripture through dualities: the letter and the spirit, the flesh and the spirit, prophets and saints, the Old and the New Testament.[27] Yet this binary nature is ultimately a unity, for the first is but a shadow, a prefiguration, an anticipation, and the latter an illumination, a fulfillment, a transfiguration. As Gregory the Great says, "The Catholic Church receives the New Testament in such a way that it does not reject the Old. She venerates the Old Testament in such a way that she is ever perceiving the spirit of the New Testament even in the fleshly sacrifices."[28] A thousand years later, Pascal follows almost exactly this exegetical model: "Jesus Christ, with whom the two *Testaments* are concerned: the *Old* as its hope, the *New* as its model, and both as their center" (S7/L388).

Now in French, *chiffre* is both a cipher and a numerical digit. In the seventeenth century, the problem of the cipher was both geometric and theological.[29] Some of the greatest minds of the day—Fludd, Gassendi, Grotius, Leibniz, Spinoza—waged fierce debates on how to reconcile the faith of religion with the rationality of science through symbolic interpretations of scripture. The polymath Blaise de Vigenère in his *Traité des chiffres et manières d'écrire* (1568) writes that "in fact all of Scripture has so much in common with numbers, it is hardly anything else than anagrams, just waiting for a few letters so that by their different transpositions and arrangements it can express an infinite diversity of senses" (in Force, *Le Problème herméneutique*, 279). Yet because human beings are flawed and feeble, many things are obscured and we are constantly beset by hermeneutic difficulties:

A cipher has two meanings [*Le chiffre a deux sens*]. When we come upon an important letter whose meaning is clear, but

where it is said that the meaning is veiled and obscure, hidden
in such a way that we might see the letter without seeing it,
and understand it without understanding it, what must we
think but that the cipher has a double meaning [*c'est un chiffre
à double sens*]? (S291/L260)

Ciphers are like shadows that refer to their gnomon—accidental
and transient, but still intelligible and measurable. It becomes
the work of the reader to make sense of them. And because ciphers are revelations given by God, humans must accept this
open invitation.

## How to read

Pascal's poetics of the aphorism consists then in nothing but this
painstaking decipherment of God's signs. In turn the reader's
hermeneutics of the aphorism consist in a painstaking decipherment of Pascal's own signs. Pascal saw the world itself as a cipher:
"A portrait brings absence and presence, pleasure and displeasure. Reality excludes absence and displeasure" (S291/L260).
Even before Derrida, Pascal knew that writing, like portraiture,
also brings absence and presence. The hundreds upon hundreds
of notes that make up the *Pensées*—composed in the author's
miniscule handwriting, virtually unpunctuated, full of abbreviations and erasures—themselves may be said to constitute a dense
network of ciphers. The ever perceptive Borges noticed that
the Brunschvicg edition records "Nature is an infinite sphere, the
center of which is everywhere, the circumference nowhere,"
whereas Tourneur in his reveals that Pascal started to write the
word *effroyable*: "a ~~frightful~~ sphere, the center of which is everywhere, and the circumference nowhere" ("Pascal's Sphere," 353).
When is the infinite ever not frightful?

One way is with a sense of perspective, which is encoded in
his theory of writing and reading: "When we read too fast or two
slowly, we understand nothing" (S75/L41, cf. S601/L723). "The

last thing we discover in writing a book is what to put in first" (s740/L976, quoted earlier); "If we look at our work immediately after completing it, we are still too much involved in it; too long afterwards and we cannot pick it up again" (s55/L21).

These remarks, taken at face value, are commonplaces. But read in light of Pascal's intense scrutiny into the unity of opposites—the two infinites, absence and presence, hidden and revealed—we see that these *sententiae* flow from the same philosophical source. Finishing or beginning, too long or too soon, too fast or too slow, parts or wholes—these are all questions of theological and aesthetic perspectives. "It is the same with pictures seen from too far or too near," he continues. "And there is only one indivisible point, which is the right place. The others are too near, too far, too high, or too low. Perspective determines that point in the art of painting. But in truth and in morality, who will determine it?" (s55/L21). Perhaps the answer is found in the precarious point between "the two abysses of the infinite and nothingness" (s230/L199). Early modern epistemology discovered that vision is possible only through the relative position of the object, the beholder, and the spatial dimensions of a given optical field. Nietzsche will ultimately elevate this episteme into his philosophy of perspectivism—truth as determined by the relative position between the individual and the world. For Pascal, the relative position always remains between the individual and God. Whatever the ratio, the task of interpretation is never-ending.

# 6

# Nietzsche

## THE FRAGMENTS OF THE UNFINISHED

The aphorism converges on two opposing poles of aesthetic creation: the complete and the incomplete. In *Human, All Too Human*, Nietzsche ponders

> the effectiveness of the incomplete [*Das Unvollständige als das Wirksame*]. – Just as figures in relief produce so strong an impression on the imagination [*die Phantasie*] because they are as it were on the point of stepping out of the wall but have suddenly been brought to a halt, so the relief-like, incomplete presentation of an idea, of a whole philosophy [*unvollständige Darstellung eines Gedankens, einer ganzen Philosophie*], is sometimes more effective than its exhaustive realization [*erschöpfende Ausführung*]: more is left for the beholder to do, he is impelled to continue working on that which appears before him so strongly etched in light and shadow, to think it through to the end, and to overcome even that constraint which has hitherto prevented it from stepping forth fully formed. (§178)

FIGURE 12. Michelangelo, *Atlas Slave*, 1530–36, marble, Accademia, Florence (Art Resource).

FIGURE 13. Medardo Rosso, *Golden Age*, 1886, wax over plaster, Fine Arts Museums of San Francisco.

This play of illumination and darkness, this tentative, inchoate genesis of the draftsman's sketch or the sculptor's mass, this profile emerging from the shadow—these are the ecstatic images Nietzsche uses to represent the power of suggestion. In truth, the aesthetics of the unfinished keeps in abeyance the melancholic evanescence of beauty and its inevitable decay, since it arrests things at a fixed point in the midst of flux. I imagine Nietzsche's words to be the prose equivalent of Michelangelo's *Atlas Slave* (1525–30) or the sculptures of Medardo Rosso (1858–1928), which capture so evocatively forms coming into being, figures emerging into fullness of flesh (see figs. 12 and 13).

In particular, Nietzsche's image of the "figure … on the point of stepping out of the wall" suggests a temporal punctum that can only be intersected by two axes—the line of the artist, judiciously suspended, as she unfurls her creation; and that of the viewer, who must reanimate this vision. More precisely, the deliberate *chiaroscuro* of the philosopher-artist can only be rendered visible by the light of the reader's imagination. Thus "effectiveness," *Wirksame*, works only if there is a dialectic between production and reception, genesis and hermeneutics. We will return to this idea of *Wirksame* in a moment, but for now we can say that Nietzsche establishes here a tripartite relationship that will be paradigmatic henceforth for all his work: his aesthetic process, his philosophical project, and his audience.

For a thinker as self-reflective as Nietzsche, there is no doubt that this entry is a metacommentary on his own writings. It is fitting that he does so in *Human, All Too Human* (1878), for this work of 638 aphorisms ushered in his "middle period" and marked a break with his early philological studies.[1] In 1879–80 there were two sequels: "Assorted Opinions and Maxims" and "The Wanderer and His Shadow" in 758 aphorisms. But before Nietzsche started publishing his own aphorisms, he was studying those of the ancients. While still a student at the University of Leipzig, his first publication was in the prestigious *Das Rheinisches Museum für Philologie* (1867) on the reception of the sayings of Theognis. As a professional classicist, he engaged deeply with Diogenes Laertius, the master collector of the sayings and anecdotes of the ancient philosophers, publishing three papers on him, and also writing "On the Apophthegmata and Their Collection."[2]

Nietzsche's philology on fragments became a philosophy of fragments when he abandoned his profession as a classicist in the late 1870s. Rather than just studying aphorisms, he started producing them.[3] In the most productive stretch of his life, from *Human, All Too Human* (1878) to *Ecce Homo* (1888), he composed thousands upon thousands of pithy sayings and maxims. The fragmentary form became the preferred style for the rest of his life. The prophet in *Thus Spoke Zarathustra* (1883) speaks in enigmatic dithyrambs reminiscent of the wisdom literature of antiquity. All of his subsequently published works are aphoristic in one way or another: *Daybreak* (1881, 575 aphorisms); *The Gay Science* (1882, 383 aphorisms and reflections); *Beyond Good and Evil* (1886, 296 aphorisms and reflections). Though *On the Genealogy of Morals* (1887) does not bear an ostensibly aphoristic style, in its preface he writes that the third essay is but a commentary on the aphorism prefixed to it: "People find difficulty with the aphoristic form [*In andern Fällen macht die aphoristische Form Schwierigkeit*]: this arises from the fact that today this form is *not taken seriously enough.* Aphorism, properly stamped and molded, has not been 'deciphered' when it has simply been read; rather, one has then to begin its *exegesis,* for which is required an art of exegesis. I have offered in the third essay of the present book an example of what I regard as 'exegesis' in such a case—an aphorism is prefixed to this essay, the essay itself is a commentary on it" (Preface §8).[4] *Twilight of the Idols*, published in 1889, the year of his mental collapse, begins with a section of forty-four "Maxims and Arrows."

"The aphorism, the apothegm [*Der Aphorismus, die Sentenz*], in which I am the first master among Germans, are the forms of eternity [*Formen der „Ewigkeit"*]," declares Nietzsche. "My ambition is to say in ten sentences [*Sätzen*] what everyone else says in a book—what everyone else does not say in a book" (*Twilight of the Idols*, "Expeditions of the Untimely Man" §51).[5] Nietzsche's aphoristic form becomes his way of training his readers not to subscribe to a doctrine or a particular Nietzschean view of life, but rather to create and craft their own philosophy of life. They must "continue working on that which [is] so strongly etched in light and shadow, to think it through to the end" [*zu Ende zu denken*], as the entry in *Human, All Too Human* urges (§178). In a late notebook, Nietzsche writes that "in books of aphorisms [*Aphorismenbüchern*] like mine there are plenty of forbidden, long things and chains of thoughts between and behind short aphorisms, some of which would be questionable enough for Oedipus and his sphinx" (*KSA* 11:579). He will not spoon-feed his readers, for

he intends for them to engage in a hermeneutic agon, an existential struggle as perilous as a tragic hero's encounter with the The-
ban monster.[6] If, as we saw in chapter 2, Socrates thought that
the best method for engaging in philosophy was the dialectic—
intense, difficult, aporetic conversations with the leading young
citizens of Athens—Nietzsche's method is more like Heraclitus'—
intense, difficult, aporetic maxims and arrows that strike at the
heart of the reader, either quickening or seizing their habits of
thought. The reader is required to do as much work in its interpretation as the author does in its production, to investigate what
is "between and behind" his sharp words.

"At long last the horizon appears free to us again ... all the
daring of the lover of knowledge is permitted again.... and the sea,
*our* sea, again lies open again!" Nietzsche proclaims in *The Gay
Science* (§343). We have already encountered the images of the
horizon and vast waters in Confucius, Heraclitus, Socrates, and
Bacon. For Nietzsche, only aphoristic writings can express such
infinite freedom of going beyond the horizon. For one who phi-
losophizes with a hammer, he deliberately avoids the grand, all-
encompassing narratives of a *Critique*, a *Phenomenology*, or a
*World as Will and Representation* and uses instead a multitude of
short forms to express his most explosive ideas. Struggling with
these elephantine treatises makes one tired, bent, crooked. For his
"philosophy of the future," another method is necessary, one that
would capture the healthy, throbbing, "free spirit" of the new: the
"exuberant, floating, dancing, mocking, childish, and blissful art"
(*Gay Science* §107). The aphorism is precisely this genre.

Nietzsche thus proposes a radical hermeneutics that bridges
writing and ethics: he wants his readers ultimately to stop reading, stop interpreting, and start living. "We do not belong to
those who have ideas only among books, when stimulated by
books. It is our habit to think outdoors—walking, leaping, climb-
ing, dancing, preferably on lonely mountains or near the sea where
even the trails become thoughtful" (*Gay Science* §366). Is not a

well-wrought aphorism, supple and limber, precisely that which walks, leaps, climbs, and dances? Who can really read Hegel outdoors anyways?

## Writing in blood

Nietzsche's aphoristic form is incredibly variegated: there are maxims, epigrams, exegeses, reflections, or mini-essays not unlike those of Pascal, Lichtenberg, Goethe, Schlegel's *Athenaeum Fragments*, or Schopenhauer.[7] The question remains why, after the early period, Nietzsche decisively turns against conventional prose—the scientific monograph of his philological profession or the polemical essays of his *Untimely Meditations*—and adopts instead the aphoristic form.

There is an easy, though not entirely satisfactory, biographical answer to this. Biographers claim that Nietzsche's turn toward the aphorism was due to his debilitating health.[8] He had frequent migraines and vomiting as well as poor eyesight. He contracted diphtheria and dysentery during his two-month service (1870) in the Franco-Prussian War. He was simply incapable of writing or thinking for extended periods of time. A year after the publication of *Human, All Too Human*, he resigned from his chair of classical philology at the University of Basel and began his lifelong wanderings: his mother's house in Naumburg, Wagner's Bayreuth, Sorrento, Nice, Sils-Maria, Leipzig, Genoa, Sicily, Recoaro, Rome, Messina, Florence, Venice, Turin, Jena, and finally back to his mother's house where he died under the care of his sister.[9] Might not the syncopated leaps and bounds of the aphoristic style reflect the free flight of his peripatetic existence?

As it happens, in 1882 Nietzsche acquired a typewriter—or more precisely, a Danish Malling Hansen Writing Ball. From this purchase Friedrich A. Kittler claims that Nietzsche's thinking "changed from argument to aphorisms, from thoughts to puns, from rhetoric to telegram style" (*Gramophone, Film, Typewriter,*

203). However attractive it may be to attribute stylistic and cognitive transformations to the latest writing apparatus, I want to resist such technological determinism.[10] Kittler cites Nietzsche: "Our writing tools are also working on our thoughts" (201). But it is important that he claims scribal apparatus to be "also working," that is, a *co-temporary* of thought, not *dictating* it. After all, the syntax of Henry James, another famous early adopter of the typewriter, became ever more luxuriant and expansive.[11] First, Nietzsche bought a typewriter because of his frequent migraines and bouts of nausea that rendered him incapable of long stretches of thinking or writing, not the other way around. Second, his aphoristic, telegraphic style appears already in *Human, All Too Human* (1878), which predates his typewriting phase by four years. Third, Nietzsche stopped using his writing ball after about five months and reverted to his notebooks. All his subsequent major books were composed in these voluminous pages. Furthermore, aesthetically speaking, the typewriter seems contrary to the "incomplete presentation of an idea" that he so treasured, for its end scripts are neat, unidirectional, perfectly spaced rows, betraying none of the energies, nuances, cadences that handwriting does. In other words, "the effectiveness of the incomplete" is best presented in the messy pages of a continuous notebook rather than the unbound, anonymous lines of a typescript.

It is of course a truism that the form reflects the content of a work, which in turn reflects life: but in this case Nietzsche's fragmentary, kaleidoscopic style reflects not so much the influence of technology or his poor health (which is not so apparent in his published writings) as it does his ludic, peripatetic, postmetaphysical psyche. In *Ecce Homo,* he discusses whether place and climate affect the tempo of the human spirit's metabolism, "to communicate a state, an inward tension of pathos, by means of signs.... I have many stylistic possibilities—the most multifarious art of style [*Möglichkeiten des Stils—die vielfachste Kunst des Stils*] that has ever been at the disposal of one man" ("Why I Write Such

Good Books" §4).[12] The aphorisms, written in this "multifarious art of style" where "profundity and high spirits go tenderly hand in hand," capture the swirling energies of Nietzsche's thoughts.

Aphorisms are therefore one of the most durable literary forms:

> Praise of aphorisms [*Lob der Sentenz*]: A good aphorism [*Eine gute Sentenz*] is too hard for the tooth of time and is not consumed by all millennia, although it serves every time for nourishment: thus it is a great paradox of literature, the intransitory amid the changing [*das Unvergängliche inmitten des Wechselnden*], the food that always remains esteemed, like salt, and never loses its savor, as even that does. (*Human, All Too Human,* "Assorted Opinions and Maxims" §168)

Similarly, Zarathustra states:

> Whoever writes in blood and aphorisms [*Wer in Blut und Sprüchen schreibt*] does not want to be read, but to be learned by heart. In the mountains the shortest way is from peak to peak, but for that one must have long legs. Aphorisms should be peaks [*Sprüche sollen Gipfel sein*]—and those who are addressed should be great and tall. (*Thus Spoke Zarathustra, First Part,* "On Reading and Writing")

These are rich images. Here aphorisms are not fragments of discourse but the hard-earned achievement, the pinnacle that withstands "the tooth of time." In German culture, the mountain has evocative associations as the topography of mystery and revelations of the divine.[13] Both Nietzsche and his alter ego Zarathustra exalt in its elevated, cold, solitary atmosphere. The former spent large parts of his life in Sils-Maria, and the latter spent ten years alone meditating in its caverns. The mountain is the "intransitory amid the changing." The mountain's peaks tower over the craggy slopes, but without the latter's support there would be no such elevation. Scaling the solid mass of the slopes, one might say, represents the author's triumph in reducing the preponderance of thoughts into one single aphorism. In turn, the "tall and lofty" readers need not arduously climb every step to reach the top—they dance and leap from "peak to peak," refreshed by the alpine air.

## Metaphysician or moralist?

As Blanchot reminds us, Nietzsche considered himself the last philosopher. But this means that he is *still* a philosopher (*Infinite Conversation,* 141). Even if he sought to end or replace metaphysics, he nevertheless prolongs a metaphysical way of thinking. Nietzsche affirms that "Nothing exists apart from the whole" (*Twilight of the Idols,* "The Four Great Errors" §8). At the same time, "we should get rid of the whole, unity ... we must shatter the universe, unlearn our respect for the Whole" (*Will to Power* §1062). These are just two of his innumerable contradictory statements. Blanchot proposes an elegant solution: "The fragmentary speech does not know contradiction, even when it contradicts. Two fragmentary texts may be opposed: they are simply posed one after another, one without relation to the other.... If thought is not only a going beyond, if the affirmation of Eternal Return is understood (first) as a failure of this going beyond, then does fragmentary speech open us to this 'perspective,' does it not permit us to speak in this sense?" (153–54, 158). And since the Eternal Return unfolding in time results in endless repetition, fragments cannot but repeat this repetition, paradoxically becoming continuous, and thereby whole.

Robert B. Pippin, *contra* Blanchot, has argued that Nietzsche is better understood not as one of the last great metaphysicians, nor as metaphysics' destroyer, but as the last of the great French moralists who were intensely interested in psychology and human foibles (*Nietzsche, Psychology and First Philosophy,* 7–11). Indeed, in Nietzsche's oeuvre there are some forty-eight references to Montaigne, ninety-eight to Pascal, and twenty-seven to La Rochefoucauld.[14] Their unsentimental concision was refreshing to Nietzsche. He shares with them the ability to coolly pierce through illusions, hypocrisy, and conventions with pungent witticisms. "What interests Nietzsche in 'essays' or 'maxims' or 'pensées,'" Pippin suggests, "is that they are presented without, and with no hidden reliance on, a 'deeper' philosophical theory of human nature or of reason or of anything else" (10).

Indeed, in *Ecce Homo*, the seventeenth-century moralists are highly praised: "There is a small number of old Frenchman to whom I return again and again. I believe only in French culture and consider everything else in Europe today that calls itself 'culture' a misunderstanding." Yet like with most things in his life, this was a deeply ambivalent relationship. What Nietzsche admires in Pascal is his recognition of the wretchedness of the human condition. What he faults him is that he falls back all too easily on Christianity as a means of salvation: "I do not read but *love* Pascal, as the most instructive victim of Christianity, murdered slowly, first physically, then psychologically" ("Why I am so clever" §3). The faith of Pascal "resembles in a gruesome manner a continual suicide of reason—a tough, long-lived, wormlike reason that cannot be killed all at once and with a single stroke" (*Beyond Good and Evil* §46). Even worse, he takes "abundant, over-abundant enjoyment at one's own suffering," wallowing in "desensualization, decarnalization, contrition, Puritanical spasms of penitence, vivisection of the conscience, and *sacrifizio dell'intelletto*" (*Beyond Good and Evil* §229).

### Wirksame

Nietzsche found a more kindred spirit in another figure—Heraclitus. His most sustained examinations of the Greek thinker are found in his lecture notes on *The Pre-Platonic Philosophers* (ca. 1869–72) and the incomplete long essay "Philosophy in the Tragic Age of the Greeks (ca. 1873)." It is not difficult to see the two thinkers' affinities.[15] First, Nietzsche sees Heraclitus as a visionary. He is an "entirely different form of a superhuman [*übermenschlich*] self-glorification.... He sees outside himself only error, illusion, an absence of knowledge—but no bridge leads him to his fellow man, no overpowering [*übermächtig*] feeling of sympathetic stirring binds them to him" (*PPP*, 55). Second, Nietzsche's understanding of Heraclitus' "the oneness and eternal lawfulness of nature's processes" marks the first step in the development of his own doctrine of the Eternal Return.[16] Third, Nietzsche's aesthetics of the ludic, demonstrated most prominently in *The Gay Science,* has a prehistory in Heraclitus' fragment of the child playing with dice (DK B52). Nietzsche is fond of this image, and describes in depth this *paideia* as a "newly awakened drive to play [*Spieltrieb*] now wills once more his *setting into order* (*diakosmesis*)" (*PPP*, 72). Finally, Nietzsche overturns the entire reception history of Heraclitus when he declares that "dissatisfied people are also responsible for the numerous complaints about the obscurity of Heraclitus' style. The fact is that hardly anyone has ever written with as lucid and luminous a quality" (*PTAG*, 64).

For our purposes, what is of interest is Nietzsche's reading of Heraclitus' concept of *time* by way of Schopenhauer. He writes in "Philosophy in the Tragic Age of the Greeks" that Heraclitus "repeatedly said of it [time] that every moment in it exists only insofar as it has just consumed the preceding one, its father, and is then immediately consumed likewise." If one accepts this postulate, one must agree with Heraclitus to conclude that "the whole nature of reality [*Wirklichkeit*] lies simply in its acts [*Wirken*] and that for it there exists no other sort of being." To elucidate this, Nietzsche turns to a long passage in *The World as Will and Representation*:

> Only by way of its acts does [reality] fill space and time. Its activity upon the immediate object conditions the intuitive perception in which alone it has existence. The consequence of the activity of any material object upon another is recognized only insofar as the latter now acts differently from what it did before upon the immediate object. Reality consists of nothing other than this. Cause and effect [*Wirkung*] in other

words make out the whole nature of materiality: its being is its activity. That is why in German the epitome of all materiality is properly called *Wirklichkeit* [actuality], a word much more apt than *Realität*. That upon which it acts is likewise invariably matter; its whole being and nature consists only in the orderly changes which one of its parts produces in another. *Wirklichkeit* therefore is completely relative, in accordance with a relationship that is valid only within its bounds, exactly as is time, exactly as is space. (1.1.4 = *PTAG*, 53–54)

From this Nietzsche concludes that "The everlasting and exclusive coming-to-be [*Das ewige und alleinige Werden*], the impermanence of everything actual [*die gänzliche Unbeständigkeit alles Wirklichen*], which constantly acts and comes-to-be but never is, as Heraclitus teaches it, is a terrible, paralyzing thought" (*PTAG*, 54).

I believe this passage written around 1873 illuminates "the effectiveness of the incomplete" with which we began this chapter. In *Human, All Too Human*, published in 1878, the German for "effectiveness" is *das Wirksame*. In "Philosophy in the Tragic Age of the Greeks" Nietzsche uses at least four forms of *Wirk—Wirken, Wirkung, Wirklichkeit,* and *Wirklichen*—to describe Schopenhauer's and Heraclitus' concept of Eternal Becoming.[17] Eternal Becoming is an important concept for Nietzsche not only because it is ultimately transfigured to his prized doctrine of the Eternal Return in the later writings, but also because there is a sentence that repeats verbatim what is said already in *The Pre-Platonic Philosophers*: "Eternal Becoming possesses something at first terrifying and uncanny: the strongest comparison is to the sensation whereby someone, in the middle of the ocean or during an earthquake, observes all things in motion" (*PPP*, 64 = *PTAG*, 54).

My sense is that by the time he composes *Human, All Too Human,* Nietzsche realizes that the aesthetics of the unfinished is the most stylistically effective (*Wirksame*) because it is able to capture the reality (*Wirklichkeit*) of time that is an ever "exclusive coming-to-be, the impermanence of everything actual" (*Das ewige und alleinige Werden, die gänzliche Unbeständigkeit alles Wirklichen*).[18] In other words, "becoming," the unfolding of things in time, can be best expressed through the aesthetics of the unfinished. Only through this can the "terrible, paralyzing thought" of Heraclitean flux be cured. The artist cannot replicate *in toto* the Kantian sublime found in nature as in "the middle of the ocean" or "during an earthquake." Rather, what she can do is record the sense of temporality by bringing figures to a "halt, so the relief-like, incomplete presentation of an idea, of a whole philosophy [*unvollständige Darstellung eines Gedankens, einer ganzen Philosophie*], is sometimes more effective than its exhaustive realization." This in fact is already anticipated in "Philosophy in the Tragic Age of the Greeks" when he says:

> Only aesthetic man can look thus at the world, a man who has experienced in artists and in the birth of art objects how the struggle of the many can yet carry rules and laws inherent in itself, how the artist stands contemplatively above and at the same time actively [*wirkend*] within his work, how necessity and random play, oppositional tension and harmony, must pair to create a work of art [*wie Nothwendigkeit und Spiel, Widerstreit und Harmonie sich zur Zeugung des Kunstwerkes paaren müssen*]. (62)

The aesthetics of the unfinished carries precisely the "rules and laws inherent in itself" and represents precisely the dialectic between "necessity and random play, oppositional tension and harmony." What is new in *Human, All Too Human* is that Nietzsche brings in the value of hermeneutics, for it becomes the reader's duty to realize ("more is left for the beholder to do, he is impelled to continue working [it]"), to bring into *Wirklichkeit* the artist's intention. Schopenhauer and Heraclitus first "so strongly etched in light and shadow" the idea of the Eternal Becoming (*Ewige Werden*); Nietzsche now must "think it through the end" into the Eternal Return (*Ewige Wiederkunft*).

In sum, the *Wirksame* of aphorisms resides in these moments of philosophical and philological "play," *Spiele*. Schiller is illuminating on this matter: "From this play of *the freely associated ideas*, which is still of a wholly material kind, and to be explained by purely natural laws, the imagination, in its attempt at a free form, finally makes the leap to aesthetic play" (*Letters on the Aesthetic Education of Man*, 174). We may thus say that Nietzsche's aphorism is a Janus-faced play of aesthetic forms: he inherits the genre from classical antiquity, French classicism, and Schopenhauer, yet he also anticipates the fragmentary poetics of the modernists and deconstructionists. This "play of the freely associated ideas" is afforded by his "most multifarious art of style."

## Fragments and systems

We must now ask: do Nietzsche's fragments ever coalesce into a system? In a letter sent to his publisher sometime in the mid-1880s, he writes, "I now need profound tranquility, for many, many years to come, because I am facing the elaboration of my entire system of thought" (*Sämtliche Briefe* 7:297). Is he unwittingly turning into another lugubrious German thinker like Kant or Schopenhauer? How can we reconcile this to what he proclaims in *Twilight of the Idols*: "I distrust all systematizers [*Systematikern*] and avoid them. The will to a system [*Der Wille zum System*] is a lack of integrity" ("Maxims and Arrows" §26)?

To better understand Nietzsche's aversion to systems, we must turn to the *Athenaeum Fragments*, early Romanticism's crucial meditation on fragments and systems. As Rodolphe Gasché suggests, the Romantic fragment is a response to Kant's transcendental idea of totality—*Ganzheit* and *Allheit* ("Foreword," Schlegel, *Philosophical Fragments*, xxviii). The heart of the problem is *Darstellung*—the adequate representation of ideas; the only possible manner of representation is in parts. This is what was implicit in Kant; the Romantics theorized and elevated this to the cult of the fragment.[19] Schlegel writes, "A. You say that fragments are the real form of universal philosophy. The form is irrelevant. But what can such fragments do and be for the greatest and most serious concern of humanity, for perfection of knowledge? B. Nothing but a Lessingean salt against spiritual sloth, perhaps a cynical *lanx satura* in the style of old Lucilius or Horace, or even the *fermenta cognitionis* for a critical philosophy, marginal glosses to the text of the age" (*Athenaeum Fragments* §259).

Kant had defined critical philosophy as "what first raises ordinary knowledge to the rank of science," consisting of nothing less than "the science of the relation of all knowledge to the essential ends of human reason" (*Critique of Pure Reason* A832/B860). This requires the architectonic construction of a system, for "without systematic unity, our knowledge cannot become science; it will be an aggregate." A Kantian would regard an assemblage of aphorisms as a mere "unconnected and rhapsodistic state" without any scientific value (A839/B867).[20] Conversely, a system is that which allows the operation of reason to "find for the conditioned knowledge given through the understanding the unconditioned whereby its unity is brought to completion" (A308/B364).[21]

The Jena Romantics questioned this unity. For them, ideas are "infinite, independent, unceasingly moving in themselves, godlike thoughts" (*Ideas* §10), which cannot be grasped by the faculty of the human intellect. Writing certainly expresses some of the pure thought of reason, but since writing cannot possibly capture such totality, the exercise of approximation leads, by necessity, to the production of literary fragments. In other words, the limits of the Kantian "presentability of ideas" result in the Romantic theory of fragmentation.[22] For Schlegel, the aphorism is the perfect antidote to the epistemic urge for system building. Yet fragments are also generative: inasmuch as they probe the relationships between parts and their totality, the many and the one, they express not only the aftermath of a philosophical inquiry but also its emergence: "One can only become a philosopher, not be one. As soon as one thinks one is a philosopher, one stops becoming one" (*Athenaeum* §54).

The Romantics see systems in fragments: "Aren't all systems individuals just as all individuals are systems at least in embryo and tendency?" (*Athenaeum* §242), and fragments in systems: "Even the greatest system is merely a fragment" (Schlegel, *Literary Notebooks* §930). Either way, "It's equally fatal for the mind to have a system and to have none. It will simply have to decide to combine the two" (*Athenaeum* §53). Hence the fragment as hedgehog.

### Nachlass

It is not difficult to situate Nietzsche as a late descendant of the Romantics.[23] He asks in *Human, All Too Human II*, "Do you think this work must be fragmentary [*Stückwerk*] because I give it to you (and have to give it to you) in fragments [*Stücken*]?" ("Assorted Opinions and Maxims" §128). In *Beyond Good and Evil,* he notes that "individual philosophical concepts ... grow up connected and related to one another; however suddenly and arbitrarily they appear.... They nonetheless belong just as much to a system as do the members of the fauna of a continent" (§20). So how do you reconstruct the development or unity of his thoughts, how do you map such intellectual biodiversity?

I believe that Nietzsche's philosophical idea of a system operates in tandem with his posthumous fragments as philological artifacts. His *Nachlass* can be divided roughly into three kinds. The first comprises the authorized manuscripts completed before his collapse in 1889: *Ecce Homo, Nietzsche Contra Wagner*, and *The Antichrist.* The second are dubbed *Schriften*, primarily his unpublished lectures and writings from the time he was a professor at Basel, such as "On Truth and Lies in an Extra-Moral Sense," *The Pre-Platonic Philosophers,* and "Philosophy in the Tragic Age of the Greeks." The third consists of Nietzsche's 106 notebooks

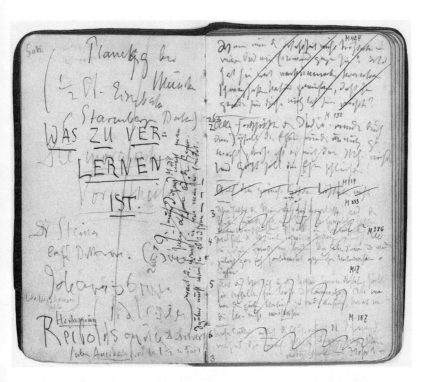

**FIGURE 14.** Nietzsche, octavo notepad (9.5 × 16.5 in.) bound in brown linen cover, 116 pages, notes on *Daybreak*, summer 1880. www.nietzschesource.org/dfga/n-v-3 (Klassik Stiftung Weimar, Goethe- und Schiller-Archiv, 2016).

from 1870 to 1888, varying from almost completed essays, annotated outlines, deleted passages, marginalia, to single sentences or just lists of topics. He reused old notebooks, writing from front to back and then from back to front so that it is difficult to decipher their chronology (see fig. 14).[24]

Faced with such a mass of published and unpublished materials, an editor is confronted with the decision of whether to publish the *Nachlass* chronologically, alongside the contemporary works, as Giorgio Colli and Mazzino Montinari do in their authoritative *Kritische Gesamtausgabe,* or relegate it to later volumes, which is what they do in the abridged *Kritische Studienausgabe*.[25] Is an author's work everything he or she has written? Is *Werke* the process or the product?

It is clear that in Nietzsche's final years he did have a culminating work in mind with the title *The Will to Power: Attempt at a Revaluation of All Values*. This work, edited and published posthumously by his sister, Elisabeth Förster-Nietzsche, purportedly represents Nietzsche's unfinished masterpiece. As is well known, she was a German nationalist and virulent anti-Semite, and attempted to establish an ill-fated "Aryan" colony in Paraguay with her husband, Bernhard Förster.[26] Upon his death, Elisabeth returned to Germany to tend to her incapacitated brother and became his literary executor. In her later years, she supported the Nazi party. It is no surprise, then, that her edition of her brother's work distorts his affinities with nationalism, racism, and fascism. Her *Wille zur Macht*, edited with Peter Gast, artificially organizes his notes by topics, numbers, and culls them into 1,067 fragments, roughly one-third of the 1883–88 notebooks. It is universally recognized as a work of dubious scholarship.[27]

Examining anew Nietzsche's manuscripts in Weimar, Mazzino Montinari observes that from 1885 to 1888 he drafted various outlines with chapter summaries of a final system. But in late August to early September 1888, various letters by Nietzsche attest that he had definitively abandoned his *magnum opus*. By the time of his collapse in 1889, Montinari concludes, he had finished all that he wanted to do: "The unity (even if not 'systematic' in the conventional sense) of Nietzsche's attempt is evident from the entirety of the unpublished writings that have already become well known in their actual, unsystematic form" ("Nietzsche's Unpublished Writings from 1885–88," 84).

How to properly interpret Nietzsche's final writings has been a matter of scholarly debate ever since. Do you give equal weight to the polished aphorisms in his published works and the fragmented jottings in his notebooks? There are perhaps three prevailing interpretive paradigms. One view assumes that Nietzsche took so much care in the presentation of his books that his published writings should take priority since they represent his authorized statements. Another view, which Heidegger maintains, is that his unpublished notebooks actually contain his deeper, undiluted, "Heraclitean" ideas. A third holds that one should take everything Nietzsche wrote and consider both the unity and the development of his thoughts.

To take Nietzsche's notebooks as having the same value as the published works is to posit that "the thinking of the thoughts"—the process—is as important as the thoughts—the product.[28] Yet this panoptic view destroys the carefully crafted self-presentation of the author. Nietzsche explains that "most thinkers write badly because they communicate to us not only their thoughts but also the thinking of their thoughts" (*Human, All Too Human* §188). Moreover, he warns against the biographical fallacy: "The worst readers of maxims are the friends of their author when they are exercised to trace the general observation back to the particular event to which the maxim owes its origin: for through this prying they render all the author's efforts null and void, so that, instead of philosophical instruction, all they receive (and all they deserve to receive) is the satisfaction of a vulgar curiosity" (*Human, All Too Human*, "Assorted Opinions and Maxims" §129).

Yet the value of reading notes and drafts is that they allow us a glimpse into the proverbial "workshop of a great thinker." For Walter Benjamin, "To great writers, finished works weigh lighter than those fragments on which they work throughout their lives.... For the genius each caesura, and the heavy blows of fate, fall like gentle sleep itself into his workshop of labor. About it he draws a charmed circle of fragments" ("One Way Street," in *Selected Writings*, 1:446). And for Giorgio Agamben, "Every written work can be regarded as the prologue (or rather, the broken cast) of a work never penned, and destined to remain so, because later works, which in turn will be the prologues or the moulds for the other absent works, represent only sketches or death masks" (*Infancy and History*, 3). A work, even if it appears to be the most polished and perfect masterpiece, is never innocently complete, for the writer conceals in her study the deletions, drafts, and still-borns that never made it to the light of day.

## Children and fruits

By now we are quite familiar with the concept of the unfinished, and it might seem redundant to cite yet another passage of Nietzsche on the incomplete. Repetition and the unfinished, however, are both about the reiterative process of infinite becoming and closely related to the doctrine of eternal recurrence. For Deleuze, repetition has the "power of beginning and beginning again" (*Difference and Repetition,* 136).[29] With that in mind, let us read this entry from *Human, All Too Human*:

> Uncompleted thoughts [*Nicht fertig gewordene Gedanken*]. – Just as it is not only adulthood but youth and childhood too that possess value in themselves and not merely as bridges and thoroughfares, so incomplete thoughts also have their value [*die nicht fertig gewordenen Gedanken ihren Werth*]. That is why one must not torment a poet with subtle exegesis but content oneself with the uncertainty of his horizon, as though the way to many thoughts still lay open. Let one stand on the threshold; let one wait as at the excavation of a treasure: it is as though a lucky find of profound import were about to be made. The poet anticipates something of the joy of the thinker at the discovery of a vital idea and makes us desire it, so that we snatch at it; he, however, flutters by past our heads, displaying the loveliest butterfly wings—and yet he eludes us. (§207)

This passage is a brilliant demonstration of Nietzsche's skill as a coiner of images—the aesthetics of the unfinished cannot be articulated analytically but only expressed through a series of lyrical analogies: juvenescence, the promise of the horizon, the archaeologist's eureka moment, the poet's dream, the butterfly's flight.[30] These vivid metaphors of larvae and lava forcefully show that

Nietzsche's own "uncompleted thoughts" must "possess value in themselves" and not be reckoned as only drafts that must be discarded once the final project is completed, for any notion of a final project might well be a myth anyways.

Yet in the preface to *On the Genealogy of Morals*, he employs one more image that suggests otherwise: fruits. Commenting on the long gap between his first two books, Nietzsche writes that time makes ideas "riper, clearer, stronger, more perfect." "Our ideas, our values, our yeas and nays, our ifs and buts," he continues, "grow out of us with the necessity with which a tree bears fruit—related and each with an affinity to each, and evidence of *one* will, *one* health, *one* soil, *one* sun" (Preface §2). Nietzsche helps us gloss this horticultural imagery in *Human, All Too Human*: "Something said briefly can be the fruit and harvest of much long thought [*Etwas Kurz-Gesagtes kann die Frucht und Ernte von vielem Lang-Gedachten sein*]: but the reader who is a novice in this field, and has as yet reflected on it not at all, sees in everything said briefly something embryonic, not without censuring the author for having served him up such immature and unripened fare" ("Assorted Opinions and Maxims" §127). This arboreal metaphor is appropriate: Nietzsche's aphorisms are both seeds and fruits, seeds that contain the potential of full flourishing, seeds implanted in the reader's mind to germinate, and fruits that are the sweet produce of the author's thoughts after a long Indian summer. (See the discussion of Jesus' and Erasmus' mustard seeds in chapter 4.) The inclusion of "harvest" suggests the wider ambit of an entire field or orchard, or an entire season. While fruits as a completed product might seem contrary to the "uncompleted thoughts" entry that praises the intrinsic value of "youth and childhood," are children, too, not the fruits of the womb? And the purpose of fruits is, after all, the propagation of the species. They renew season after season—their *telos* is their repetition. *This* perhaps is the primal will-to-power: the desire to reproduce, to flourish, to expand and fill the earth with the harvest of one's words.

## The distance between thoughts and words

The self-reflexive nature of Nietzsche's writings, as we have explored them, begs the question of the development of his thoughts. Now we have to go a level deeper and think about the tenuous continuity between inner thoughts, speech, and writing. Nietzsche's interest in the production of thought—the movement from ideas in our minds to ideas expressed in writing—is repeated throughout the course of both his published and unpublished works, yet it is never theorized systematically. *The Gay Science:* "Even one's thoughts one cannot reproduce entirely in words" (§244). *Ecce Homo:* "I am one thing, my writings are another matter" ("Why I Write Such Good Books" §1). *Beyond Good and Evil:* "One no longer loves one's insights enough once one communicates it" (§160). Four years before his collapse in Turin, Nietzsche writes in a letter to his close friend Franz Overbeck: "My philosophy, if that is what I am entitled to call what torments me down to the roots of my nature, is no longer communicable, at least not in print" (*Writings from the Late Notebooks,* x). Finally, perhaps most suggestive of all, this penetrating insight from *Twilight of the Idols*: "We have already grown beyond [*darüber*] whatever we have words for; in all talking there lies a grain of contempt [*Gran Verachtung*].... The speaker has already vulgarized [*vulgarisirt*] himself by speaking" ("Expeditions of an Untimely Man" §26).

In a passage remarkably similar to Nietzsche's thoughts, Schopenhauer writes:

> The actual life of a thought lasts only until it reaches the point of speech: there it petrifies and is henceforth dead but indestructible, like the petrified plants and animals of prehistory. As soon as our thinking has found words it ceases to be sincere or at bottom serious. When it begins to exist for others it ceases to live in us, just as the child severs itself from its mother when it enters into its own existence. (*Essays and Aphorisms*, "On Books and Writing" §5)

Schopenhauer's vexation with language is a paradox: the journey from inner thoughts to outward expression—in a word, communication—is one of deep inauthenticity. It leads to dispossession and "petrification." So is silence the only way to express sincerity and seriousness? This impossibility would ultimately lead to Schopenhauer's famous tragic sense of life. For Nietzsche, in his attempt to overcome nihilism, it means embracing the figural nature of language, as explored in the early essay "On Truth and Lies in an Extra-Moral Sense."[31] The figural nature of things is that which allows us to glimpse the "horizon," "the threshold," the archaeologist's "treasure" chest, for therein awaits the promise of fulfillment.

A fragment from late 1887 or early 1888 states: "I maintain the phenomenality of the inner world, too, everything of which we become conscious is arranged, simplified, schematized, interpreted through and through—the actual process of inner 'perception,' the causal connection between thoughts, feelings, desires, between subject and object, are absolutely hidden from us—and are perhaps purely imaginary" (*Will to Power* §477). For Schopenhauer and Nietzsche, the idea of language as the medium between the inner and external self is at best a shaky one. Nietzsche denies any transparency between intention and expression, since there is always something lost in the movement between the two. That is not to say that they deny any relationship, only a derivative one. Nietzsche's, and to an extent Schopenhauer's, concept of the "will"—this instinctual drive, this ceaseless striving for motion— cannot be rationalized in language.[32]

In short, Schopenhauer and Nietzsche propose that within our souls there are thoughts, passions, and feelings that are before and beyond words. This gesture toward the inefficacy of language is not the same as the mystic's apophasis, for it is not an acknowledgment of the ineffable infinitude of the divine in the face of the human; rather, it suggests that there is nothing but a gossamer link between our unconsciousness and language. Hence it is not difficult to see how this would ultimately lead to psychoanalysis.

This abyss of meaning is prior to the deconstructive view of language, for it posits not so much that language is a system intrinsically indeterminate and contingent but rather that consciousness, or, more precisely, the instinctual preconscious inner lifeworld of individuals, cannot be completely comprehended or articulated in language. As such, the interpretation of aphorisms as a search for origins—either the etiology of their historical meaning or the author's mind—is a tragic mistake, since origins are always already irretrievably lost.

## Farewell to books

We began our investigation of Nietzsche's aphorisms by reading them as expressions of "the effectiveness of the incomplete." Next we moved on to consider how they are also "blood" and "peaks," "the intransitory amid the changing," "forms of the eternal." Then we came to the basic interpretive problem of how to distinguish Nietzsche's *Nachlass* from his published aphorisms. Finally, we discussed the extent to which any notion of expression is fraught with difficulties, since speech, much less writing, can only approximate inner life. What, then, finally is the value of aphorisms for Nietzsche? For one simple but powerful reason: they are quick to read.

Reading too much erodes your capacity for original thinking: "I have seen this with my own eyes: gifted natures with a generous and free disposition, 'read to ruin' in their thirties—merely matches that one has to strike to make them emit sparks— 'thoughts.' Early in the morning, when day breaks, when all is fresh, in the dawn of one's strength—to read a book at such a time is simply depraved!" (*Ecce Homo*, "Why I Am so Clever" §8).

The danger of excessive reading, Nietzsche thinks, is that it leads to an idolatry of the book: we confuse the explication of text for the interpretation of life. The final goal of reading aphorisms is not so much to penetrate their inner meaning (something that Nietzsche seems to deny anyway) but rather to use them as a springboard to other lines of inquiry. "I don't write treatises [*Abhandlungen*]," he continues, "they're for jackasses and magazine readers [*Esel und Zeitschriften-Leser*]" (*KSA* 11:579). For this reason, readers should, like Roman builders, plunder from older writers in order to build their own edifices: "*Error of the philosophers. –* The philosopher believes that the value of his philosophy lies in the whole, in the building: posterity discovers it in the bricks with which he built and which are then often used again for better building: in the fact, that is to say, that that building can be destroyed and *nonetheless* possess value as material" (*Human, All Too Human*, "Assorted Opinions and Maxims" §201).[33] This practice is by no means original to Nietzsche. Montaigne encapsulates the entire Renaissance practice of imitation by admitting that his work is no more than a careful spoliation of previous texts and thinkers.[34] Ultimately, there must be a coproduction of meaning between the aphorist and the reader.

For Nietzsche, readers must create at last their own values, for "nobody can get more out of things, including books, than what he already knows" (*Ecce Homo*, "Why I write such good books" §1). The ideal reader, in contrast, is one who "turns into a monster of courage and curiosity; moreover, supple, cunning, cautious; a born adventurer and discoverer" (§3). "Ultimately, the individual derives the values of its acts from itself; because it has to interpret in a quite individual way even the words it has inherited. Its interpretation of a formula at least is personal, even if it does not create a formula; as an interpreter, the individual is still creative" (*Will to Power* §767). Perhaps Nietzsche would say that any textual explication of an aphorism is both vulgar and pedantic. Too much hermeneutics becomes a logorrhea, an excess verbiage of the spirit. True interpretation is internal, silent, and lived. "The book which, after demolishing everything, fails to demolish itself will have exasperated us to no purpose," says E. M. Cioran, a great admirer of Nietzsche (*All Gall Is Divided*, 8). When you understand an aphorism, you no longer read but think; you no longer think but live.

For this reason, my favorite aphorism of all is: "What good is a book that does not even carry us beyond [*über*] all books?" (*Gay Science* §248).

# Epilogue

## A CIRCLE

We need no reminders that we live in a digital world of ceaseless clicks, swipes, and likes. The short forms that we encounter today come more likely from the glow of the illuminated screen than the inert pages of a book: tweets, memes, GIFs. Aphorisms seem appropriate yet ill-matched to this cultural climate of the short attention span. They are quick to read, of course, but because of their hermeneutic density, they also suspend our demand for instant gratification. In 2012 an unsigned editorial post of *n+1* smartly characterized internet writing as having two styles: the logorrhea of the blogs and the terseness of Twitter: "The tweet is a literary form of Oulipian arbitrariness, and the straitjacket of the form has determined the schizophrenia of the content" ("Please RT"). Against our insatiable appetite for what's next, we are made to both linger on and scroll quickly through this microform.

Ending with Twitter might seem too predictable, too over-determined, but every book is a product of its time. The company was founded in 2006, launching the now ubiquitous platform of the 140-character short form (now enlarged to 280). It is not

difficult to see Twitter as a digital descendant of the analog aphorism. But the ecosystem of twitterature embraces more: it is a
vehicle also for journalism, advertising, corporate communication, self-promotion, political campaigns, experimental poetry,
micro short stories, collaborative works, and rewritings of the
classics.[1] Though I have yet to find an author whose tweets possess the hermeneutic depths of the aphorisms I have discussed
(though I don't doubt that many are out there), I am nevertheless
fascinated by its communicative possibilities.

In terms of my theory of the aphorism, tweets come before,
after, and against long-form publications. Sometimes they function as headlines or clickbaits that link to longer forms of continuous writing. And in terms of my central conceptual paradigm—
fragments and systems—Twitter offers both on an exponentially
larger and faster scale. Tweets exist as quantifiable bytes of data,
complete fragments like Schlegel's hedgehog, but taken as an
aggregate (the cunning foxes of multiple updates) they offer the
illusion of intimacy at a distance, all the while being stored in a
"cloud," a gigantic system of virtual storage whose material body
is nowhere but presence everywhere. Whereas before you had
to be a member of the cultural elite for anyone to pay attention to
you, now anyone can be a French *moraliste*, as long as you have
followers. Not only that, your distribution is instantaneous. Anyone with an account can "follow" or "retweet." Today, social
media is how you get attention, from your closest friends to the
anonymous masses. In this sense, the Kantian *system* should be
replaced by the term *network,* for the former implies an architectonic coherence and the other a limitless, centerless flow of information. Taken together, Twitter becomes the largest archive
of the present the world has ever seen.

So far, I have deliberately suspended discussions of the political implications of aphorisms. Through Twitter's real-time circulation, digital posts have become powerful instruments of protest
from Turkish coups to anti–Wall Street encampments to political
demonstrations in Tahrir Square.[2] And the irony of writing this

book in the age when a demagogue has tweeted his way into the presidency has not escaped me. His 24/7 rants have been aptly described as "the oracular communiqués of a deranged minor god" (Purdy, "What I had lost was a country").

In early China, direct criticism of the ruler was not possible. Instead, ministers would remonstrate through poetic allusions— an apposite verse launched at the opportune moment of crisis would reveal the truth through a moral principle.[3] This is the strategy that President Obama followed in his response to white-supremacist violence in Charlottesville, Virginia, in the summer of 2017. In a series of three tweets, he wrote, "No one is born hating another person because of the color of his skin or his background or his religion.... People must learn to hate, and if they can learn to hate, they can be taught to love.... For love comes more naturally to the human heart than its opposite. – Nelson Mandela."

These words are from the last chapter of the anti-apartheid leader's autobiography, *Long Walk to Freedom* (622). As he narrates his release from prison to the day of his inauguration as president of South Africa, he reflects on the possibility of healing after decades of racial oppression. While Mandela's hopeful words are embedded in the eloquent texture of his prose, as an excerpt they easily become aphoristic. Here is one moral authority quoting another moral authority, indirectly but unmistakably criticizing the current political authority. The interpretation that Mandela's words demands is an ethical one and an exhortation to action. Obama's tweet quickly became the most liked and one of the most retweeted tweets of all time.[4]

Likes and retweets are ways for people to give instantaneous approval and feedback. The singular utterance of the tweet thus becomes dialogic through the comment box that spawns immediate commentarial and subcommentarial traditions on a page that can be scrolled down infinitely. The more "followers" you garner, the more authority and the wider circulation you have. The daily fragments of thoughts and opinions coalesce into a system that reveals the psyche of the individual and the collective spirit of the internet. As with the transition from orality to text, scroll to codex, manuscript to print, tweets can proliferate in innumerable iterations across various media. The analog page of Mandela's book, published in 1994, is effortlessly transposed to the digital screen in 2017. Weighed with moral urgency, it is made intensely relevant.

## Exhaustion

While I was working on this book, I kept returning to two aphorisms: Nietzsche's "What good is a book that does not even carry us beyond all books?" and Calvino's "I dream of immense cosmologies, sagas, and epics all reduced to the dimension of an epigram." As I conclude, I want to ask: Is the urge to produce aphorisms a way of curbing the excessive production of words, or does it exacerbate it?

There are still too many epigrams. Too many books. Too many tweets.

The topoi of "too many books" and "nothing new under the sun" are connected and have long genealogies. Heraclitus: "Much learning does not teach one to have intelligence; for it would have taught Hesiod and Pythagoras, and again, Xenophanes and Hecataeus" (DK22 B40). Ecclesiastes: "For in much wisdom is much vexation, / and those who increase knowledge increase sorrow" (1:18). Laozi: "He who knows has no wide learning; he who has wide learning does not know. The sage does not hoard" (*Daodejing* §81). Seneca: "In reading of many books is a distraction" (*Ep.* 1.2.3). Marcus Aurelius: "Forget your books; no more hankering for them; they were no part of your equipment" (2.2). Dogen: "You should stop searching for phrases and chasing after words. Take the backward step and turn the light inward" (*Treasury of the True Dharma Eye,* 907). Pascal: "All the good maxims already exist in the world: We just fail to apply them" (S458/L540). Vauvenargues: "A truly new and truly original book would be one

which made people love old truths" (*Réflections et maximes* §400).
Goethe: "What was discovered long ago is buried again; how
hard Tycho tried to show that comets were regular structures, a
fact known to Seneca long ago" (*Maxims and Reflections* §123).
Thoreau: "What the first philosopher taught the last will have to
repeat" (*Journal*, 1:123). Schopenhauer: "The art of *not* reading
is a very important one. It consists in not taking an interest in
whatever may be engaging the attention of the general public at
any particular time" ("On Books and Writing" §16); André Gide:
"Everything has been said before, but since nobody listens we
have to keep going back and beginning all over again" ("Le traité
du Narcisse," 1); Canetti: "The great writers of aphorisms read as
if they had all known each other well" (*Human Province*, 34).

I am reminded of what Jean-Luc Nancy says near the beginning of *The Birth to Presence*: "A moment arrives when one can
no longer feel anything but anger, an absolute anger, against so
many discourses, so many texts that have no other care than to
make a little sense, to redo or to perfect delicate works of signification" (5). I often have this feeling of vertiginous exhilaration—
excitement, agitation, frustration, despair—whenever I enter a
bookstore or the library or even surf on Amazon.com: all the
oceans of texts and mountains of books that I'll never have time
to read. I always want to write about epics and encyclopedias but
end up working on ruins, fragments, aphorisms.

### Zengo

It seems almost a cliché nowadays to suggest an Asian alternative
to this surfeit of mostly Western discourse. And it is true that the
West has always turned to Asian aesthetics as an antidote to modern technology.[5] But since I am an Asian-American teaching early
modern European literature in Asia, I have some personal interest in this intercultural exchange.

One winter my wife and I had a brief stopover in Kyoto on our
way back from Singapore to the United States for the Christmas

holidays. We visited many temples, monasteries, and shrines. In some hall of every dwelling there invariably hangs an ink scroll of a Zen aphorism, called *zengo* (禅語). *Zengo* are written in the way of the brush, *shodo* (書道). They are closely related to the *koan* (公案), paradoxical questions that the master poses to the beginning novice during practice in order to break through the rational mind's cascades of affirmations and negations. There are eight-, seven-, six-, five-, four-, three-, two-, and one-character *zengo*. Some of my favorites are:

庭前柏樹子
*Teizen no hakujushi*
"The cypress tree in the front garden"

日日是好日
*Nichi-nichi kore kō-nichi*
"Every day is a good day"

無根樹
*Mukonju*
"Rootless tree"

放下著
*Hōgejaku*
"Let it go!"

如是
*Nyoze*
"Thus"

不識
*fushiki*
"Don't know"

知足
*chisoku*
"Know enough"[6]

These sayings, easily parodied, find their way onto some dozen Twitter sites that broadcast a daily dose of Zen wisdom. But in whatever media they are transmitted, contemplation of their meaning—memorizing and assimilating them to daily life—is central to Zen practice. In the hushed silence of the hall, the ink traces of the scroll aid the mind in achieving a state of clarity and stillness. The founder of the Soto school of Zen, Master Dogen, states: "To study the Buddha Way is to study the self, to study the self is to forget the self, and to forget the self is to be enlightened by the ten thousand things" (*Treasury of the True Dharma Eye,* 30).

How did these single-line Zen aphorisms come to be? In order to answer this question, we have to trace, very briefly, a vast swath of cultural history, starting with the origins of Indic sutra, proceeding to Chinese brush painting, before finally arriving back at Zen meditation.

## Origins of *sūtra*

In Sanskrit, *sūtra* is one equivalent word for "aphorism," and it is one of the most important genres of writing in South Asia.[7] In a series of groundbreaking studies beginning in the 1940s, Louis Renou explored its origins and development.[8] He hypothesized that the word derived from weaving, cognate with "suture"; thus sutra is a "guiding thread" or a "rule." When strung together, single sutras come to constitute a unifying sutra. So sutra refers to both the integral text as well as an individual unit of line. Renou categorized two types of sutras: an earlier one—descriptive, normative, brief—related to Vedic rituals, roughly corresponding to *śruti,* "that which is heard"; and a later one—argumentative, dialectical, structured—related to the philosophical schools, roughly corresponding to *smṛti,* "that which is remembered" ("Sur le genre du sūtra," 165). So again we have oracular originals followed by a deluge of commentary, revealed writings mixed with discursive ones, fragments and systems.

Pāṇini's grammar (ca. fourth century BCE) is widely considered the pinnacle of the philosophical schools, and its main feature is brevity (Skr. *Lāghava*).[9] Similar to Erasmus' theory of adages, sutras should have a general applicability, descriptive exactness, and authoritativeness. This is how Madhvācārya, the thirteenth-century founder of the school of Dvaita Vedānta, defines it:

> A *sutra* consists of a small number of syllables, (of) intelligible (sentences), contains the essence, "faces all sides" (does not focus attention on one subject), is free from (exclamatory and laudatory) insertions, (and is) irreproachable. (Houben, "*Sūtra* and *Bhāsyasūtra*," 288)

If we substitute aphorism for sutra, Erasmus, Schlegel, or Nietzsche would have no problem accepting this definition. Like Western and Chinese aphorisms, sutras necessitate commentary, or *bhāsyasūtra*. A fifth-century CE subcommentator declares, "A sutra needs to be supplemented whence we supply a remaining part of the sentence" (278). A tenth-century commentator elaborates, "[What is indicated] need not be explicitly stated by a Sūtra-author, for Sūtra-authors do not explicitly state what is indicated through meaning" (289). So again we have a finite, fixed aphorism that germinates into massive forests of exegesis.

Now one of the most important commentaries on Pāṇini's grammar is by Patañjali. According to tradition (now disproved by scholarship), he also wrote the *Yoga Sūtra* in a sort of Buddhist-hybrid Sanskrit, a text that was virtually forgotten until it was rediscovered by Westerners in the nineteenth century.[10] As is typical of any sutra, it is accompanied by a vast apparatus of commentaries and glosses. It has meant many things to many people. Nevertheless, its teaching can be distilled in its second sutra:

> Yoga is the stilling of the changing states of the mind.
>
> *Yogas citta-vrtti-nirodhah.* (16)

From just this one verse it is easy to see how Buddhist meditation—and its Zen manifestation—cross-fertilized with this spiritual tradition.[11] The Buddha, after all, received many years of training from different communities and meditated the entire night before he became enlightened. Bodhidharma, the fifth- to sixth-century CE monk who transmitted Chan (Zen) Buddhism to China, meditated facing a wall for nine years. In contrast to the myriad discursive interpretations that we have encountered in the previous pages, Zen meditation (*zazen*) is ultimately nonhermeneutic, a practice of emptying the mind: no thinking, just sitting, just breathing. The irony is that instructions on how to meditate still require plenty of explanations.[12]

In Buddhism, the Sanskrit *sūtra* is conflated with the Pali *sutta*.[13] According to tradition, sutras or suttas are the written transmission of the Buddha's oral teaching. The Pali Canon of the Sutta-piṭaka is made up of four major collections, the long sayings (*dīgha*), the middle-length sayings (*majjhima*), the grouped sayings (*samyutta*), and the numbered sayings (*aṅguttara*) (Norman, *Pāli Literature*, 30–95). The fundamental texts of the Mahayana tradition are in the Tripiṭaka, the "three baskets." Scholars point out that, remarkably, the general doctrines in both the surviving Chinese and Pali texts are mostly in agreement.[14] And like the case of early Christianity, oral recitation lives alongside and commingles with its textual transmission.

## One single stroke

Anyone who's ever looked at Buddhist scriptures will know that they are not short at all. Impressively prolix, sutras are multithreaded bodies of work—like the 250,000-line *Perfection of Wisdom Sutra*; but they are also composed of individual strands that can exist on their own. Indeed, the making of excerpts is highly encouraged. The *Mahāprajñāpāramitā Sūtra*, some 100,000 lines and part of the *Perfection of Wisdom*, is reduced to the *Heart Sutra* of 260 Chinese characters. The *Heart Sutra* is further reduced to the mantra, "Form is emptiness and emptiness is form" (色即是空, 空即是色). In detaching a singular thread of the sutra from the vast warp and woof of Buddhist scriptures, we encounter the old problem of the autonomous saying and its assemblage.

The copying of sutras as merit for salvation has long been an Indic practice. As Buddhism traveled eastward, this merged with the distinctively Chinese art of calligraphy. And as Chan/ Zen developed in China and traveled to Japan, it absorbed this refined art of the literati and entered into ritualized practice. Chinese theories of calligraphy had already emphasized, on one hand, painstaking preparation—the rubbing of the ink stick on the ink stone, the correct placement of the paper, the arrangement of the brushes, correct lighting and posture; on the other, the spontaneous power of the hand—the elastic control of moisture, speed, and pressure that contribute to the liveliness of the composition.[15] In Japanese, the term *bokuseki* (墨跡, "ink traces") expresses the calligraphic style of bold, dynamic strokes reduced to their purest essences. The distance between the spontaneity of the artist and the slow rumination of art cannot be any greater—or closer.

This aesthetic corresponds well with the strict discipline and intense concentration of a Zen monk. The Song dynasty literatus Huang Tingjian wrote, "I used to say of writing that brushwork in characters is like insight in the sayings of the Chan masters" (Brinker, *Zen Masters*, 100). Having absolute immediacy, admitting of no correction, *bokuseki* embody the calligrapher's state of meditative consciousness or *samadhi*. On one hand, *zengo* are not grasped by employing the rational intellect but by transcending it. On the other, they are a condensation of centuries of scriptures, teachings, and transmissions, from the source texts such as the *Gateless Barrier*, *The Blue Cliff Record*, and the *Treasury of the True Dharma Eye*. These, too, begin with a gnomic apothegm followed by commentary.

In one branch of Buddhist metaphysics, the whole universe is envisioned as a vast textual sutra, and each particle of dust con-

FIGURE 15. Nakahara Nantenbō (1839–1925), "Enso with a poem, 'If that moon falls, I will give it to you. Now try to take it,'" 1922/23, ink on paper, National Gallery of Victoria, Melbourne.

tains within itself the whole world. There are no more fragments, no more systems, for "there is no moment or place that is not sutras. The sutras are written in letters of the supreme principle and of the secular principles," "one character contains unlimited meanings; one single stroke contains innumerable truths."[16] This becomes the principle that allows the reduction of entire sutras into one *zengo*, a verse into a word. One word contains within it an infinitude of meaning. Finite aphorism, infinite signification. Indeed, for Zen, and for Buddhism in general, language is but the finger that points to the moon. And once the river has been crossed, the proverbial raft—assembled from the rickety timber of aphorisms—is no longer necessary. Silence pervades.

In the meandering trajectory from Sanskrit to Pali to Chinese and Japanese, we see once again how aphorisms function as agents of cultural and personal change, adapting to their material and social circumstances, changing with their societies and speakers, all the while maintaining their inner claim to be carriers of truth.

Given that the preceding pages have already treated so many aphorisms with so many interpretations, it seems a good idea to end with these single-word aphorisms, unexplicated:

靜
*jing*
"Stillness"

黙
*Moku*
"Silence"

無
*Mu*
"Emptiness"

○
*Ensō*
"Circle"

# ACKNOWLEDGMENTS

This book was written during the sometimes halcyon, sometimes hectic days between my wife's pregnancy and my daughter's first birthday. Having an infant around the house meant that the intense concentration required for reading epics or philosophical tracts was all but impossible, so I had to resort to a much shorter form.

The thinking behind it all, however, probably began when I was a freshman at the Santa Fe campus of St. John's College, when we read Heraclitus and Parmenides in our morning Greek-language tutorial and Plato and Aristotle in our evening seminar. Then at the Annapolis campus, in my junior and senior years, we read Pascal and La Rochefoucauld; Kant, Hegel, and Nietzsche. In New Mexico my tutors were Frank Pagano, Susan Stickney, and Matthew Davis; and in Maryland, Stephen Larsen, the late Douglas Allanbrook, Thomas May, and Joseph MacFarland. From them I learned how to ask questions.

At Princeton as a graduate student, I read Erasmus, Bacon, and other humanists with Leonard Barkan, Anthony Grafton, and Jeff Dolven; Nietzsche with Alexander Nehamas; and early Chinese thought with Martin Kern and Willard Peterson. From them I learned how to be a scholar.

At Stanford as a postdoctoral fellow, I taught Nietzsche with Joshua Landy, Lanier Anderson, and Sepp Gumbrecht, and the European epic with Robert Pogue Harrison and Marisa Galvez. From them I learned how to teach.

During the early stage of thinking, I was sustained by some lively, intense conversations with Robert Pogue Harrison in a seafood restaurant by Lago Bracciano outside Rome (he then subsequently invited me to talk about the project on his podcast, *Entitled Opinions*); Haun Saussy at the London Review of Books Café; Paul Fry and Brigitte Peucker at the P. S. Café Petit in Tiong Bahru; Ann Blair and David D. Hall at the Rare Books School seminar at the Houghton Library; Glenn Most and Michael Puett at the Ancient Wisdom workshops at Humboldt-Universität; Sean McCann at the Royals Bistro at NUS U-Town; and Gavin Flood at the Agora Café, where we went every week after our world religious poetry course. From them I learned how to have good conversations.

I tried out bits and pieces of the book at the American Comparative Literature Association, the Renaissance Society of America, Bodleian Libraries' Centre for the Study of the Book, Underwood College at Yonsei University, and Yale-NUS. From these audiences I learned how to give talks.

It was at Yale-NUS that the book was written. I'm happy to have friends such as Mira Seo, Matthew Walker, Shaoling Ma, Geoff Baker, Paro Kulkarni, Robin Hemley, Mate Rigo, and leaders such as Tan Tai Yong, Pericles Lewis, Steven Bernasek, Charles Bailyn, Joanne Roberts, and Rajeev Patke. From them I'm learning how to be a colleague.

I thank Scott Cook, Glenn Most, Michael Puett, Matt Walker, Luke Parker, Phillip Horky, Eric MacPhail, Paul Fry, and Guy Stroumsa, who all read individual chapters. In the process of writing, Stephen Moore, Clio Doyle, and Emily Dalton were my copyeditors. From them I'm learning how to write.

From the moment of contact to production, Anne Savarese has been superb: timely, efficient, ever-encouraging. The two readers' reports she commissioned were nothing short of brilliant: they saved me from many errors, deepened the book's textual engagement, and raised its theoretical reach. As the physical book came into being, I appreciated the professional and generous work of Thalia Leaf, Ellen Foos, Daniel Simon, and Thomas Broughton-Willett. From them I'm learning how to be an author.

As the book came to a close, Roman Larson taught me the new meaning of some old aphorisms. From him I'm learning how to be a friend.

This book is dedicated to Melissa, with whom I live out my daily aphorisms, and Julia, our living, breathing little book of aphorisms. From them I'm learning how to be human.

I am grateful to all.

# NOTES

A *note on citations and convention*: Numbers preceded by § refer to the numeric order of the aphorism rather than the page number; numbers with a colon (5:2) refer to the book or chapter followed by the section or subdivision; a pure number (4) refers to the page number. All translations from Greek and Latin texts, unless otherwise noted, are from the Loeb Classical Library, following the abbreviations established in the *Oxford Classical Dictionary*, 4th ed. Greek texts are reproduced in the block quotes; in the body text, they are transliterated. All scripture is from the New Revised Standard Version; all Plato from the *Complete Works* edited by John M. Cooper and all Aristotle from the *Complete Works* edited by Jonathan Barnes. All other translations are found in the bibliography, and all unattributed translations are mine.

Throughout I will use the gender-neutral "they" or "their" to refer to the hypothetical singular reader.

## Introduction: A Line

1. The full title of the 1665 first edition is *Réflexions ou sentences et maximes*, but they are conventionally called just *maximes*. The first term has religious as well as Cartesian connotations; the second is usually moral or legal judgment; and the third, as Ian Maclean has argued, becomes in La Rochefoucauld descriptive rather than prescriptive ("La Rochefoucauld, Little Learning and the Love of Truth," 304–5). See also Francis Goyet, "L'origine logique du mot maxime."

2. See also his "L'expérience du proverbe," and Haun Saussy's discussion in *Ethnography of Rhythm*, 17–26.

3. See Ludwik Sternbach, *Subhāṣita, Gnomic, and Didactic Literature*.

4. See Michael V. Fox, "Ancient Near Eastern Wisdom Literature."

5. On the difficulty of calling these texts philosophy, see Wiebke Denecke, *The Dynamics of Masters Literature*, 1–32.

6. See Hans Armin Gärtner's erudite entry, "Gnome," in *Brill's New Pauly*, with a rich bibliography. Old English riddles are found in the Exeter Book and examined in Dieter Bitterli's *Say What I Am Called*.

7. As Jonathan Barnes does in his introductory account in *Early Greek Philosophy*, xi. For a social history of proverbs, fables, *gnōmai*, and *exemplae*, see Teresa Morgan, *Popular Morality in the Early Roman Empire*, 84–121.

8. See Han Baltussen, *Philosophy and Exegesis in Simplicius.*

9. See Barry Taylor, "Medieval Proverb Collections."

10. But see Mary Franklin-Brown's analysis in *Reading the World.* Whereas an earlier generation of scholars, such as Émile Mâle, saw encyclopedias as well ordered as the soaring cathedrals of the period (6), she sees them as "heterotopias," drawing on the concept of Foucault (216–18). Her analysis of the *Speculum Maius* is in ch. 5.

11. See Timothy Billing's translation of Ricci's *On Friendship.*

12. On Wittgenstein's style, see Stanley Cavell's classic, "The *Investigations'* Everyday Aesthetics of Itself."

13. For theoretical reflections, see William Tronzo, ed., *The Fragment;* for historical analysis, see Clifford Siskin, *System: The Shaping of Modern Knowledge.*

14. See my *Poetics of Ruins in Renaissance Literature,* ch. 2. I discuss Petrarch in ch. 3.

15. Rodolphe Gasché makes the connection of *Darstellung* to fragments in his foreword to Schlegel's *Philosophical Fragments,* esp. xi.

16. Although the aesthetics of the unfinished is usually seen as a Romantic topos, it goes before and beyond it. Vasari in his *Lives of the Artists* remarked on Michelangelo's Medici *Madonna* that "though the parts are unfinished, what is left roughed out and full of chisel marks reveals, in the imperfection of the sketch, the perfection of the work" (*nella imperfezione della bozza la perfezione dell'opera,* 2:902). Paul Valéry writes in "au Sujet du Cimetière Marin," "a work is never truly completed, but abandoned" (*Il n'y a pas d'oeuvre achevée, il n'y a que des oeuvres abandonnées*).

17. Schleiermacher himself expressed his theory of hermeneutics in "Die Aphorisimen von 1805 und 1809/10" before laying out his comprehensive *Outline of the 1819 Lectures. Hermeneutics and Criticism* was published four years after Schleiermacher's death in 1838.

18. See André Lardinois, "Modern Paroemiology and the Use of Gnomai in Homer's *Iliad.*"

19. Brooke Holmes argues that with the emergence of interpretations of somatic symptoms from the sixth century BCE onward, the human body becomes a site of empirical knowledge (*The Symptom and the Subject,* 84–120). Symptoms lie at the "threshold of seen and unseen," and by explaining the causes of the diseases hidden inside a person, physicians developed a new ethics of care (126). Jacques Jouanna in *Hippocrates* examines his relationship with the Presocratics (259–89) and the fifth-century "birth of the human sciences" (210–42).

## Chapter 1: Confucius

1. There are many sound translations of the *Analects*: see James Legge, Arthur Waley, D. C. Lau, Burton Watson, E. Bruce Brooks and A. Taeko Brooks, Roger T. Ames and Henry Rosemont Jr., and Simon Leys. I have benefited most from the recent translations by Edward Slingerland and Annping Chin, because they include many of the traditional commentaries. All quotations are from Slingerland (at times slightly

modified), which follows the Chinese text of Cheng Shude 程樹德, regarded as having the most extensive annotations in a modern edition. For a state-of-the-field survey, see Oliver Weingarten, "Recent Monographs on Confucius and Early Confucianism."

2. In the *Balanced Discussions,* Wang Chong gives a different account, stating that the original *Analects* had more than a hundred chapters. See Tae Hyun Kim and Mark Csikszentmihalyi, "History and Formation of the Analects," 2, and in general John Makeham, "The Formation of *Lunyu* as a Book."

3. Maurizio Scarpari, *Il confucianesimo*, 31–37 provides a good account.

4. See Scott Cook's important *The Bamboo Texts of Guodian*. Dirk Meyer's *Philosophy on Bamboo* argues that the pervasive use of bamboo and ink during the second half of the first millennium BCE enabled an efflorescence of philosophical activity.

5. Michael Hunter's *Confucius Beyond the* Analects is an exhaustive study that distinguishes the Kongzi of the *Lunyu* and the other "Kongzis" depicted in the other multitudinous texts. See pages 39–45 for a list of all the extant sources, which run to the dozens. Also helpful is *Concise Companion to Confucius,* edited by Paul Goldin, with the first three chapters by Hunter, Cook, and Weingarten.

6. See *Confucius and the* Analects *Revisited*, edited by Hunter and Martin Kern.

7. See John Makeham's magisterial *Transmitters and Creators*, a study of the commentarial tradition from the Han to the Qing dynasties; John Henderson's stimulating *Scripture, Canon, and Commentary* is a cross-cultural approach.

8. For the formation of the Confucian canon, see Michael Nylan, *The Five "Confucian" Classics,* and Daniel K. Gardner, *The Four Books.*

9. This inverse ratio is also true for the *Spring and Autumn Annals*, whose composition Mencius attributes to Confucius. As a 241-year chronicle of the minor state of Lu, it lists, season-by-season, important births, deaths, accessions, sacrifices, harvests, wars, peace treaties, the earthly and celestial phenomena of the realm. While cumulatively the text is massive, each unit of text seems on its surface as short and dry and factual as a telephone book. So enormous rationale had to be conjured in order to find a deeper meaning out of it. The *Commentary of Zuo* (左傳) and the *Commentary of Gong Yang* (公羊) are such enterprises.

10. What Foucault says about sixteenth-century Europe is true for traditional China too: "The task of commentary can never, by definition, be completed. And yet commentary is directed entirely towards the enigmatic, murmured element of the language being commented on: it calls into being, below the existing discourse, another discourse that is more fundamental and, as it were, 'more primal.' … There can be no commentary unless, below the language one is reading and deciphering, there runs the sovereignty of an original Text" (*The Order of Things,* 45).

11. Lionel Jensen, *Manufacturing Confucianism*, explores how the figure of the Master was invented by the Jesuits.

12. See in general the forthcoming edited volume by Glenn W. Most and Michael Puett, *Rethinking Wisdom Literature.*

13. These are the *Spring and Autumn Annals* (*Chunqiu,* 春秋), *Book of Poetry* (*Shijing,* 詩經), *Book of Documents* (*Shangshu,* 尚書), *Records of Rituals* (*Liji,* 禮儀), and the *Classic of Changes* (*Yijing,* 易經).

14. See *From Max Weber* on the organization of bureaucracy, 196–244; sociology of charismatic authority, 245–52, his analysis of the Chinese literati, 416–44. Also Randall Collin's thousand-page *The Sociology of Philosophies*, explaining the development of philosophical schools in China, Greece, and India through the complex network of "interaction ritual chain," which creates "argumentative communities" across generations.

15. Martin Kern cautions that "in thinking about the early 'Masters,' we also must once and for all abandon the traditional approach that treats the 'Masters' as the personal authors of these eponymous texts" ("The 'Masters' in the *Shiji*," 336).

16. For a brief, reliable history, see Kogen Mizuno, *Buddhist Sutras*.

17. See Mark Lewis, *Writing and Authority*, 297–99.

18. See Henderson, *The Construction of Orthodoxy and Heresy*.

19. See John Brough, "Thus Have I Heard."

20. A. C. Graham's *Disputers of the Tao* provides clear philosophical analyses of these schools.

21. See chapter 18, *lunshuo* 論說. *Weiyan* 微言 is already attested in the *Hanshu*, but it is developed into a sophisticated theory in Liu Xie.

22. The *Analects* "constructs nothing theoretically, nor does it reveal anything mystically. Its intention is not to direct our behavior from the outside, by shaping it to the teachings of a doctrine, but to favor its adaptation in relation to a circumstance. This wisdom guides us toward an ever more intimate reconciliation with what each situation expects from us in order to create a proper balance. And it does so in an eminently variable way" (*Detour and Access*, 195–96). Jullien's thoughts are provocative but controversial in sinology. Lewis cites him approvingly in *Writing and Authority* (395, n.117) and follows his line of argument: "The hermeneutics of the *Lun yu*, which is closely tied to the enunciatory structure of the text, shaped the Chinese understanding of the sage intellect and the authoritative text. A suspicion of the ultimate reliability of language and the possibility of fixed definitions, a denial of absolute and unchanging truths or rules, the location of meaning and authority within the endlessly adaptable wisdom of the sage mind, the preference for locating truth within particular propositions that suggested broader truths, the tendency to privilege the indirect over the explicit, all these traits appeared within the writing and reading of the *Lun yu* and became central to later notions of wisdom" (*Writing and Authority*, 86).

23. There are accounts of the Master's itinerant journeys in *Zhuangzi* and Sima Qian, chapter 47.

24. This is my own rendering, which I prefer to Daniel K. Gardner's "On Reading." See also his *Zhu Xi's Reading of the* Analects.

25. For example, "Learning is like a chase in which, as you fail to catch up, you fear to lose what you have already gained" (8.17); "Every day I examine myself on three counts: in my dealings with others have I in any way failed to be dutiful? In my interactions with friends and associates, have I in any way failed to be trustworthy? Finally, have I in any way failed to repeatedly put into practice what I teach?" (1.4).

26. See Susan Cherniack, "Book Culture and Textual Transmission in Sung China," and Ann M. Blair, *Too Much to Know*.

27. See part 2 of Makeham's *Transmitters and Creators,* "Commentary as Philosophy: Huang Kan's *Lunyu yishu,*" 79–170.

28. See, among others, Peter K. Bol, *Neo-Confucianism in History.*

29. This is true for commentaries on the *Book of Songs* as well: they moved from specific, grammatical explanations of individual odes to general aesthetic treatises such as the *Wenfu* and *Wenxindiaolong.*

30. The Ming iconoclast Li Zhi 李贄 (1527–1602) would write: "After Yan Hui passed away, Confucius's subtle words were cut short, sagely learning died out, and [genuine] Confucianism was no longer transmitted" (*A Book to Burn and a Book to Keep (Hidden),* 17, trans. modified).

31. Sarah Allen's *The Way of Water and Sprouts of Virtue,* esp. 29–62, explores how water was the paradigm for conceptualizing cosmic principles in early China. Her gloss of *Analects* 9.17 is on 35–36.

32. See James I. Porter's magisterial *The Sublime in Antiquity.*

# Chapter 2: Heraclitus

1. The critical editions of Heraclitus include Miroslav Marcovich, *Heraclitus;* G. S. Kirk, *Heraclitus: The Cosmic Fragments;* T. M. Robinson, *Heraclitus;* and Charles Kahn, *The Art and Thought of Heraclitus.* By far the most exhaustive is that of Serge Mouraviev's *Heraclitea,* an edition with twenty projected volumes. Eleven have been published so far. Here I use the most recent Loeb edition of André Laks and Glenn W. Most (at times silently modified). The first reference (DK) is to the widely accepted ordering by Hermann Diels and Walther Kranz, the second (LM) refers to Laks and Most's unique numbering.

2. Paolo Valesio's *Novantiqua* is essentially a 300-page exegesis of this fragment.

3. Even scholars today call early Greek thinking "Presocratic philosophy," a prelude to Plato; the "Presocratic" implies a teleology, and the word "philosophy" was a contested term before Plato and Aristotle. For a history of the term's construction, see André Laks, *The Concept of Presocratic Philosophy.* For a portrait of the intellectual world, see Maria Michela Sassi, *The Beginnings of Philosophy in Greece.* Early Greek philosophy is particularly well served by a number of splendid anthologies. First and foremost is Diels and Kranz, *Die Fragmente der Vorsokratiker,* translated by Freeman in *Ancilla to the Pre-Socratic Philosophers.* More recent ones include Patricia Curd, *A Presocratics Reader;* Richard D. McKirahan, *Philosophy Before Socrates;* G. S. Kirk, J. E. Raven, M. Schofield, *Presocratic Philosophers;* Daniel W. Graham, *Texts of Early Greek Philosophy;* and Jonathan Barnes, *Early Greek Philosophy.* Though Guy Davenport's *7 Greeks* is not a scholarly translation, it is poetic and supple and should not be ignored.

4. One may make a counterargument that Parmenides' poem presents a series of arguments, but its very form—a composite of visionary myth, philosophical treatise, scientific cosmology, all in dactylic hexameter, the meter of the epics—suggests that he must wrap his thoughts in verse. Moreover, while deduction is certainly present

in the early mathematicians (for example, Hippocrates of Chios) and, from a different angle, Parmenides, neither are usually assumed to practice discursive or dialectical philosophy. I thank Philip Horky for suggesting this line of argument to me.

5. See Uvo Hölscher, "Paradox, Simile, and Gnomic Utterance in Heraclitus," and Lisa Maurizio, "Technopaegnia in Heraclitus and the Delphic Oracles."

6. Vernant, "Myth and Thought among the Greeks," 387.

7. There is much work on this topic. The most impressive, and recent, is Peter Struck, *Divination and Human Nature*.

8. See Giovanni Manetti, *Theories of the Sign in Classical Antiquity*, for a semiotic approach; and in general Struck, *Birth of the Symbol*, for a history of ideas approach, with special attention to allegory.

9. See Michael Scott, *Delphi*, 9–30 for a description of the ritual.

10. "Poetry thus arrived on the scene as the form structuring those ambiguous words that people came to hear to help them make decisions about their lives, words whose meaning they often appreciated only when it was too late" (Calasso, *The Marriage of Cadmus and Harmony*, 144).

11. See Andrea Nightingale, "Sages, Sophists, and Philosophers," and Johannes Engels, *Die sieben Weisen*.

12. The maxim is discussed elsewhere in the Platonic corpus: see *Charmides* 164d, *Protagoras* 343b, *Phaedrus* 229e, *Philebus* 48c, *Laws* II.923a.

13. Two recent reinterpretations are Most, "Heraclitus Fragment B123 DK," and Graham, "Does Nature Love to Hide? Heraclitus B123 DK."

14. To be more precise, Odysseus at this point has revealed his identity, but the question remains as to how truthful he is in his retelling of his voyages.

15. See also his later 1966–67 *Heraclitus Seminar* conducted with Eugene Fink. The point about Aristotle's gloss of *legein* as *apophainesthai* is so important for Heidegger that it already appears in the subsection of the second part of the introduction to the 1927 *Being and Time*, "Concept of Logos," 28.

16. John Burnet, *Early Greek Philosophy*, 133n; Martin L. West, *Early Greek Philosophy and the Orient*, 124–29; Jonathan Barnes, *Presocratic Philosophers*, 59.

17. Kirk, *The Cosmic Fragments*, 39; Marcovich, *Heraclitus*, 113; Graham, *Explaining the Cosmos*, 132–33; Enrique Hülsz, "Heraclitus on *Logos*," 291–92. See Mark A. Johnstone's "On *Logos* in Heraclitus," esp. 5–9; and Robinson's "Heraclitus and *logos*— again" for the background of the debate.

18. See Gavin Flood, *The Truth Within*. I will explore the task of searching within oneself in the next chapter with the *Gospel of Thomas*.

19. Heraclitus, in the words of Anthony A. Long, inquired into the "deepest reaches of selfhood" (*Greek Models of Mind and Self*, 8). Long argues that before Plato, Heraclitus is the only thinker from whose writings we can recover some theory of the soul (83). In "Heraclitus on Measure and the Explicit Emergence of Rationality," Long goes so far as to say that "Heraclitus discovered an idea and ideal of rationality by incorporating such notions in his logos, something that no one, to the best of our knowledge, had done before" (202). See also Martha Nussbaum, "*Psyche* in Heraclitus."

20. Except Nietzsche, who explicitly declares that "dissatisfied people are also responsible for the numerous complaints about the obscurity of Heraclitus' style. The fact is that hardly anyone has ever written with as lucid and luminous a quality" (*Philosophy in the Tragic Age of the Greeks*, 64). See chapter 6.

21. Scholars are divided on whether Heraclitus had a coherent argument. Kahn holds that he was the "first major prose author of Greece," and that his lost work was "genuinely literary prose." ("Philosophy and the Written Word," 114, 111). See also the introduction to his *Art and Thought of Heraclitus*. Diels' *Die Fragmente der Vorsokratiker*, Kirk's *The Cosmic Fragments*, and Marcovich's *Heraclitus* all stress the obscure nature of his thoughts. Hölscher's "Paradox, Simile, and Gnomic Utterance in Heraclitus" states that Heraclitus depends on "intuition and simile" rather than rigorous logic. Jaap Mansfeld's "Myth, Science, Philosophy" also sees little argument or logic in Heraclitus. For a judicious summary of the critical debates, see Herbert Granger, "Argumentation and Heraclitus' Book," 1–3.

22. In the stimulating "Aphorism and Argument," Jonathan Barnes ponders the relationship between the gnomic pithiness of the short saying and philosophy's penchant for particles and connectives.

23. In a very different context, at the consummation of Wagner's *Tristan und Isolde*, Tristan says, "*Tristan du, ich Isolde, nicht mehr Tristan!*" and Isolde replies, "*Du Isolde, Tristan ich, nicht mehr Isolde.*" Their individual identities dissolve and merge into one (act 2, scene 3).

24. See in general Hadot, *Veil of Isis*.

25. For Nicholas of Cusa, this will become *coincidentia oppositorum*—the principle in which finite beings can grasp the infinite.

26. See David Sider, "The Fate of Heraclitus' Book in Later Antiquity."

27. For analytic reconstructions, see Gregory Vlastos, "On Heraclitus," and Edward Hussey, "Epistemology and Meaning in Heraclitus."

28. See Harold F. Cherniss's still valuable *Aristotle's Criticism of Presocratic Philosophy*.

29. For some methodological reflections, see Mansfeld, "Doxography of Ancient Philosophy."

30. Kahn, *Art and Thought of Heraclitus*, 25.

31. Mouraviev presents a précis of his multidecade work and a reconstruction in "Le livre d'Héraclite 2500 ans après. L'état actuel de sa reconstruction." Kahn admits that "the present arrangement is largely my own contrivance, the result of much trial and error, and it has no special title to historical authenticity" (*Art and Thought of Heraclitus*, 6). Laks and Most state, "Our own order (like other, different ones before ours) aspires only to suggest possible associations and to gather together, for convenience of consultation, fragments that seem to form thematic groupings" (*Early Greek Philosophy: Early Ionian Thinkers, Part 2*, 114).

32. *Herakleitos der dunkle, von Ephesos, dargestellt aus den Trümmern seines Werkes und den Zeugnissen der Alten* (*Heraclitus the Obscure, of Ephesus, Depicted on the Basis of the Ruins of His Work and the Testimonia of the Ancients*), published in the *Museum der Alterthums-Wissenschaft*, edited by Friedrich August Wolf and Philipp Buttmann, 1807.

33. Ineke Sluiter in "Obscurity" gives its typology from unintentional to intentional.

## Chapter 3: *The Gospel of Thomas*

1. Translation by Marvin Meyer from *The Nag Hammadi Scriptures*, 140–56. The numbers in parentheses refer to the numbered *logion*.

2. See also John 8:52, "If any one keeps my *logos*, he will never taste death."

3. See Mt. 13:49, 25:32; Lk. 6:22; Acts 13:2, 19:9; Rom. 1:1; Gal. 1:15, 2:12.

4. The *Gospel of Thomas* has been the subject of numerous studies in the past two decades. I have benefited particularly from April DeConick, *Seek to See Him* and her *Voices of the Mystics;* Marvin Meyer, *Secret Gospels;* Jon Ma Asgeirsson, "Arguments and Audience(s) in the *Gospel of Thomas*"; Nancy Dorian, *The Gospel of Thomas*; Stevan L. Davies, *The Gospel of Thomas and Christian Wisdom;* Stephen J. Patterson, Hans-Gebhard Bethge, and James M. Robinson, *Fifth Gospel;* Stephen J. Patterson, *The Gospel of Thomas and Christian Origins*; Risto Uro, *Thomas;* and Richard Valantasis, *The Gospel of Thomas.*

5. "*Pap oxy* 1 preserves the Greek original of *Gos. Thom.* 28–33, *Pap. Oxy. 654* the first seven sayings, and *Pap. Oxy 655* sayings 37–40" (Helmut Koester, *Ancient Christian Gospels,* 76).

6. On the authorship question, see Patterson, *The Fifth Gospel*, 29–32.

7. See the *Acts of Thomas*, a third-century text.

8. For the relationship between the proverbial literature and Q, see Ronald A. Piper, *Wisdom in the Q-Tradition*; James G. Williams, *Those Who Ponder Proverbs;* and Patterson, "Wisdom in Q and *Thomas.*" John Dominic Crossan in *In Fragments* offers a systematic classification of Jesus' short sayings by different genres, compounds, dialogues, stories, and models. He argues that these short sayings are distinct from Jesus' parabolic teachings. Also of interest is volume 55 of *Semeia: Early Christianity, Q and Jesus.*

9. See *Ancient Education and Early Christianity*, edited by Matthew Ryan Hauge and Andrew W. Pitts.

10. The question of Gnosticism is a contentious one. Those who use the Gnostic category include James Robinson, ed., *The Nag Hammadi Library;* Willis Barnstone and Marvin Meyer, *The Gnostic Bible;* and Bentley Layton, *The Gnostic Scriptures.* Those who avoid the term include Michael Allen Williams, *Rethinking Gnosticism;* and Karen L. King, *What Is Gnosticism?* DeConick, Davies, Dunderberg, and Uro discuss the designation in their works.

11. The original verb "says" is in the present tense, though the Meyer translation renders it in the past.

12. See Werner Kelber's argument, much influenced by Derrida, in *The Oral and the Written Gospel.*

13. There is some philological debate whether the phrase should be punctuated "Thus have I heard: at one time the Blessed one was staying at Savatthi" or "Thus heard

I on one occasion: the Buddha was staying..." The difference is whether "at one time" modified the subject or the accusative object. See John Brough, "Thus Have I Heard."

14. See Gérard Vallée, *A Study in Anti-Gnostic Polemics,* and Geoffrey S. Smith, *Guilt by Association.* For a theoretical overview, see Jacques Berlinerblau, "Toward a Sociology of Heresy, Orthodoxy, and *Doxa.*"

15. See Robinson's preface to *The Nag Hammadi Scriptures,* xi–xii. For the problem of *Thomas* as an "apocryphal" scripture and the Patristics' canonization of the four Gospels, see Koester, *Ancient Christian Gospels,* 14–19, 360–430.

16. Stroumsa in *The Scriptural Universe of Ancient Christianity* (125–26) builds upon Weber's paradigm.

17. Pierre Bourdieu writes, "Orthodoxy, straight, or rather straightened, opinion, which aims, without ever entirely succeeding, at restoring the primal state of innocence of doxa, exists only in the objective relationship which opposes it to heterodoxy, that is, by reference to the choice—*hairesis,* heresy— made possible by the existence of *competing possibles*" (emphasis in original, *Outlines of a Theory of Practice,* 169).

18. See William P. Brown, *Character in Crisis*; James L. Crenshaw, *Old Testament Wisdom*; John J. Collins, *Jewish Wisdom in the Hellenistic Age;* and Michael V. Fox, ed., *Essays on the Art of the Aphorism.*

19. For a study of the topos of the hiding of the face of God (*histîr pānîm*) in the Hebrew Bible, see Samuel E. Balentine, *The Hidden God.* For the Jewish origins of the esoteric traditions in early Christianity, see Stroumsa, *Hidden Wisdom.* For concealment in Gnostic, esoteric, and mystical traditions, see DeConick and Grant Adamson, eds., *Histories of the Hidden God.*

20. See the discussion in Davies, *Gospel of Thomas and Christian Wisdom,* 37–39.

21. See Henri de Lubac, *Medieval Exegesis,* and Erich Auerbach, "Figura."

22. The bibliography on parables is vast. The tip of the iceberg, from the literary perspective, is Frank Kermode, *The Genesis of Secrecy*—see ch. 2, "Hoti's Business: Why Are Narratives Obscure?"—and Joshua Landy, *How to Do Things with Fiction,* 43–68.

23. The theologian Richard Kearney has written that "hermeneutics is a lesson in humility (we all speak from finite situations) as well as imagination (we fill the gaps between available and ulterior meanings)" (*Anatheism,* xvi).

24. Benjamin also writes, "Proverbs cannot be applied to situations. Instead, they have a kind of magical character: they transform the situation" ("On Proverbs," *Selected Writings,* 2:2:582).

25. Davies, *Gospel of Thomas and Christian Wisdom,* 41.

26. See Courcelle's magisterial three-volume *Connais-toi toi-même.* Hans Dieter Betz has two very helpful articles, "The Delphic Maxim γνωθι σαυτον in Hermetic Interpretation" and "The Delphic Maxim 'Know Yourself' in the Greek Magical Papyri." Patterson synthesizes their findings in his chapter "Jesus Meets Plato" in *The Gospel of Thomas and Christian Origins,* 33–60.

27. Cf. "If anyone keeps my word, that person will never taste death" (John 8:42). This insistence on "taste" is without a doubt a reference to Adam and Eve's eating from the Tree of Good and Evil.

28. See Gavin Flood, *The Truth Within*.

29. For the presence of the *Gospel of Thomas* in Clement, see Alain Le Boulluec, "De *l'Evangile des Egyptiens* à *l'Evangile selon Thomas* en passant par Jules Cassien et Clément d'Alexandrie," and Salvatore Lilla, *Clement of Alexandria*.

30. The counter reading would be that this is Heraclitus' critique of gold-seekers— the futility of their task.

31. The critical edition is Miroslav Marcovich, *Hippolytus*.

32. See Catherine Osborne, *Rethinking Early Greek Philosophy*, and Jaap Mansfeld, *Heresiography in Context,* ch. 1.

33. See his synoptic *Philosophy as a Way of Life*.

## Chapter 4: Erasmus and Bacon

1. Between the 1508 and the final 1536 editions, others appeared in Basel in 1515, 1517/18, 1520, 1523, 1528, 1530. For the publication history, see Margaret Mann Phillips, *The "Adages" of Erasmus*; John N. Grant, "Erasmus' Adages," in *The Collected Works of Erasmus*, 30:1–84; and William Barker's introduction to his selection, *The Adages of Erasmus*, ix–xlvii.

Important works on the *Adages* include Kathy Eden, *Friends Hold All Things in Common*; Jacques Chomarat, *Grammaire et rhétorique chez Érasme*; Lisa Jardine, *Erasmus*; Eric MacPhail, *Dancing around the Well*; Daniel Kinney, "Erasmus' *Adagia*"; and Thomas M. Greene, "Erasmus' 'Festina lente.' "

2. The standard editions of Erasmus' works are now the Amsterdam edition of *Opera omnia* and *The Collected Works of Erasmus* published by the University of Toronto Press. In this chapter, the English translation is cited by volume and page number, followed by the internal section and line numbers.

3. I.e., *Calvitiae encomium* 22 = fragment 13 Rose. I thank my colleague Steven Green for helping me with this translation.

4. See my *Poetics of Ruins in Renaissance Literature*, ch 1.

5. *amicorum communia omnia* (I i 1); *dulce bellum inexpertis* (IV i 1); *festina lente* (II i 1); *caecus caeco dux* (I viii 40); *una hirundo non facit ver* (I vii 94); *bis dat qui cito dat* (I viii 91); *quot homines, tot sententiae* (I iii 7); *leonem ex unguibus aestimare* (I ix 34); *in aqua scribis* (I iv 56); *tempus omnia revelat* (II iv 17); *nosce teipsum* (I vi 95); *ne quid nimis* (I vi 96); *multa novit vulpes, verum echinus unum magnum* (I x 18).

6. In Erwin Panofsky's eloquent formulation, "The Middle Ages had left antiquity unburied and alternately galvanized and exorcised its corpse. The Renaissance stood weeping at its grave and tried to resurrect its soul" (*Renaissance and Renascences in Western Art*, 113).

7. For the impact of proverbs on Netherlandish visual culture, see Walter S. Gibson, *Figures of Speech*.

8. See Seneca's simile of the bees in epistle 84, which became proverbial in the Renaissance, explored in G. W. Pigman III's much-cited "Versions of Imitation in the Renaissance."

9. See these seminal works that have shaped the field: Thomas M. Greene, *The Light in Troy*; Ann Moss, *Printed Commonplace-Books and the Structuring of Renaissance Thought*; Francis Goyet, *Le sublime du 'lieu common'*; Terence Cave, *The Cornucopian Text*; Mary Thomas Crane, *Framing Authority*; Jeff Dolven, *Scenes of Instruction,* ch. 3; Natalie Zemon Davis, "Proverbial Wisdom and Popular Errors"; George K. Hunter, "The Marking of *Sententiae* in Elizabethan Printed Plays, Poems, and Romances."

10. See Ian Mclean, *Interpretation and Meaning in the Renaissance*, 202.

11. See Thomas Rütten, "Hippocrates and the Construction of 'Progress' in Sixteenth- and Seventeenth-Century Medicine."

12. Some of them include the sayings of Sextus Empiricus, which capture so well Montaigne's vacillations: ου καταλαμβανω, "I do not understand"; επεχω, "I stop"; and σκεπτομαι, "I examine." See Alain Legros, *Essais sur poutres.*

13. See George A. Kennedy's translations in *Progymnasmata.*

14. One of my favorite *apophthegamata* is by the eighteenth-century Frenchman Nicolas Chamfort: "A poet consulted Chamfort on what he thought about a distich, 'Excellent,' he said, 'except for its length'" (*Caractères et Anecdotes* §1248).

15. See Peter Mack, *Renaissance Argument*, 117–29, 244–56.

16. The image of gems is also discussed in MacPhail, *Dancing around the Well,* ch. 2.

17. See Albertus Magnus (attributed), *Book of Minerals.*

18. Osip Mandelstam has an entomological metaphor: "A quotation is not an excerpt. A quotation is a cicada. It is part of its nature never to quiet down" (*Selected Poems,* 108).

19. See Robert P. Crease, *Prism and the Pendulum,* 59–76.

20. Maryanne Cline Horowitz in *Seeds of Virtue and Knowledge* studies how the Stoics' biological images for rationality—sparks and seeds—had far-reaching influence on the idea of the human good from antiquity to the Renaissance.

21. See Jill Kraye, "Pagan Philosophy and Patristics in Erasmus and His Contemporaries"; in general, Jerry H. Bentley, *Humanists and Holy Writ,* and Erika Rummel, *Humanist-Scholastic Debate in the Renaissance and the Reformation.*

22. See H. J. De Jonge, "Erasmus' Method of Translation in His Version of the New Testament."

23. *medium ostendere digitum* (II iv 68); *in canis podicem inspicere* (II ii 36).

24. For *lectio divina,* see Jean Leclercq, *The Love of Learning and the Desire for God,* 5–7.

25. See Jean Céard, "La Censure tridentine et l'édition Florentine des *Adages* d'Érasme."

26. In the *Birth of Tragedy,* Nietzsche writes that the Alexandrian man is "basically a librarian and proof-reader, sacrificing his sight miserably to book-dust and errors" (§18). He discusses the antiquarian mode of history in "The Use and Abuse of History for Life."

27. MacPhail discusses some of these passages in a different context in *Dancing around the Well,* 116–33.

28. Susan Sontag, America's Barthes, writes in her diary that "an aphorism is aristocratic thinking: this is all the aristocrat is willing to tell you; he thinks you should get it fast, without spelling out all the details. Aphoristic thinking constructs thinking as an obstacle race: the reader is expected to get it fast, and move on. An aphorism is not an argument; it is too well-bred for that" (*As Consciousness Is Harnessed to Flesh,* 512).

29. See Ann M. Blair's wonderful *Too Much to Know.*

30. Where available, I use the ongoing *Oxford Francis Bacon* (*OFB*), ed. Rees, Trapp, Jardine, and Vickers. For the *Novum organum,* I have also consulted the editions by Peter Urbach and John Gibson as well as that by Lisa Jardine and Michael Silverthorne. For all other works, I use the Victorian *Works of Francis Bacon,* ed. Spedding, Ellis, and Heath (1889–1901) which is precritical.

31. See Hans Blumenberg, *Shipwreck with Spectator,* followed by Paolo Rossi, *Naufragi senza spettatore,* and Eric MacPhail, "The Submersion of Tradition."

32. For a portrait of this world, see Jennifer Summit, *Memory's Library.*

33. In general, I have benefited from reading Stephen Gaukroger, *Francis Bacon and the Transformation of Early-Modern Philosophy* and his *The Emergence of a Scientific Culture*; Lisa Jardine, *Francis Bacon*; and Paolo Rossi, *Francis Bacon.*

34. Peter Harrison, *The Bible, Protestantism, and the Rise of Natural Science.* Responding to Harrison, Richard Serjeantson proposes that Bacon is the first to articulate an explicitly "interpretive" vision of nature in "Francis Bacon and the 'Interpretation of Nature' in the Late Renaissance." He reminds us that the subtitle of *Novum Organum* is *sive indicia vera de interpretatione naturae,* "or, True Indications on the Interpretation of Nature."

35. I am hardly the first to study Bacon's use of aphorisms, though I believe I am unique in considering it in connection to the uncompleted nature of *Instauratio magna*: see Stephen Clucas, "'A Knowledge Broken'"; Brian Vickers, *Francis Bacon and Renaissance Prose,* ch. 3; James Stephens, "Science and the Aphorism"; Alvin Snider, "Francis Bacon and the Authority of Aphorism"; Lisa Jardine, introduction to Francis Bacon, *New Organon,* xvii–xxi; Sister Scholastica Mandeville, "The Rhetorical Tradition of the Sententia, with a Study of Its Influence on the Prose of Sir Francis Bacon and of Sir Thomas Browne."

36. This is not to suggest that he was not interested in human history. He published biographies of Henry VII (1622) and Henry VIII (1621).

37. See Neal Ward Gilbert, *Renaissance Concepts of Method.* Recent scholars have cautioned that the use of the "scientific method" for Bacon is anachronistic. Graham Rees and Maria Wakely state: "As for 'method,' Bacon never used the term in *Novum organum* or anywhere else, to mean 'scientific method'" (*OFB* 11:lxxii).

38. See Walter J. Ong's classic *Ramus, Method, and the Decay of Dialogue.*

39. In general, Bacon makes no distinction between aphorisms and axioms. In *Advancement of Learning,* the proverbs of Solomon are called both; in the *New Atlantis,* the greatest achievement of the "interpreters of nature" is the production of "general observations, aphorisms, and axioms."

40. Alastair Fowler gives bibliographic information on the inscriptions, engraver, and printer in *The Mind of the Book*, 127–31.

41. See Didier Maleuvre, *The Horizon*, 4.

42. Rees and Wakely provide an exhaustive publication and manuscript history in the introductions to volumes 11–13 of the *OFB*.

43. Daniel Garber entertains one reading of the *Sylva*: "One might think of it as a Baconian natural history, rearranged to look like a popular miscellany, and larded with elements of the fantastic and lurid to draw the reader in, like a comic-book version of a classic novel" ("Merchants of Light and Mystery Men," 103). While he finds this appealing, he ultimately rejects it and proposes instead that the *Sylva* represents the messy, inchoate stages of constructing a natural history, where the course of investigation is neither orderly nor systematic.

44. This vision was the inspiration for the founding of the Royal Society in 1660. One could argue that terse articles in the early decades of the *Philosophical Transactions of the Royal Society* are an outgrowth of Bacon's aphoristic philosophy.

45. Guido Giglioni explore the topos of *selva* in "From the Woods of Experience to the Open Fields of Metaphysics," 247.

46. For a discussion of this imagery, see Peter Pesic, "Wrestling with Proteus," and its controversy, "Proteus Rebound."

# Chapter 5: Pascal

1. The entire publication history is based on three caches of documents preserved today in the Bibliothèque nationale de France. The first is the so-called "Recueil original," containing some 741 fragments in Pascal's own hand, attached randomly onto folio sheets in 1711. Nonetheless, this is the only autograph collation that exists (fond français 9202). Étienne Périer supervised two transcriptions in 1662–63: the "Première Copie" (fond français 9203) and "Seconde Copie" (fond français 12449). See discussion in Pol Ernst, *Les Pensées de Pascal, géologie et stratigraphie*; Jean Mesnard, *Les Pensées de Pascal;* Anthony R. Pugh, *Composition of Pascal's Apologia*.

2. These categories were hotly debated in the generation after Pascal in the "Quarrel between the Ancients and Moderns." As Bernard Fontenelle noted in his "Sur la poésie en général," "Order, clarity, correctness [*L'ordre, la clarté, la justesse*], which were once qualities rare even among the best writers, are now much more common." And Charles Perrault in his *Parallèle des Anciens et des Modernes* declared that the legacy of Descartes has made the modern literary style "clear, precise [*nette*], and methodical" (translated and discussed in Larry F. Norman, *Shock of the Ancient*, 155, 162). The clarity of French became proverbial, reaching its apotheosis in Antoine Rivarol's 1783 prizewinning essay "De l'universalité de la langue française," which haughtily proclaimed: *Ce qui n'est pas clair n'est pas français*, "What is not clear is not French." See Marc Fumaroli, "The Genius of the French Language," 588–90 on Gallic Cartesianism, and 604–6 on Rivarol's claims.

3. See Marie Pérouse, *L'invention des 'Pensées' de Pascal.*

4. On the influence of the *Logic* on the organization of the *Pensées,* see Antony McKenna, *Entre Descartes et Gassendi,* 59. In general, Tad M. Schmaltz, "What Has Cartesianism to Do with Jansenism?"

5. See Michel Le Guern, *Pascal et Descartes;* Vincent Carraud, *Pascal et la philosophie,* ch. 3; Jean-Luc Marion, *Sur le prisme métaphysique de Descartes,* ch. 5; Roger Ariew, "Descartes and Pascal."

6. The commonly accepted edition is Philippe Sellier, having superseded that of Louis Lafuma. There are good English translations by Honor Levi, A. J. Krailsheimer, and Roger Ariew. I chose Ariew's translation because of its relative literal fidelity to the French, and he follows Sellier's numbering.

But since the Lafuma is still read, the parenthetical letters and numbers indicate the ordering established by Sellier (S) and Lafuma (L). Most French editions print a concordance in the back. Dominique Descotes and Gilles Proust offer digital facsimiles of the manuscripts and copious annotations at www.penseesdepascal.fr.

7. See Jean Laporte, *Le Coeur et la raison selon Pascal.*

8. Works on the moralists include Paul Bénichou, *Morales du grand siècle;* Louis Van Delft, *Les Moralistes. Une apologie;* Bérangère Parmentier, *Le Siècle des moralistes;* Anthony Levi, *French Moralists.* Georges Van Den Abbeele explores their relationship with Descartes in "Moralists and the Legacy of Cartesianism."

9. See the discussion in Jean Lafond, *Moralistes du XVIIe Siècle,* 63–65, and Richard Parish, "Seventeenth-century Religious Writing," 333–42.

10. For an introduction, see Jean-Pierre Chantin, *Le Jansénisme.*

11. See Davidson and Dubé, *A Concordance to Pascal's 'Pensées.'* Work on Pascal's sense of order is extensive; see Hugh M. Davidson, *The Origins of Certainty;* ch. 2, Ernst, *Approches pascaliennes,* 17–47; Pugh, *The Composition of Pascal's 'Apologia,'* ch. 1; Peter Bayley, "A Reading of the First *Liasse*"; Dominique Descotes, *L'Argumentation chez Pascal,* 47–103; Frank Mariner, "The Order of Disorder"; Nicholas Hammond, *Playing with Truth,* 50–78.

12. For Pascal's views on the fallibility of language, see Louis Marin, *La Critique du discours,* ch. 6, and Sara E. Melzer, *Discourses of the Fall.*

13. Cf. "When words are repeated in a discourse and, in trying to correct them, we find them so appropriate that we would be spoiling the discourse to do so, we must leave them, for this is the sign of it. And here we are dealing with envy, which is blind and does not realize that such repetition is not a defect here. For there is no general rule" (s452/L515).

14. See Léon Brunschvicg, *Descartes et Pascal lecteurs de Montaigne.* For Montaigne's style, see Jean Starobinski's illuminating *Montaigne in Motion.*

15. Mesnard in a short eight-page meditation, "Pourquoi les *Pensées* de Pascal se présentent-elles sous forme de fragments?" argues against Lucien Goldmann's idea of the tragic infinity (in *La culture du XVIIe siècle,* 363–70). For Goldmann, "Chercher le 'vrai' plan des *Pensées* nous paraît ainsi une entreprise antipascalienne par excellence, une entreprise qui va à l'encontre de la cohérence du texte, et méconnaît implicitement ce qui constitue aussi bien son contenu intellectuel que l'essence de sa

valeur littéraire. Il peut y avoir un plan logique pour un écrit rationaliste, un ordre de la persuasion pour un écrit spirituel; il n'y a, pour une œuvre tragique, qu'une seule forme d'ordre valable, celui du fragment, qui est recherche d'ordre, mais recherche qui n'a pas réussi, et ne peut pas réussir, à l'approcher" (*Dieu caché,* 220). Mesnard on the other hand distinguishes between the work's presentation in fragments and its composition: "Le fragment a pour lui une fonction dynamique. Il est élément d'un tout dans lequel il est destiné à entrer, soit tel quel, soit après réajustement, pour rendre l'adaptation plus parfaite. Il n'y a donc pas contradiction entre l'écriture fragmentaire et la construction d'un ordre, bien au contraire. Comme l'architecte dessine la courbe d'une moulure ou la disposition d'un escalier en fonction de son plan d'ensemble. La maison n'en recevra pas moins, le moment voulu, sa toiture" (367). My subsequent discussion will show that I am more on Goldmann's side. Mesnard's analogy of the architect is telling, because it is paradigmatically Cartesian in its insistence on a structured discourse through the analogy of a building, and perhaps an allusion to the head engraving of the 1670 Port-Royal edition. I believe that faced with the immensity of the universe and the divine, any human construction would collapse. For Pascal, the architectonics of thought rest on very shaky grounds indeed.

16. See Louis Lafuma, *Histoire des Pensées de Pascal, 1656–1952,* and Antony McKenna, *De Pascal à Voltaire, 1670–1734.*

17. Carraud provides an illuminating précis of the notions of *l'infini* in *Pascal et la Philosophie,* 393–450.

18. See Judith V. Field, "The Infinitely Great and the Infinitely Small in the Work of Girard Desargues." The connection between Desargues and Pascal is made by João Cortese, "Infinity between Mathematics and Apologetics."

19. This fragment appropriately serves as the epigraph to Paul de Man's *Allegories of Reading.*

20. The chasm between the "God of the Philosophers" and the "God of Abraham" finds a deconstructive stance in *God Without Being,* in which Jean-Luc Marion accuses theology (and philosophy) of idolatry in their obsession with the metaphysics of being, whereas the "God of Abraham" is the God of pure love, incarnate in Jesus, a God without the objectification of being. Marion's purpose is "to bring out the absolute freedom of God with regard to all determinations, including, first of all, the basic condition … of Being" (xx). Marion, of course, wrote his first books on Cartesian epistemology and theology.

21. Daniel Heller-Roazen, *The Fifth Hammer,* 135–40.

22. Blumenberg, *Shipwreck with Spectator,* 19.

23. See the discussion in Christopher D. Johnson, *Hyperboles,* 437–42.

24. Hall Bjørnstad gives a stimulating history of the critical reception in "Twice Written, Never Read."

25. For the intellectual genesis of the work, see Mitchell Cohen, *The Wager of Lucien Goldmann,* 154–200.

26. See Hélène Michon, *L'ordre du Coeur,* 139–72, 241–356; Michel de Certeau, *Mystic Fable,* 2:194–211; and Dawn M. Ludwin, *Blaise Pascal's Quest for the Ineffable.*

Johnson argues for Pascal as "the Baroque's most eloquent apologist for the *via nega-tiva*" (in *Hyperboles,* 425).

27. See Henri de Lubac, *Medieval Exegesis,* and Erich Auerbach, *"Figura."*

28. *Sup. Cant.,* c. 7. Cited in de Lubac, *Medieval Exegesis,* 1:244.

29. See Pierre Force, *Le Problème herméneutique chez Pascal.*

## Chapter 6: Nietzsche

1. Though it is a break, it is not a complete disavowal or departure. See James I. Porter's *Nietzsche and the Philology of the Future,* which argues that his early classical scholarship actually formed the foundations to his metaphysics of culture.

2. *De Laertii Diogenis fontibus* (part 1, 1868, and part 2, 1869), *Analecta Laertiana* (1870), and *Beiträge zur Quellenkunde und Kritik des Laertius Diogenes* (1870). For a publication history, see William H. Schaberg, *The Nietzsche Canon,* 8–19. Discussed in Jonathan Barnes, "Nietzsche and Diogenes Laertius."

3. Nietzsche's aphoristic style has been remarked in some of the most influential studies of the field. The first sentence of Karl Löwith's *Nietzsche's Philosophy of the Eternal Recurrence of the Same* reads: "Nietzsche's philosophy is neither a unified, closed system nor a variety of disintegrating aphorisms, but rather a system in apho-risms" (11). For Walter Kaufmann, though his texts appear to be an "anarchy of atoms" (74), "a glittering mosaic of independent monads" (91), he attempts to reconstruct an overarching argument in *Nietzsche.* Arthur Danto in *Nietzsche as Philosopher* tartly notes of *Human, All Too Human*: "Nietzsche was a B-plus aphorist [?!], but how many aphorists of any grade do we encounter?" (236).

Gilles Deleuze explains that "Understood, formally, an aphorism is present as a *fragment*; it is the form of pluralist thought; in its content it claims to articulate and formulate a *sense.* The sense of a being, an action, a thing—these are the objects of the aphorism" (*Nietzsche and Philosophy,* 31). For Sarah Kofman, "The aphorism is an invitation to dance: it is the actual writing of the will to power, affirmative, light and innocent," reconciling "the opposition between play and seriousness, surface and depth, form and content, spontaneous and considered, amusement and work" (*Nietz-sche and Metaphor,* 115). Jacques Derrida in *Spurs / Éperons* uses the utterly ordinary note "I have forgotten my umbrella" to demonstrate the radical indeterminacy of Nietzsche's texts (122–35). Alexander Nehamas writes that "Nietzsche's stylistic plu-ralism is another facet of his perspectivism: it is one of his essential weapons in his effort to distinguish himself from the philosophical tradition as he conceived it" (*Nietzsche,* 20).

More specifically, Paul Franco in *Nietzsche's Enlightenment,* ch. 1, investigates how *Human, All Too Human* is a pivotal transition in his thought. Werner Stegmaier in *Nietzsches Befreiung der Philosophie* considers the aphorisms in *The Gay Science.* Eva Strobel's *Das "Pathos der Distanz"* focuses on the late period. J. Hillis Miller makes stimulating remarks in "Aphorism as Instrument of Political Action in Nietzsche," as does Jill Marsden's "Nietzsche and the Art of the Aphorism." Joel Westerdale's *Nietz-*

*sche's Aphoristic Challenge* provides a very helpful account of aphorisms in the development of his complete career.

My modest contribution to this vast field is to insist that Nietzsche's thoughts on the nature of the unfinished, the becoming, and the contradictions of thinking are part and parcel of his theory and practice of the aphorism.

4. See John T. Wilcox, "What Aphorism Does Nietzsche Explicate in *Genealogy*, Essay III?" and "That Exegesis of an Aphorism in *Genealogy* III."

5. Nietzsche uses *Sentenz* and *Aphorismus* more or less interchangeably. Miller, in drawing out the juridical connotations of *Sentenz*, remarks that "An aphorism lays down the law, even the law against itself, as in the judge's 'sentencing' of a criminal" ("Aphorism as Instrument," 73)

6. Christa Davis Acampora's *Contesting Nietzsche* sees *agon* as a central motif in his work and demonstrates how struggles, contests, battles are ultimately nourishing for life.

7. Hans Krüger notes the explosion of publications of aphorisms notes in the late eighteenth century: Ernst Platner, *Philosophischen Aphorismen* (Leipzig, 1776–82); Ignaz Felner, *Aphorismen oder Fragmente zum Denken und Handeln* (Basel, 1789); Johann Friedrich Baumann translated from the English *Aphorismen und Fantasien eines Britten*; Nicolaus Müller translated *Aphorismen aus Voltaire, Rousseau und Raynald* (*Über den Aphorismus als philosophische Form*, 30). Gerhard Neumann's *Ideenparadiese* is a monumental 850-page study of the form from Lichtenberg to Novalis to Schlegel to Goethe; Friedermann Spicker's *Der Aphorismus* focuses on the eighteenth to nineteenth century; Harald Fricke's *Aphorismus* is a general taxonomic introduction.

8. This is Rüdiger Safranski's diagnosis, in *Nietzsche*, 155–76. Curt Paul Janz's three-volume *Nietzsche* in German is considered the definitive biography.

9. See Paolo D'Iorio's evocative *Nietzsche's Journey to Sorrento*.

10. To be fair, Kittler does as well, which is why I was surprised to read this reductive sentence in an otherwise groundbreaking work.

11. See Matthew Schilleman, "Typewriter Psyche."

12. The interpretation of this aphorism forms the first chapter of Nehamas' *Nietzsche*.

13. See *Heights of Reflection*, edited by Sean Ireton and Caroline Chaumann.

14. According to the index in *KSA* 15:329, 339, 322. See discussion in Brendan Donnellan, *Nietzsche and the French Moralists*.

15. He is discussed over ninety times (*KSA* 15:312–13). Nietzsche used Jacob Bernay's edition of *Die Heraklitischen Briefe* (1869). For Nietzsche and the Presocratics, see the edited collections by Anthony K. Jensen and Helmut Heit, *Nietzsche as a Scholar of Antiquity*, esp. Heit's "Nietzsche's Genealogy of Early Greek Philosophy"; Paul Bishop, ed., *Nietzsche and Antiquity;* Glenn W. Most, "Friedrich Nietzsche between Philosophy and Philology"; and Porter's reading in *Nietzsche and the Philology of the Future*, 225–50. Deconstructive readings include Kofman, "Nietzsche and the Obscurity of Heraclitus," and Steven Ungar, "Parts and Holes."

16. Nietzsche's Eternal Return is notoriously difficult to understand. His thoughts are presented obliquely in *The Gay Science* 109 and 341 and allegorically in *Zarathustra*

III.2.13. Löwith in *Nietzsche's Philosophy of the Eternal Recurrence of the Same* and, more recently, Paul S. Loeb in "Eternal Recurrence" take Nietzsche to offer a cosmological account of time and fate. Lawrence J. Hatab in *Nietzsche's Life Sentence* holds that it is deeply "existential," namely, the ability to embrace all of life even to an endless repetition. In any case, I hold that Nietzsche's engagement with Heraclitus' Eternal Becoming is highly relevant.

17. See the many entries with the form *Wirk* in Jacob and Wilhelm Grimm's *Deutsches Wörterbuch* for its polyvalent senses.

18. Robin Small notes that Nietzsche's concept of *Wirklichkeit* might be influenced by African Spir's *Forschung nach der Gewissheit in der Erkenntnis der Wirklichkeit* ("Investigation into Certainty in the Knowledge of Reality"), a copy of which he borrowed from the University of Basel library in 1873, before acquiring his own in 1877. Small remarks that there are many similarities between Spir's work and *Human, All Too Human* (*Nietzsche and Rée*, 67–68).

19. In general see Martha B. Helfer, *Retreat of Representation*. See also Matthew Bell, "The Idea of Fragmentariness in German Literature and Philosophy, 1760–1800," and Christopher Kubiak, "Sowing Chaos."

20. A major reevaluation of the two philosophers appears in the three-volume *Nietzsche's Engagements with Kant and the Kantian Legacy*, edited by Marco Brusotti, Herman Siemens, João Constâncio, and Tom Baily.

21. Recently, Clifford Siskin offers a genealogy in *System: The Shaping of Modern Knowledge*. He traces its eminence in the Enlightenment, from Galileo to Newton, though, surprisingly, he does not discuss German idealism's attempts to encapsulate modern knowledge into a single philosophical paradigm. For Siskin, a system, whether it is the solar system, a computer program, or a sonnet, is "a form that works physically in the world to mediate our efforts to understand it" (12).

22. See Nancy and Lacoue-Labarthe, *The Literary Absolute*, ch. 1.

23. See Judith Norman, "Nietzsche and Early Romanticism."

24. *Nietzsche Source* (www.nietzschesource.org/facsimiles/dfga) is a "digital facsimile reproduction of the entire Nietzsche estate, including first editions of works, manuscripts, letters and biographical documents."

25. Montinari gives the history of the *KSA* in "The New Critical Edition of Nietzsche's Works." Alan D. Schrift, the current editor of the Stanford University Press series, in "Translating the Colli-Montinari *Kritische Studienausgabe*," gives a candid account of the vexations and delays of the volumes.

26. See Safranski, *Nietzsche*, 304–17.

27. See Karl Schlechta, *Der Fall Nietzsche*. The renowned translators Walter Kaufmann and R. J. Hollingdale, before access to the archive was possible, reprint the ordering. The most recent English edition, edited by Rüdiger Bittner, follows the Colli-Montinari text and is ordered chronologically as *Writings from the Late Notebooks*.

28. There should be a study on the epistemology and *poiesis* of the artistic, philosophical, and scientific notebook from Leonardo to Nietzsche to Valéry, etc. For the artistic (a)practice of the unfinished, see the magnificent Met exhibit catalog *Unfinished*, edited by Kelly Baum, Andrea Bayer, and Sheena Wagstaff.

29. Deleuze's *Difference and Repetition* inverts the conventional idea of repetition as difference over time experienced in a succession of moments: identity persists but is now understood as a simulacra in which the "different related to different *by* means of difference itself" (299). "Eternal return cannot mean the return of the Identical because it presupposes a world (that of the will to power) in which all previous identities have been abolished and dissolved. Returning is being, but only the being of becoming. The eternal return does not bring back 'the same,' but returning constitutes the only Same of that which becomes" (41). I think this is reflected in Nietzsche's style.

30. I am reminded of this very *unaphoristic* passage in Proust, when the narrator encounters Albertine for the first time:

> The aurora of adolescence with which the faces of these girls still glowed ... shed its light on everything around them and, like the fluid painting of certain Primitives, brought out in relief the most insignificant details of their daily lives against a golden background. Their faces were for the most part blurred with this misty effulgence of a dawn from which their actual features had not yet emerged. It is so short, that radiant morning time, that one comes to like only the very youngest girls, those in whom the flesh, like a precious leaven, is still at work. (*Remembrance of Things Past* 1:966)

31. See Paul de Man's influential reading in *Allegories of Reading,* 103–59.

32. For an analytical account of Nietzsche's theory of the unconscious, see Paul Katsafanas, *The Nietzschean Self,* where he argues that "conscious mental states are those with conceptual content, whereas unconscious mental states are those with nonconceptual content" (46).

33. Characteristic of Nietzsche's plurality of views, there is an equal and opposite aphorism to every aphorism: "The worst readers are those who behave like plundering troops: they take away a few things they can use, dirty and confound the remainder, and revile the whole" ("Assorted Opinions and Maxims" §137).

34. In "Defense of Seneca and Plutarch" (II:32), the French essayist acknowledges that his book is "built up purely from their spoils" (*The Complete Essays,* 545).

## Epilogue: A Circle

1. See, for example, Eric Jarosinski @NeinQuarterly. In 2012, then a junior faculty member at Penn, he started a Twitter feed called "A Compendium of Utopian Negation," featuring a monocled Adorno as the avatar, spouting aphorisms like "Signifying nothing is harder than it looks"; "For Shakespeare, please press 1. For Cervantes, please press 2. For Kafka, please hang up. And press 3"; "No, some of us will never be happy. That's why there's still hope"; "The #dislikebutton. Formerly known as Schopenhauer"; "We regret to inform you about tomorrow. It's another day"; "To tweet: human. To delete: divine." These tweets have now become a book, *Nein: A Manifesto.*

2. See Zeynep Tufekci, *Twitter and Tear Gas.*

3. See David Schaberg, *A Patterned Past,* ch. 1.

4. Jonah Engel Bromwich, "Obama's Charlottesville Response, Boosted by Nostalgia, Becomes Most-Liked Tweet Ever."

5. See R. John Williams, *The Buddha in the Machine.*

6. See Shozo Sato, *Shodo,* which arranges the *zengo* by order of the number of characters. Shodo Harada, a Rinzai priest, has also many beautiful examples with commentary in *Moon by the Window.*

7. See Ludwik Sternbach, *Subhāṣita, Gnomic, and Didactic Literature.*

8. With Jean Filliozat, *L'Inde classique* (1947); *Histoire de la langue sanskrite* (1956); "Sur le genre du Sūtra dans la littérature sanskrite" (1963).

9. See Henry Smith, "Brevity in Pāṇini."

10. See David Gordon White, *The Yoga Sutra of Patanjali,* 10. Interestingly, according to White, the individual sutras in the *Yoga Sutra* have no verbs (cf. Pascal's *Mémorial*). As such the medium and the message of the sutra aspire to a timelessness in their truth claims.

11. See Johannes Bronkhorst, *Two Traditions of Meditation in Ancient India.*

12. See, for example, Carl Bielefeldt, *Dogen's Manuals of Zen Meditation.*

13. "The etymology of the Pali term *sutta* is unclear; it was later Sanskritized as *sutra*, but this refers to a concise, technical piece of prose very different from the *suttas*. In fact, it is more likely that the word is derived from the Vedic *sūkta*, which means 'that which is well-spoken'" (Daniel Veidlinger, "Sutta (Pāli/Theravada Canon)").

14. Etienne Lamotte, *History of Indian Buddhism,* 156.

15. See Susan Bush, ed., *Early Chinese Texts on Painting* and *The Chinese Literati on Painting.*

16. The first quotation is from Kūkai, "Hokkai jōshin" 法界浄心, translated in Fabio Rambelli, *Buddhist Materiality,* 116. The second from Dogen, *Treasury of the True Dharma Eye,* 538.

# BIBLIOGRAPHIC ESSAY

Since this book deals with the intersection between philosophy, philology, and hermeneutics, I have learned a great deal from Pierre Hadot's *Philosophy as a Way of Life*, Alexander Nehamas' *The Art of Living*, and Michel Foucault's "Self Writing." The recent efflorescence of philology has been spearheaded by Sheldon Pollock, Benjamin A. Elman, and Kevin Ku-ming Chang's edited volume *World Philology*, Werner Hamacher's *Minima Philologia*, and James Turner's *Philology: The Forgotten Origins of the Modern Humanities* (see my state-of-the-field report, "The Many Returns of Philology"). For hermeneutics, the best guide I have found is Peter Szondi, *Introduction to Literary Hermeneutics*.

In English, the closest general theory of the aphorism is Gary Saul Morson's *The Long and Short of It: From Aphorism to Novel*. Morson's work, which was quite stimulating at the early stages of my thinking, differs from mine in several ways. His taxonomic range is wider, treating what he calls apothegms, dicta, sardonic maxims, witticisms and "witlessisms," whereas mine is restricted to the more enigmatic, fragmentary, and gnomic. A charming appeal of his work is that he offers sweeping, breezy synthesis with chatty, general classifications. My historical range is broader; I do more close-reading of authors with more sustained attention to antiquity. As a specialist of Tolstoy, he is ultimately interested in the role of aphorisms in the narrative structure of novels, as the subtitle of the book suggests. I am ultimately more interested in aphorisms as philosophical fragments and systems, and their hermeneutic inexhaustibility.

Conceptually my book is closest to Heinz Krüger's *Über den Aphorismus als philosophische Form*, a dissertation completed shortly before his early death in January 1956 at the age of forty and not published until 1988 by a Munich publisher, edition text + kritik. Adorno, his *Doktorvater*, wrote a moving foreword. Krüger, too, was interested in the relationship between the literary form of "fragments" and the philosophical content of "systems." Much influenced by his teacher's negative dialectical aesthetics, the organizing principles of his book are the categories of aphorisms as forms of *Lebensphilosophie* ("life philosophy"), *Offenes und geschlossenes Denken* ("open and closed thoughts"), *Nichtwissens* ("not knowing"), and *Die Ausnahme* ("the exception"). As with most works in European languages, the emphasis is on his own national literature.

Georg Christoph Lichtenberg (1742–1799)—professor of experimental physics at the University of Göttingen, hypochondriac, and hunchback—had some distinguished admirers: Goethe, Schopenhauer, Nietzsche, Kierkegaard, Kraus, Wittgenstein. For more than three decades, he keep scribbling in what he called his *Sudelbücher*, from the obsolete English "Waste Books." He purpose was, like Sterne in *Tristram Shandy*, to write "a book wherein I write everything, as I see it or as my thoughts suggest it to me." This was accomplished by "a strict attention to one's own thoughts and sensations," thereby "the most strongly individualized expression of the same, through carefully chosen words ... one writes down immediately" so as to preserve a "store of observations" (II.169/g207). What was preserved is a swirling *Wunderkammer* of anecdotes, musings, epigrams, maxims, mathematical problems, physics equations, weather, laboratory and stock market reports, travel receipts, romantic gossip, sketches of hypothetical experiments and distorted faces, and much else. J. P. Stern calls his particular observations an "inversion of the categorical imperative" (*Lichtenberg*, 229). See Lorraine Daston's elegant entry, "1789, June 2, The Disciplines of Attention," in *A New History of German Literature*.

Before his death in 1832, Goethe was planning a publication of his collected maxims, composed in quiet moments in the midst of an astonishingly productive life. He had gathered his jottings under the folders labeled *Späne* ("shavings") and *Gnomen* ("gnomes"). *Elective Affinities* (1809) and *Wilhelm Meister's Journeyman Years* (1821, 1829) contain many aphorisms, but ironically, they are often misunderstood by the characters who write them. And so what is unique with Goethe's aphorisms is their multiple publication histories and the different frameworks he puts around them. "The obscurity of certain maxims is only relative: it doesn't do to make everything that is obvious to a practitioner crystal-clear to a listener" (§1068). "Surely the world is quite full enough of riddles for us not to need to turn the simplest phenomena into riddles too?" (§81). These are translated by Elisabeth Stopp in *Maxims and Reflections*.

Hugo von Hofmannsthal's 1902 short story "The Letter," from the young promising (fictional) writer Lord Chandos to Francis Bacon, dated 1603, explains the lack of his literary productivity through a probing inquiry into his crisis with the efficacy of language. I find it poignant that before his intellectual collapse, he had intended to "put together a collection of maxims like Julius Caesar's—you remember that Cicero mentions it in one of his letters":

> My plan here was to assemble the most remarkable utterances which I had collected during my travels in my dealings with the learned men and clever women of our time, with exceptional individuals from among the general public.... In this way I wished to combine beautiful classical and Italian aphorisms and reflections with whatever else I had run across in the way of intellectual baubles in books, manuscripts, and conversations. (*The Lord Chandos Letter,* 119)

In other words, Lord Chandos' ambition was a reduction of the plentitude of history and experience into a finite, bound collection. It is precisely the impossibility of this reduction that precipitated his mental breakdown. At the end of modernity and beginning of modernism, and as a semi-autobiographical testament on his abandoning of lyric poetry, Hofmannsthal reaches back to the reputed founder of modern science, Francis Bacon, to explore the limits of language as the medium to express truth.

As a visiting fellow at the Bodleian Libraries, Oxford, in the Trinity term of 2015, I was given access to the manuscript and typescript of Kafka's Zürau aphorisms, written in his sister Ottla's house between September 1917 and April 1918. The gripping history of how the text got from Prague to Israel to Switzerland to the UK deserves more than a *New Yorker* article. The conservators have immaculately preserved the writings in two shoe-sized gray boxes. They contain his autograph script, notecard-sized (12 × 8.7 inches), then a typescript, all enveloped in clear plastic film, gently cradled in gray foam (Bodleian MS Kafka 43 & Kafka 47). I would gladly have written a chapter on this had not Paul North's splendid *The Yield: Kafka's Atheological Reformation* appeared later that fall.

The German critic André Jolles published in 1929 *Simple Forms: Legend, Saga, Myth, Riddle, Saying, Case, Memorabile, Fairytale, Joke.* It has often been seen as a precursor to morphology and narratology, especially Vladimir Propp. Jolles defines a *saying* as "the literary form that encloses an experience, without preventing it from continuing to be an individual detail in a world characterized by dispersion. It binds this world within itself without thereby removing it from the empirical world" (124).

Farther afield, Wolfgang Mieder is probably the world's most prolific expert on proverbs, phraseology, and paremiology, having edited and authored over a hundred books on the subject. His methodology is primarily linguistics and folklore. The sociologist Murray S. Davis has a charming account of the genre's psychological and social effects in "Aphorisms and Clichés: The Generation and Dissipation of Conceptual Charisma." James Geary's *The World in a Phrase: A History of Aphorisms* and *Geary's Guide to the World's Great Aphorists* are entertaining surveys for the general reader. Besides *Bartlett's Familiar Quotations*, there are the *Yale Book of Quotations*, edited by Fred R. Shapiro, and the *Oxford Book of Aphorisms*, edited by John Gross.

Bendt Alster's *Proverbs of Ancient Sumer: The World's Earliest Proverb Collections* is a two-volume edition of all extant Old Babylonian Sumerian proverbs. They are mostly found on school tablets and thus have a didactic purpose for scribes in training. In Egypt, proverbs are found in the genre of "practical instructions" in which a father gives advice to his son. See Hellmut Brunner, *Die Weisheitsbücher der Ägypter: Lehren für das Leben,* and Miriam Lichtheim, *Late-Egyptian Wisdom Literature in the International Context.* Seven thousand Akan proverbs are gathered by Peggy Appiah, Kwame Anthony Appiah, and Ivor Agyeman-Duah in *Bu Me Be*, with an introduction by K. A. Appiah that discusses their philosophical import with some attention to Paul Grice's theory of meaning.

Much more work should be done on classical aphorisms. Karl Bielohlawek's *Hypotheke und Gnome* dates from 1940. There are surveys by Joseph Russo, "Prose Genres for the Performance of Traditional Wisdom in Ancient Greece: Proverb, Maxim, Apothegm" and "The Poetics of the Ancient Greek Proverb." No recent book-length treatment existed in English until Nikolaos Lazaridis' *Wisdom in Loose Form: The Language of Egyptian and Greek Proverbs in Collections of the Hellenistic and Roman Periods.* Collections, however, are very robust: Von Leutsch and Schneidewin's *Corpus paroemiographorum Graecorum*; Otto's *Die Sprichwörter und sprichwörtlichen Redensarten der Römer*; Walther and Schmidt's *Lateinische Sprichwörter und Sentenzen des Mittelalters.* Tosi's *Dizionario delle sentenze latine e greche: 10,000 citazioni dall'antichità al Rinascimento nell'originale e in traduzione, con commento storico, letterario e filologico* makes him the twentieth-century Erasmus.

The gnomologia is a major genre in the formative stages of Arabic literature. *A Treasury of Virtues* is a collection attributed to 'Ali ibn Abi Talib (d. 40 H/661 CE) and compiled by the Fatimid jurist and scholar al-Quda'i (d. 454 H/1062 CE). 'Ali was the cousin and son-in-law of the Prophet Muhammad, the first Shia imam, and the fourth Sunni caliph. A shorter compilation, *One Hundred Proverbs,* is attributed to the eminent writer al-Jahiz (d. 255 H/869 CE). Both are translated with the facing originals in the NYU Library of Arabic series. Dimitri Gutas in *Greek Wisdom Literature in Arabic Translation* translates and annotates *Mukhtar min Kalam al-hukama al-arbaah al-akabir,* "A Selection from the Sayings of the Four Great Philosophers" ascribed to Pythagoras, Socrates, Plato, and Aristotle. In Persian literature, aphorisms— *matal* (plural *amtāl*)—are also numerous. See the informative entry "Aphorism" by Paul Sprachman in the *Encyclopædia Iranica.*

The *Proverbios morales* written in Spanish by Santob de Carrión, the pen name of Rabbi Shem Tov Ibn Ardutiel ben Isaac, documents the complex cultural interactions between Christians and Jews in pre-1492 Spain. He begins by declaring, "I wish to speak, concerning the world and its ways and my doubts [*dubd*] about it, very truthful words" (v. 213–16). In his skepticism he anticipates Montaigne, according to T. A. Perry in his translation and study *The Moral Proverbs of Santob de Carrión.*

In Italian, Einaudi's Meridiani has published two volumes of *Scrittori italiani di aforismi,* edited by Gino Ruozzi, ranging from Alberti to Leonardo, Guicciardini, Campanella, Tesauro, Vico, Algarotti, Leopardi, Tommaseo, Dossi, Bufalino, Sgalambro, and Pontiggia. For noteworthy criticism, consult *Teoria e storia dell'aforisma,* also edited by Ruozzi, and *La brevità felice: Contributi alla teoria e alla storia dell'aforisma,* edited by M. A. Rigoni. Both are arranged chronologically and provide useful appraisals of primary texts and secondary bibliography. Ruozzi ends with a witty essay by the ubiquitous Umberto Eco, which is basically a catalog of his favorite aphorisms.

In the course of research, I was deeply impressed by the aphorisms of Joseph Joubert (1754–1824). He never published anything in his lifetime, and his writings only appeared after an edition by no less a personage than Chateaubriand. I am particularly struck by Joubert's sensitivity when it comes to exploring the relationship between thinking, speaking, and writing: "When we speak, we write what we are saying in the air." "Thought forms in the soul the same way clouds form in the air." "The mind is the atmosphere of the soul." "Our ideals, like pictures, are made from lights and shadows." "Luminous words, like those drops of light we see in fireworks." "A poetic vapor, a dense cloud that resolves itself into prose." "To penetrate a thought and to produce a thought are almost the same action." "I love blank paper more than ever, and I no longer wish to give myself the trouble of expressing carefully any thoughts but those worthy of being written upon silk or upon bronze." "The worst thing about new books is that they keep us from reading the old ones." "The number of books is infinite." Above all, he wished that all space and time would be concentrated in one pure drop of light, in one essential word: "Luminous point. Seek it in everything."

Blanchot in an equally luminous meditation, "Joubert and Space," says we should read his thoughts not grouped by banal topics like "family and society," "wisdom and virtue," "truth and errors" (50; or as I have done in the last paragraph, as a interlinked sequence of thoughts) but in the chronological order in which they were written. "Thoughts recover once again their dailiness and touch ordinary life, liberate themselves from it, and liberate from it another day, another rarity that shows through here and there" (51). It is through the rhythm of the quotidian that the "brief rift of a clarity" shines through. For Blanchot, Joubert is an "early version of Mallarmé" (56).

Paul Valéry would wake up every morning at five o'clock to dedicate himself to a writing exercise that required dictating precisely whatever was on his mind. Eventually, over the course of fifty years, these *études* would fill 261 notebooks or some 30,000 pages of jottings, scientific formulas, mathematical equations, sketches, diagrams, delicate little watercolors, prose poems, and, of course, aphorisms. Jean Paulhan, best known as the publisher of *La Nouvelle Revue Française*, has some very stimulating thoughts on proverbs gathered from his three-year stay in Madagascar in "Sacred Language" and "L'expérience du proverbe." The polymath Pascal Quignard has a brief, lyrical, impressionistic book on La Bruyère, *Une gêne technique à l'égard des fragments*. Jacques Derrida has "Fifty-two Aphorisms for a Foreword" and "Aphorisms Countertime," in *Psyche: Inventions of the Other*, vol. 2. In the first, he writes, "If there is a truth of architecture, it appears doubly allergic to the aphorism: it is produced as such, for the most part, outside of discourse. It concerns an articulated organization, but a mute articulation" (117). In the second, he writes, "The aphorism or discourse of dissociation: each sentence, each paragraph dedicates itself to separation, it shuts itself up, whether one likes it or not, in the solitude of its proper duration" (128).

Alain Montandon's *Les formes brèves* and Bernard Roukhomovsky's *Lire les formes brèves* are both slim, elegant, and of an introductory nature. As their titles suggest, their ambits are wider than just the aphorism. They are also interested in epigrams, anecdotes, proverbs, and, in Montandon's case, short poetry (limerick, idyll, haiku, the Spanish *greguería*). Éric Tourrette in *Les formes brèves de la description morale* is also interested in a wider range of forms that include quatrains, maxims, and other short notes. Marie-Paule Berranger in *Dépaysement de l'aphorisme* studies the exquisite cadavers, automatic writing, and other ludic forms of the discontinuous by Dada and surrealist authors. There are many useful edited volumes: Lafond, *Les Formes brèves de la prose et le discours discontinu* (*XVIe–XVIIe Siècles*); Pelegrin, *Les formes brèves*; Ortemann, *Fragment(s), fragmentation, aphorisme poétique*.

Ben Grant's *The Aphorism and Other Short Forms* examines the fragment, proverb, maxim, haiku, epigram, and quotation. Published in Routledge's New Critical Idiom series, it is more of a textbook survey, similar to Montandon and Roukhomovsky, though it has a good discussion of Derrida.

It is no accident that with the advent of Twitter there is also a resurgent interest in the short form. The writing guru Alan Ziegler has recently edited a collection entitled *Short: An International Anthology of 500 Years of Short-Short Stories, Prose Poems, Brief Essays, and Other Short Prose Forms* (2014). See also David Shields' *Life Is Short—Art Is Shorter: In Praise of Brevity* (2015), James Lough's *Short Flights: Thirty-Two Modern Writers Share Aphorisms of Insight, Inspiration, and Wit* (2015) and Brian Dillon, *Essayism* (2018). In the twentieth century, proponents of the form include Karl Kraus (Austrian, 1874–1936), Antonio Porchia (Spanish, 1886–1968), Malcolm de Chazal (Mauritian, 1902–1981), Stanisław Jerzy Lec (Polish, 1909–1966), and Nicolás Gómez Dávila (Colombian, 1913–1994). Exciting practitioners of the craft today include Sarah Manguso (*300 Arguments: Essays*, 2017), S. D. Chrostowska (*Matches: A Light Book,* 2015), Valeria Luiselli (*Sidewalks,* 2010), Maggie Nelson (*Bluets*, 2009), Don Paterson, (*Best Thought, Worst Thought*, 2008), and James Richardson (*Vectors*, 2001).

Not surprisingly, there are many reviews of these on the internet. I've enjoyed reading Sarah Manguso, "In Short: Thirty-six Ways of Looking at the Aphorism," Stephen Burt, "It's Suddenly Understandable: On Aphorism, Lyric, and Experiment," Kristen Martin, "In Praise of the New Aphorism, No Longer Just for Great Men," Ryan Ruby, "The Long History of a Short Form," and Sharon Dolin, "Making a Space for Aphorism: Exploring the Intersection between Aphorism and Poetry."

Chinese proverbs are known as *chengyu*, 成語, one-word four-character phrases that encapsulate an ancient story or classical allusion. As a graduate student at Princeton learning classical Chinese, I read them in their *locus classicus* in the historiographies of Sima Qian and Ban Gu. But I first encountered them when I was growing up in Hong Kong in the 1980s. My favorite TV show was a weekly cartoon—*Animated Gallery of Proverb* (*chengyu donghualang*, 成語動畫廊)—that presented their etiologies by a panda scholar and YY, a red robot. It then became a series of graphic books and is now available on YouTube.

# BIBLIOGRAPHY

Acampora, Christa Davis. *Contesting Nietzsche.* Chicago: University of Chicago Press, 2013.

Adorno, Theodor. *Minima Moralia: Reflections on a Damaged Life.* Translated by E. F. N. Jephcott. London: Verso, 1974.

Agamben, Giorgio. *Infancy and History: The Destruction of Experience.* Translated by Liz Heron. London: Verso, 1993.

Albertus, Magnus (attrib.). *Book of Minerals.* Translated by Dorothy Wyckoff. Oxford: Clarendon Press, 1967.

Allen, Sarah. *The Way of Water and Sprouts of Virtue.* Albany: State University of New York Press, 1997.

Alster, Bendt. *Proverbs of Ancient Sumer: The World's Earliest Proverb Collections.* 2 vols. Bethesda, MD: CDL Press, 1997.

Appiah, Peggy, ed. *Bu Me Be: Akan Proverbs.* With Ivor Agyeman-Duah. Introduction by Kwame Anthony Appiah. Accra: Centre for Intellectual Renewal, 2000.

Aristotle. *Aristoteles pseudepigraphus.* Edited and translated by Valentin Rose. Leipzig: B. G. Teubner, 1863.

———. *The Complete Works: The Revised Oxford Translation.* 2 vols. Edited by Jonathan Barnes. Princeton: Princeton University Press, 1984.

Asgeirsson, J. Ma. "Arguments and Audience(s) in the *Gospel of Thomas* (Part I)." *Society of Biblical Literature Seminar Papers* 36 (1997): 47–85.

———. "Arguments and Audience(s) in the *Gospel of Thomas* (Part II)." *Society of Biblical Literature Seminar Papers* 37 (1998): 325–42.

Auerbach, Erich. "Figura" (1938). In *Time, History, and Literature: Selected Essays of Erich Auerbach,* edited by James I. Porter and translated by Jane O. Newman, 65–113. Princeton: Princeton University Press, 2014.

Augustine. "Of True Religion." In *Augustine: Earlier Writings,* translated by John H. S. Burleigh, 218–83. Philadelphia: Westminster Press, 1953.

Bacon, Francis. *The New Organon.* Edited by Lisa Jardine and Michael Silverthorne. Cambridge: Cambridge University Press, 2000.

———. *Novum Organum; with Other Parts of the Great Instauration.* Translated by Peter Urbach and John Gibson. Chicago: Open Court, 1994.

———. *The Oxford Francis Bacon.* Edited by Graham Rees, J. B. Trapp, Lisa Jardine, and Brian Vickers. 16 vols. Oxford: Oxford University Press, 1996–.

————. *The Works of Francis Bacon.* Edited by James Spedding, Robert Leslie Ellis, and Douglas Denon Heath. 15 vols. London: Longman, 1861.

Badiou, Alain. "French." In *Dictionary of Untranslatables*, edited by Barbara Cassin and translated by Steven Rendall et al., 349–54. Princeton: Princeton University Press, 2014.

Balentine, Samuel E. *The Hidden God: The Hiding of the Face of God in the Old Testament.* Oxford: Oxford University Press, 1983.

Baltussen, Han. *Philosophy and Exegesis in Simplicius: The Methodology of a Commentator.* London: Bloomsbury, 2013.

Ban Gu. *Hanshu.* Beijing: Beijing chubanshe, 1962.

Barnes, Jonathan. "Aphorism and Argument." In *Language and Thought in Early Greek Philosophy*, edited by Kevin Robb, 91–109. La Salle, IL: Hegeler Institute, 1983.

————. *Early Greek Philosophy.* Harmondsworth: Penguin Books, 1987.

————. "Nietzsche and Diogenes Laertius." *Nietzsche-Studien* 15 (1986): 16–40.

————. *The Presocratic Philosophers.* London: Routledge and K. Paul, 1979.

Bartlett, John, and Justin Kaplan. *Bartlett's Familiar Quotations: A Collection of Passages, Phrases, and Proverbs Traced to Their Sources in Ancient and Modern Literature.* Boston: Little, Brown, 2002.

Barthes, Roland. "La Rochefoucauld." In *New Critical Essays*, 3–22. Translated by Richard Howard. New York: Hill and Wang, 1980.

Baum, Kelly, Andrea Bayer, and Sheen Wagstaff, eds. *Unfinished: Thoughts Left Visible.* Exhibition catalog. New York: Metropolitan Museum of Art, 2016.

Bayley, Peter. "A Reading of the First *Liasse.*" In *Convergences: Rhetoric and Poetic in Seventeenth-Century France: Essays for Hugh M. Davidson*, edited by David Lee Rubin and Mary B. McKinley, 196–207. Columbus: Ohio State University Press, 1989.

Bell, Matthew. "The Idea of Fragmentariness in German Literature and Philosophy, 1760–1800." *Modern Language Review* 89, no. 2 (1994): 372–92.

Bénichou, Paul. *Morales du grand siècle.* Paris: Gallimard, 1948.

Benjamin, Walter. *Illuminations.* Translated by Harry Zohn. New York: Schocken Books, 1968.

————. *Origin of German Tragic Drama.* Translated by John Osborne. London: Verso, 1998.

————. *Selected Writings.* 4 vols. Edited by Marcus Bullock and Michael W. Jennings. Cambridge, MA: Harvard University Press, 2003–2006.

Bentley, Jerry H. *Humanists and Holy Writ: New Testament Scholarship in the Renaissance.* Princeton: Princeton University Press, 1983.

Berlinerblau, Jacques. "Toward a Sociology of Heresy, Orthodoxy, and *Doxa.*" *History of Religions* 40, no. 4 (2001): 327–51.

Berranger, Marie-Paule. *Dépaysement de l'aphorisme.* Paris: J. Corti, 1988.

Betz, Hans Dieter. "The Delphic Maxim γνωθι σαυτον in Hermetic Interpretation." *Harvard Theological Review* 63, no. 4 (1970): 465–84.

————. "The Delphic Maxim 'Know Yourself' in the Greek Magical Papyri." *History of Religions* 21, no. 2 (1981): 156–71.

Bielefeldt, Carl. *Dogen's Manuals of Zen Meditation*. Berkeley: University of California Press, 1990.

Bielohlawek, Karl. *Hypotheke und Gnome: Untersuchungen über die griechische Weisheitsdichtung der vorhellenistischen Zeit*. Leipzig: Dieterich, 1940.

Bishop, Paul, ed. *Nietzsche and Antiquity: His Reaction and Response to the Classical Tradition*. Rochester, NY: Camden House, 2004.

Bitterli, Dieter. *Say What I Am Called: The Old English Riddles of the Exeter Book and the Anglo-Latin Riddle Tradition*. Toronto: University of Toronto Press, 2009.

Bjørnstad, Hall. "Twice Written, Never Read: Pascal's Memorial Between Superstition and *Superbia*." *Representations* 124, no. 3 (2013): 69–95.

Blair, Ann M. *Too Much to Know: Managing Scholarly Information before the Modern Age*. New Haven: Yale University Press, 2010.

Blanchot, Maurice. *The Infinite Conversation*. Translated by Susan Hanson. Minneapolis: University of Minnesota Press, 1993.

———. "Joubert and Space." In *The Book to Come*. Translated by Charlotte Mandell, 49–65. Stanford: Stanford University Press, 2002.

Blumenberg, Hans. *Shipwreck with Spectator: Paradigm of a Metaphor for Existence*. Translated by Steven Rendall. Cambridge, MA: MIT Press, 1997.

Bol, Peter K. *Neo-Confucianism in History*. Cambridge, MA: Harvard University Asia Center, 2008.

Borges, Jorge Luis. "Pascal's Spheres." In *Selected Non-Fictions*, edited by Eliot Weinberger, 351–53. New York: Viking, 1999.

Bourdieu, Pierre. *Outlines of a Theory of Practice*. Translated by Richard Nice. Cambridge: Cambridge University Press, 1977.

Brinker, Helmut, and Hiroshi Kanazawa. *Zen Masters of Meditation in Images and Writings*. Translated by Andreas Leisinger. Honolulu: University of Hawaii Press, 1996.

Bromwich, Jonah Engel. "Obama's Charlottesville Response, Boosted by Nostalgia, Becomes Most-Liked Tweet Ever." *New York Times*. August 16, 2017. www.ny times.com/2017/08/16/us/politics/obama-charlottesville-tweet.html

Bronkhorst, Johannes. *The Two Traditions of Meditation in Ancient India*. Stuttgart: F. Steiner Verlag, 1986.

Brough, John. "Thus Have I Heard." *Bulletin of the School of Oriental and African Studies* 13, no. 2 (1950): 416–26.

Brown, William P. *Character in Crisis: A Fresh Approach to the Wisdom Literature of the Old Testament*. Grand Rapids, MI: Eerdmans, 1996.

Burgwinkle, William E, Nicholas Hammond, and Emma Wilson, eds. *The Cambridge History of French Literature*. Cambridge: Cambridge University Press, 2011.

Burlingame, Eugene Watson. *Buddhist Parables*. Delhi: Motilal Banarsidass, 1922.

Burnet, John. *Early Greek Philosophy*. London: A. & C. Black, 1892.

Brunner, Hellmut. *Die Weisheitsbücher der Ägypter: Lehren für das Leben*. Zurich: Artemis & Winkler, 1998.

Brunschvicg, Léon. *Descartes et Pascal, Lectures de Montaigne*. Neuchatel: Éditions de la Baconnière, 1945.

Brusotti, Marco, Herman Siemens, João Constâncio, and Tom Baily, eds. *Nietzsche's Engagements with Kant and the Kantian Legacy*. 3 vols. London: Bloomsbury, 2017.

Burt, Stephen. "It's Suddenly Understandable: On Aphorism, Lyric, and Experiment." *Los Angeles Review of Books*. July 27, 2016. https://lareviewofbooks.org/article /suddenly-understandable-aphorism-lyric-experiment

Bush, Susan, and Hsio-yen Shih, ed. and trans. *Early Chinese Texts on Painting* and *The Chinese Literati on Painting*. Hong Kong: Hong Kong University Press, 2012.

Calasso, Roberto. *The Marriage of Cadmus and Harmony*. Translated by Tim Parks. New York: Vintage, 1994.

Calvino, Italo. *Six Memos for the Next Millennium*. Translated by Geoffrey Brock. New York: Vintage, 1993.

Canetti, Elias. "Confucius in His Conversations." In *The Conscience of Words*, 171–79. Translated by Joachim Neugroschel. New York: Seabury Press, 1979.

———. *The Human Province*. Translated by Joachim Neugroschel. New York: Seabury Press, 1978.

Carlston, Charles E. "Proverbs, Maxims, and the Historical Jesus." *Journal of Biblical Literature* 99, no. 1 (1980): 87–105.

Carraud, Vincent. *Pascal et la philosophie*. Paris: Presses universitaires de France, 1992.

Cave, Terence. *The Cornucopian Text: Problems of Writing in the French Renaissance*. Oxford: Clarendon Press, 1979.

Cavell, Stanley. "The *Investigations'* Everyday Aesthetics of Itself." In *The Cavell Reader*, edited by Stephen Mulhal, 369–89. Oxford: B. Blackwell, 1996.

Céard, Jean. "La Censure tridentine et l'édition Florentine des *Adages* d'Érasme." In *Actes du colloque international Érasme*, edited by Jacques Chomarat, André Godin, and Jean-Claude Margolin, 337–50. Geneva: Droz 1990.

Chamfort, Sébastien-Roch-Nicolas de. *Produits de la civilisation perfectionnée: maximes et pensées, caractères et anecdotes*. Paris: Gallimard, 1982.

Chantin, Jean-Pierre. *Le jansénisme: entre hérésie imaginaire et résistance catholique (XVIIe–XIXe siècle)*. Paris: Cerf, 1996.

Cherniack, Susan. "Book Culture and Textual Transmission in Sung China." *Harvard Journal of Asiatic Studies* 54, no. 1 (1994): 5–125.

Cherniss, Harold F. *Aristotle's Criticism of Presocratic Philosophy*. Baltimore: Johns Hopkins University Press, 1935.

Chomarat, Jacques. *Grammaire et rhétorique chez Érasme*, 2 vols. Paris: Les Belles Lettres, 1981.

Chrostowska, S. D. *Matches: A Light Book*. Brooklyn, NY: Punctum Books, 2015.

Cioran, E. M. *All Gall Is Divided*. Translated by Richard Howard. New York: Arcade, 1999.

Clement of Alexandria. *Stromata*. Translated by William Wilson. In *Ante-Nicene Fathers*, vol. 2, edited by Alexander Roberts, James Donaldson, and A. Cleveland Coxe. Buffalo, NY: Christian Literature, 1885.

Clucas, Stephen. "'A Knowledge Broken': Francis Bacon's Aphoristic Style and the Crisis of Scholastic and Humanist Knowledge-Systems." In *English Renaissance*

*Prose: History, Language and Politics*, edited by Neil Rhodes, 147–72. Tempe, AZ: Medieval & Renaissance Texts & Studies, 1997.

Cohen, Mitchell. *The Wager of Lucien Goldmann: Tragedy, Dialectics, and a Hidden God*. Princeton: Princeton University Press, 1994.

Collins, John J. *Jewish Wisdom in the Hellenistic Age*. Louisville, KY: Westminster John Knox Press, 1997.

Collins, Randall. *The Sociology of Philosophies: A Global Theory of Intellectual Change*. Cambridge: Harvard University Press, 1998.

Collins, Steven. "On the Very Idea of the Pāli Canon." *Journal of the Pali Text Society* 15 (1990): 89–126.

Confucius. *The Analects. The Four Books: Confucian Analects, the Great Learning, the Doctrine of the Mean, and the Works of Mencius*. Translated by James Legge. Shanghai: The Chinese Book Co., 1930.

———. *The Analects of Confucius*. Translated by Arthur Waley. New York: Alfred A. Knopf, 1938.

———. *The Analects*. Translated by D. C. Lau. Harmondsworth: Penguin Books, 1979.

———. *The Analects*. Translated by Simon Leys. New York: W.W. Norton, 1997.

———. *The Original Analects: Sayings of Confucius and His Successors, 0479–0249*. Translated by E. Bruce Brooks and A. Taeko Brooks. New York: Columbia University Press, 1997.

———. *The Analects of Confucius: A Philosophical Translation*. Translated by Roger T. Ames and Henry Rosemont Jr. New York: Ballantine, 1998.

———. *Analects: With Selection from Traditional Commentaries*. Translated by Edward G. Slingerland. Indianapolis: Hackett, 2003.

———. *The Analects*. Translated by Annping Chin. New York: Penguin Books, 2014.

Cook, Scott Bradley. *The Bamboo Texts of Guodian: A Study and Complete Translation*. Ithaca, NY: East Asia Program, Cornell University, 2012.

Cortese, João. "Infinity between Mathematics and Apologetics: Pascal's Notion of Infinite Distance." *Synthese* 193, no. 8 (2015): 2379–93.

Courcelle, Pierre Paul. *Connais-toi toi-même; de Socrate à saint Bernard*. 4 vols. Paris: Études augustiniennes, 1974.

Crane, Mary Thomas. *Framing Authority: Sayings, Self, and Society in Sixteenth-Century England*. Princeton: Princeton University Press, 1992.

Crease, Robert P. *The Prism and the Pendulum: The Ten Most Beautiful Experiments in Science*. New York: Random House, 2003.

Crenshaw, James L. *Old Testament Wisdom: An Introduction*. 3rd ed. Louisville, KY: Westminster John Knox Press, 2010.

Crossan, John Dominic. *In Fragments: The Aphorisms of Jesus*. San Francisco: Harper & Row, 1983.

Danto, Arthur C. *Nietzsche as Philosopher*. Expanded ed. New York: Columbia University Press, 2005.

Daston, Lorraine. "1789, June 2, The Disciplines of Attention." In *A New History of German Literature,* edited by David E. Wellbery, 434–39. Cambridge, MA: Harvard University Press, 2004.

Davenport, Guy. *Seven Greeks: Alcman, Anacreon, Archilochus, Diogenes, Heraclitus, Herodas, and Sappho.* New York: New Directions, 1995.

Davidson, Hugh MacCullough. *The Origins of Certainty: Means and Meanings in Pascal's "Pensées."* Chicago: University of Chicago Press, 1979.

Davies, Stevan L. *The Gospel of Thomas and Christian Wisdom.* New York: Seabury Press, 1983.

Davis, Murray S. "Aphorisms and Clichés: The Generation and Dissipation of Conceptual Charisma." *Annual Review of Sociology* 25, no. 1 (1999): 245–69.

Davis, Natalie Zemon. "Proverbial Wisdom and Popular Errors." In *Society and Culture in Early Modern France: Eight Essays,* 227–70. Stanford: Stanford University Press, 1975.

De Certeau, Michel. *The Mystic Fable, Volume Two: The Sixteenth and Seventeenth Centuries.* Edited by Luce Giard and translated by Michael B. Smith. Chicago: University of Chicago Press, 2015.

DeConick, April D. *Recovering the Original Gospel of Thomas: A History of the Gospel and Its Growth.* New York: T & T Clark International, 2005.

———, ed. *Seek to See Him: Ascent and Vision Mysticism in the Gospel of Thomas.* Leiden: Brill, 1996.

———. *Voices of the Mystics: Early Christian Discourse in the Gospels of John and Thomas and Other Ancient Christian Literature.* Sheffield: Sheffield Academic Press, 2001.

DeConick, April D., and Grant Adamson, eds. *Histories of the Hidden God: Concealment and Revelation in Western Gnostic, Esoteric, and Mystical Traditions.* Durham: Acumen, 2013.

De Jonge, H. J. "Erasmus' Method of Translation in His Version of the New Testament." *The Bible Translator* 37, no. 1 (1986): 135–38.

Deleuze, Gilles. *Difference and Repetition.* Translated by Paul Patton. New York: Columbia University Press, 1994.

———. *Nietzsche and Philosophy.* Translated by Hugh Tomlinson. New York: Columbia University Press, 1983.

Delft, Louis van. *Les moralistes, une apologie.* Paris: Gallimard, 2008.

De Lubac, Henri. *Medieval Exegesis: The Four Senses of Scripture.* 3 vols. Translated by Mark Sebanc. Grand Rapids, MI: W. B. Eerdmans, 1998.

De Man, Paul. *Allegories of Reading: Figural Language in Rousseau, Nietzsche, Rilke, and Proust.* New Haven: Yale University Press, 1979.

Denecke, Wiebke. *The Dynamics of Masters Literature: Early Chinese Thought from Confucius to Han Feizi.* Cambridge, MA: Harvard University Asia Center, 2010.

De Romilly, Jacqueline. "From Aphorisms to Theoretical Analyses: The Birth of Human Sciences in the Fifth Century B.C." *Diogenes* 36, no. 144 (1988): 1–15.

Derrida, Jacques. *Spurs: Nietzsche's styles / Éperons: les styles de Nietzsche.* Translated by Stefano Agosti. Chicago: University of Chicago Press, 1979.

———. *Psyche: Inventions of the Other.* Vol. 2. Translated by Peggy Kamuf and Elizabeth Rottenberg. Stanford: Stanford University Press, 2008.

Descartes, René. *The Philosophical Writings of Descartes.* Translated by John Cotting-ham, Robert Stoothoff, and Dugald Murdoch. 2 vols. Cambridge: Cambridge University Press, 1985.

Descotes, Dominique. *L'argumentation chez Pascal.* Paris: Presses universitaires de France, 1993.

Diels, Hermann, with Walther Kranz. *Die Fragmente der Vorsokratiker.* 3 vols. Berlin: Weidmann, 1934.

Dillon, Brian. *Essayism.* London: Fitzcarraldo, 2018.

Dionisotti, A. C. "On Fragments in Classical Scholarship." In *Collecting Fragments / Fragmente sammeln,* edited by Glenn W. Most, 1–33. Göttingen: Vandenhoeck & Ruprecht, 1997.

Dionysius (Pseudo-). *The Complete Works.* Translated and edited by Colm Luibhéid. New York: Paulist Press, 1987.

D'Iorio, Paolo. *Nietzsche's Journey to Sorrento.* Translated by Sylvia Gorelick. Chicago: University of Chicago Press, 2016.

Dōgen. *Moon in a Dewdrop.* Translated by Kazuaki Tanahashi. San Francisco: North Point Press, 1985.

———. *Treasury of the True Dharma Eye: Zen Master Dogen's Shobo Genzo.* Translated by Kazuaki Tanahashi. Boston: Shambhala, 2013.

Dolin, Sharon. "Making a Space for Aphorism: Exploring the Intersection Between Aphorism and Poetry." *Poets.org.* September 13, 2011. www.poets.org/poetsorg/text/making-space-aphorism-exploring-intersection-between-aphorism-and-poetry

Dolven, Jeff. *Scenes of Instruction in Renaissance Romance.* Chicago: University of Chicago Press, 2007.

Donnellan, Brendan. *Nietzsche and the French Moralists.* Bonn: Bouvier, 1982.

Dorian, Nancy. *The Gospel of Thomas: Introduction and Commentary.* Leiden: Brill, 2014.

Eco, Umberto. *The Infinity of Lists.* Translated by Alastair McEwen. New York: Rizzoli, 2009.

———. *The Name of the Rose.* Translated by William Weaver. San Diego: Harcourt Brace Jovanovich, 1983.

Eden, Kathy. *Friends Hold All Things in Common: Tradition, Intellectual Property, and the Adages of Erasmus.* New Haven: Yale University Press, 2001.

Elman, Benjamin A. *From Philosophy to Philology: Intellectual and Social Aspects of Change in Late Imperial China.* Cambridge, MA: Council on East Asian Studies, Harvard University, 1984.

Engels, Johannes. *Die sieben Weisen: Leben, Lehren und Legenden.* Munich: Beck, 2010.

Erasmus, Desiderius. *The Adages of Erasmus.* Selected by William Barker from vols. 31–36 of *The Collected Works.* Toronto: University of Toronto Press, 2001.

———. *The Collected Works of Erasmus.* 59 vols. Toronto: University of Toronto Press, 1974–.

———. *Opera omnia Desiderii Erasmi Roterodami.* "Amsterdam edition." 15 vols. Leiden: Brill, 1969–.

Ernst, Pol. *Approches pascaliennes: l'unité et le mouvement, le sens et la fonction de chacune des vingt-sept liasses titrées.* Gembloux: Duculot, 1970.

———. *Les Pensées de Pascal, géologie et stratigraphie.* Oxford: Voltaire Foundation, 1996.

Eusebius. *Ecclesiastical History.* Translated by Arthur Cushman McGiffert. Vol. 1 of *The Nicene and Post-Nicene Fathers,* edited by Philip Schaff and Henry Wace. Buffalo, NY: Christian Literature, 1890.

Farrington, Benjamin. *The Philosophy of Francis Bacon; An Essay on Its Development from 1603 to 1609.* Liverpool: Liverpool University Press, 1964.

Field, Judith V. "The Infinitely Great and the Infinitely Small in the Work of Girard Desargues." In *Desargues en son temps,* edited by Jean G. Dhombres and Joël Sakarovitch, 217–30. Paris: Librairie scientifique A. Blanchard, 1994.

Flood, Gavin D. *The Truth Within: A History of Inwardness in Christianity, Hinduism, and Buddhism.* Oxford: Oxford University Press, 2013.

Force, Pierre. *Le problème herméneutique chez Pascal.* Paris: J. Vrin, 1989.

Foucault, Michel. *The Order of Things: Archeology of the Human Sciences.* London: Routledge, 2002.

———. "Self Writing." In *Ethics: Subjectivity and Truth,* edited by Paul Rabinow, 207–21. New York: New Press, 1997.

Fowler, Alastair. *The Mind of the Book: Pictorial Title-Pages.* Oxford: Oxford University Press, 2017.

Fox, Michael V. "Ancient Near Eastern Wisdom Literature." *Religion Compass* 5, no. 1 (2011): 1–11.

———, ed. *Essays on the Art of the Aphorism,* special issue of *Journal for the Study of the Old Testament* 29, no. 2 (2004).

Franco, Paul. *Nietzsche's Enlightenment: The Free-Spirit Trilogy of the Middle Period.* Chicago: University of Chicago Press, 2011.

Franklin-Brown, Mary. *Reading the World: Encyclopedic Writing in the Scholastic Age.* Chicago: University of Chicago Press, 2012.

Freeman, Kathleen, trans. *Ancilla to the Pre-Socratic Philosophers: A Complete Translation of the Fragment in Diels, Fragmente der Vorsokratiker.* Cambridge, MA: Harvard University Press, 1948.

Fricke, Harald. *Aphorismus.* Stuttgart: Metzler, 1984.

Frye, Northrop. "The Structure of Imagery in *The Faerie Queene.*" In *Essential Articles for the Study of Edmund Spenser,* edited by A. C. Hamilton, 153–70. Hamden, CT: Archon Books, 1972.

Fumaroli, Marc. "The Genius of the French Language." In *Realms of Memory: The Construction of the French Past,* edited by Pierre Nora and Lawrence D. Kritzman and translated by Arthur Goldhammer, 3:555–606. New York: Columbia University Press, 1998.

Garber, Daniel. "Merchants of Light and Mystery Men: Bacon's Last Projects in Natural History." *Journal of Early Modern Studies* 3, no. 1 (2014): 91–106.

Gardner, Daniel K. *Four Books: The Basic Teachings of the Later Confucian Tradition.* Indianapolis: Hackett, 2007.

————. *Zhu Xi's Reading of the* Analects: *Canon, Commentary, and the Classical Tradition.* New York: Columbia University Press, 2003.

Gärtner, Hans Armin. "Gnome." In *Brill's New Pauly,* edited by Hubert Cancik and Helmuth Schneider, 2006. http://referenceworks.brillonline.com/entries/brill-s -new-pauly/gnome-e425560

Gaukroger, Stephen. *The Emergence of a Scientific Culture: Science and the Shaping of Modernity, 1210–1685.* Oxford: Oxford University Press, 2006.

————. *Francis Bacon and the Transformation of Early-Modern Philosophy.* Cambridge: Cambridge University Press, 2001.

Geary, James. *Geary's Guide to the World's Great Aphorists.* New York: Bloomsbury, 2007.

————. *The World in a Phrase: A Brief History of the Aphorism.* New York: Bloomsbury, 2005.

Gibson, Walter S. *Figures of Speech: Picturing Proverbs in Renaissance Netherlands.* Berkeley: University of California Press, 2010.

Gide, André. *"Le traité du Narcisse."* In *Le retour de l'enfant prodigue: précédé de cinq autres traités.* Paris: Gallimard, 1948.

Giglioni, Guido. "From the Woods of Experience to the Open Fields of Metaphysics: Bacon's Notion of Silva." *Renaissance Studies* 28, no. 2 (2014): 242–61.

Gilbert, Neal Ward. *Renaissance Concepts of Method.* New York: Columbia University Press, 1960.

Goethe, Johann Wolfgang von. *Maxims and Reflections.* Translated by Elisabeth Stopp. London: Penguin Books, 1998.

Goldin, Paul, ed. *A Concise Companion to Confucius.* Oxford: Wiley Blackwell, 2017.

Goldmann, Lucien. *Le dieu caché: étude sur la vision tragique dans les Pensées de Pascal et dans le théâtre de Racine.* Paris: Gallimard, 1955; translated by Philip Thody as *The Hidden God: A Study of Tragic Vision in the Pensées of Pascal and the Tragedies of Racine.* London: Verso, 2016.

Goyet, Francis. "L'origine logique du mot maxime." In *Logique et littérature à la Renaissance,* edited by Marie-Luce Demonet-Launay and André Tournon, 27–49. Paris: Champion, 1994.

————. *Le sublime du 'lieu commun': l'invention rhétorique dans l'Antiquité et à la Renaissance.* Paris: Champion, 1996.

Graham, A. C. *Disputers of the Tao: Philosophical Argument in Ancient China.* La Salle, IL: Open Court, 1989.

Graham, Daniel W. "Does Nature Love to Hide? Heraclitus B123 DK." *Classical Philology* 98, no. 2 (2003): 175–79.

————. *Explaining the Cosmos: The Ionian Tradition of Scientific Philosophy.* Princeton: Princeton University Press, 2008.

————. *The Texts of Early Greek Philosophy: The Complete Fragments and Selected Testimonies of the Major Presocratics.* Cambridge: Cambridge University Press, 2010.

Granger, Herbert. "Argumentation and Heraclitus' Book." *Oxford Studies in Ancient Philosophy* 26 (2004): 1–17.

Grant, Ben. *The Aphorism and Other Short Forms.* London: Routledge, 2016.

Greene, Thomas M. "Erasmus' 'Festina lente': Vulnerability of the Humanist Text." In *The Vulnerable Text: Essays on Renaissance Literature*, 1–17. New York: Columbia University Press, 1986.

———. *Light in Troy: Imitation and Discovery in Renaissance Poetry*. New Haven: Yale University Press, 1982.

Gross, John, ed. *The Oxford Book of Aphorisms*. Oxford: Oxford University Press, 1983.

Gutas, Dimitri. *Greek Wisdom Literature in Arabic Translation: A Study of the Graeco-Arabic Gnomologia*. New Haven, CT: American Oriental Society, 1975.

Güthenke, Constanze. "Enthusiasm Dwells Only in Specialization: Classical Philology and Disciplinarity in Nineteenth-Century Germany." In *World Philology*, edited by Sheldon Pollock, Benjamin A. Elman, and Ku-ming Kevin Chang, 265–84. Cambridge, MA: Harvard University Press, 2015.

Hadot, Pierre. *Philosophy as a Way of Life: Spiritual Exercises from Socrates to Foucault*. Edited by Arnold I. Davidson and translated by Michael Chase. Oxford: Blackwell, 1995.

———. *Veil of Isis: An Essay on the History of the Idea of Nature*. Translated by Michael Chase. Cambridge, MA: Harvard University Press, 2008.

Hamacher, Werner. *Minima Philologica*. Translated by Catharine Diehl and Jason Groves. New York: Fordham University Press, 2015.

Hammond, Nicholas. *Playing with Truth: Language and the Human Condition in Pascal's Pensées*. Oxford: Clarendon Press, 1990.

Harada, Shodo. *Moon by the Window: The Calligraphy and Zen Insights*. Boston: Wisdom Publications, 2011.

Harrison, Peter. *The Bible, Protestantism, and the Rise of Natural Science*. Cambridge: Cambridge University Press, 1998.

Hatab, Lawrence J. *Nietzsche's Life Sentence*. New York: Routledge, 2005.

Hauge, Matthew Ryan, and Andrew W. Pitts, eds. *Ancient Education and Early Christianity*. London: Bloomsbury, 2016.

Hegel, Georg Wilhelm Friedrich. *Lectures on the Philosophy of World History, Volume I: Manuscripts of the Introduction and the Lectures of 1822–1823*. Edited and translated by Robert F. Brown and Peter C. Hodgson. Oxford: Clarendon Press, 2011.

Heidegger, Martin. *Being and Time*. Translated by Joan Stambaugh. Albany: State University of New York Press, 1996.

———. *Early Greek Thinking*. Translated by David Farrell Krell and Frank A. Capuzzi. New York: Harper & Row, 1975.

———. *Off the Beaten Track*. Edited and translated by Julian Young and Kenneth Haynes. Cambridge: Cambridge University Press, 2002.

Heidegger, Martin, and Eugene Fink. *Heraclitus Seminar*. Translated by Charles H. Seibert. Evansville, IL: Northwestern University Press, 1979.

Helfer, Martha B. *The Retreat of Representation: The Concept of Darstellung in German Critical Discourse*. Albany: State University of New York Press, 1996.

Heller-Roazen, Daniel. *The Fifth Hammer: Pythagoras and the Disharmony of the World*. New York: Zone Books, 2011.

Henderson, John B. *The Construction of Orthodoxy and Heresy: Neo-Confucian, Islamic, Jewish, and Early Christian Patterns*. Albany, NY: State University of New York Press, 1998.

———. *Scripture, Canon, and Commentary: A Comparison of Confucian and Western Exegesis*. Princeton: Princeton University Press, 1991.

Henderson, John B., and On-Cho Ng. "The Commentarial Tradition." In *Dao Companion to the Analects*, edited by Amy Olberding, 37–53. Dordrecht: Springer, 2014.

Heraclitus. *The Art and Thought of Heraclitus*. Translated by Charles Kahn. Cambridge: Cambridge University Press, 1979.

———. *Heraclitea*. Edited by Serge Mouraviev. 11 vols. Sankt Augustin: Academia, 1991–.

———. *Heraclitus: The Cosmic Fragments*. Translated by G. S. Kirk. Cambridge: Cambridge University Press, 1962.

———. *Heraclitus: Fragments*. Edited by T. M. Robinson. Toronto: University of Toronto Press, 1997.

———. *Heraclitus: Greek Text with a Short Commentary*. Translated by M. Markovich. Mérida, Venezuela: Los Andes University Press, 1967.

Hippocrates. *Hippocratic Writings*. Edited by G. E. R. Lloyd and translated by John Chadwick and W. N. Mann. Harmondsworth: Penguin Books, 1983.

Hippolytus. *Refutation of All Heresies* and *The Pedagogue*. Vol. 5 of *Ante-Nicene Fathers*. Edited by Alexander Roberts, James Donaldson, and A. Cleveland Coxe and translated by J. H. MacMahon. Buffalo, NY: Christian Literature, 1886.

Hock, Ronald F., and Edward N. O'Neil. *The Chreia in Ancient Rhetoric: The Progymnasmata*. Atlanta: Scholars Press, 1986.

Hofmannsthal, Hugo von. *The Lord Chandos Letter*. Translated by Joel Rotenberg. New York: New York Review Books, 2005.

Holmes, Brooke. *The Symptom and the Subject: The Emergence of the Body in Ancient Greece*. Princeton: Princeton University Press, 2010.

Hölscher, Uvo. "Paradox, Simile, and Gnomic Utterance in Heraclitus." In *The Pre-Socratics: A Collection of Critical Essays*, edited by Alexander P. D. Mourelatos, 229–38. Princeton: Princeton University Press, 1994.

Homer. *The Odyssey*. Translated by Richmond Lattimore. Chicago: University of Chicago Press, 1997.

Horowitz, Maryanne Cline. *Seeds of Virtue and Knowledge*. Princeton: Princeton University Press, 1998.

Houben, Jan E. M. "*Sutra* and *Bhasyasutra* in Bhartrhari's Mahabhasya Dipika: On the Theory and Practice of a Scientific and Philosophical Genre." In *India and Beyond: Aspects of Literature, Meaning, Ritual and Thought*, edited by Dick van der Meij, 271–305. London: Kegan Paul International, 1997.

Hui, Andrew. "The Many Returns of Philology: A State of the Field Report." *Journal of the History of Ideas* 78, no. 1 (2017): 137–56.

———. *The Poetics of Ruins in Renaissance Literature*. New York: Fordham University Press, 2016.

Hülsz Piccone, Enrique, ed. *Nuevos ensayos sobre Heráclito: actas del Segundo Symposium Heracliteum*. Mexico City: Universidad Nacional Autónoma de México, 2009.

Hunter, George K. "The Marking of *Sententiae* in Elizabethan Printed Plays, Poems, and Romances." *The Library* 5, nos. 3–4 (1951): 171–88.

Hunter, Michael. *Confucius beyond the Analects*. Leiden: Brill, 2017.

Hunter, Michael, and Martin Kern, eds. *Confucius and the Analects Revisited: New Perspectives on Composition, Dating, and Authorship*. Leiden: Brill, 2018.

Hussey, Edward. "Epistemology and Meaning in Heraclitus." In *Language and Logos*, edited by Malcolm Schofield and Martha C. Nussbaum, 33–59. Cambridge: Cambridge University Press, 1982.

Ireton, Sean, and Caroline Chaumann, eds. *Heights of Reflection: Mountains in the German Imagination from the Middle Ages to the Twenty-First Century*. Rochester, NY: Camden House, 2012.

Janz, Curt Paul. *Nietzsche*. 3 vols. Munich: Carl Hanser Verlag, 1978–79.

Jardine, Lisa. *Erasmus, Man of Letters: The Construction of Charisma in Print*. Princeton: Princeton University Press, 1993.

———. *Francis Bacon: Discovery and the Art of Discourse*. Cambridge: Cambridge University Press, 1974.

Jarosinski, Eric. *Nein: A Manifesto*. New York: Grove Press, 2015.

Jensen, Anthony K., and Helmut Heit, eds. *Nietzsche as a Scholar of Antiquity*. London: Bloomsbury, 2014.

Jensen, Lionel M. *Manufacturing Confucianism: Chinese Traditions and Universal Civilization*. Durham, NC: Duke University Press, 1997.

Johnson, Christopher D. *Hyperboles: The Rhetoric of Excess in Baroque Literature and Thought*. Cambridge, MA: Harvard University Press, 2010.

Johnstone, Mark A. "On 'Logos' in Heraclitus." *Oxford Studies in Ancient Philosophy* 47 (2014): 1–29.

Jolles, André. *Simple Forms: Legend, Saga, Myth, Riddle, Saying, Case, Memorabile, Fairytale, Joke*. Translated by Peter J. Schwartz. London: Verso, 2017.

Jouanna, Jacques. *Hippocrates*. Translated by M. B. DeBevoise. Baltimore: Johns Hopkins University Press, 1999.

Joubert, Joseph. *Les carnets*. Edited by André Beaunier, André Bellessort, and Jeanne Beaunier. 2 vols. Paris: Gallimard, 1938.

Jullien, François. *Detour and Access: Strategies of Meaning in China and Greece*. Translated by Sophie Hawkes. New York: Zone Books, 2000.

Kafka, Franz. *The Zürau Aphorisms*. Translated by Michael Hoffman and Geoffrey Brock; introduction and afterword by Roberto Calasso. New York: Schocken, 2006.

Kahn, Charles H. "Philosophy and the Written Word." In *Language and Thought in Early Greek Philosophy*, edited by Kevin Robb, 110–24. La Salle, IL: Hegeler Institute, 1983.

Kant, Immanuel. *Critique of Pure Reason*. Translated by Werner S. Pluhar. Indianapolis: Hackett, 1996.

————. *Critique of the Power of Judgment*. Translated by Paul Guyer. Cambridge: Cambridge University Press, 2000.

Katsafanas, Paul. *The Nietzschean Self: Moral Psychology, Agency, and the Unconscious*. Oxford: Oxford University Press, 2016.

Kaufmann, Walter. *Nietzsche, Philosopher, Psychologist, Antichrist*. Princeton: Princeton University Press, 1974.

Kearney, Richard. *Anatheism: Returning to God after God*. New York: Columbia University Press, 2010.

Kelber, Werner H. *The Oral and the Written Gospel: The Hermeneutics of Speaking and Writing in the Synoptic Tradition, Mark, Paul, and Q*. Bloomington: Indiana University Press, 1997.

Keller, Vera. *Knowledge and the Public Interest, 1575–1725*. Cambridge: Cambridge University Press, 2015.

Kennedy, George A. *Progymnasmata: Greek Textbooks of Prose Composition and Rhetoric*. Atlanta: Society of Biblical Literature, 2003.

Kermode, Frank. *The Genesis of Secrecy: On the Interpretation of Narrative*. Cambridge, MA: Harvard University Press, 1979.

Kern, Martin. "The 'Masters' in the *Shji*." *T'oung Pao* 101, nos. 4–5 (2015): 335–62.

Kim, Tae Hyun, and Mark Csikszentmihalyi. "History and Formation of the Analects." In *Dao Companion to the Analects*, edited by Amy Olberding, 21–36. Dordrecht: Springer, 2014.

King, Karen L. *What Is Gnosticism?* Cambridge, MA: Harvard University Press, 2003.

Kinney, Daniel. "Erasmus' *Adagia*: Midwife to the Rebirth of Learning." *Journal of Medieval and Renaissance Studies* 11 (1981): 169–92.

Kirk, G. S., J. E. Raven, and M. Schofield, trans. and eds. *The Presocratic Philosophers: A Critical History with a Selection of Texts*. Cambridge: Cambridge University Press, 1983.

Kittler, Friedrich A. *Gramophone, Film, Typewriter*. Translated by Geoffrey Winthrop-Young and Michael Wutz. Stanford: Stanford University Press, 1999.

Kloppenborg, John S. *Q, the Earliest Gospel: An Introduction to the Original Stories and Sayings of Jesus*. Louisville, KY: Westminster John Knox Press, 2008.

Koester, Helmut. *Ancient Christian Gospels: Their History and Development*. Philadelphia: SCM Press, 1990.

Kofman, Sarah. *Nietzsche and Metaphor*. Translated by Duncan Large. Stanford: Stanford University Press, 1993.

————. "Nietzsche and the Obscurity of Heraclitus." *Diacritics* 17, no. 3 (1987): 39–55.

Koyre, Alexandre. *From the Closed World to the Infinite Universe*. Baltimore: Johns Hopkins University Press, 1957.

Kraye, Jill. "Pagan Philosophy and Patristics in Erasmus and His Contemporaries." *Erasmus Studies* 31, no. 1 (2011): 33–60.

Krüger, Heinz. *Über den Aphorismus als philosophische Form*. Munich: Edition Text + Kritik, 1988.

Kubiak, Christopher. "Sowing Chaos: Discontinuity and the Form of Autonomy in the Fragment Collections of the Early German Romantics." *Studies in Romanticism* 33, no. 3 (1994): 411–49.

Lacoue-Labarthe, Philippe, and Jean-Luc Nancy. *The Literary Absolute: The Theory of Literature in German Romanticism*. Translated by Philip Barnard and Cheryl Lester. Albany: State University of New York Press, 1988.

Lafond, Jean, ed. *Les Formes brèves de la prose et le discours discontinu: XVIe–XVIIe siècles*. Paris: J. Vrin, 1984.

———. *Moralistes du XVIIe siècle*. Paris: R. Laffont, 1992.

Lafuma, Louis. *Histoire des Pensées de Pascal (1656–1952)*. Paris: Éditions du Luxembourg, 1954.

Laks, André. *The Idea of Presocratic Philosophy*. Translated by Glenn W. Most. Princeton: Princeton University Press, 2018.

Laks, André, and Glenn W. Most, eds. *Early Greek Philosophy*. 9 vols. Cambridge, MA: Harvard University Press, 2016.

Lamotte, Etienne. *History of Indian Buddhism from the Origins to the Saka Era*. Translated by Sara Webb-Boin. Louvain-la-Neuve: Université Catholique de Louvain, 1988.

Landy, Joshua. *How to Do Things with Fictions*. New York: Oxford University Press, 2012.

Lao Tzu (Laozi). *Tao Te Ching*. Translated by D. C. Lau. Harmondsworth: Penguin Books, 1963.

Laporte, Jean. *Le Coeur et la raison selon Pascal*. Paris: Bibliothèque Nationale, 1983.

Lardinois, André. "Modern Paroemiology and the Use of Gnomai in Homer's *Iliad*." *Classical Philology* 92, no. 3 (1997): 213–34.

La Rochefoucauld, François. *Collected Maxims and Other Reflections*. Translated by E. H. Blackmore, A. M. Blackmore, and Francine Giguère. Oxford: Oxford University Press, 2007.

Layton, Bentley. *The Gnostic Scriptures: A New Translation*. Garden City, NY: Doubleday, 1987.

Lazaridis, Nikolaos. *Wisdom in Loose Form: The Language of Egyptian and Greek Proverbs in Collections of the Hellenistic and Roman Periods*. Leiden: Brill, 2007.

Le Boulluec, Alain. "De *l'Evangile des Egyptiens* à *l'Evangile selon Thomas* en passant par Jules Cassien et Clément d'Alexandrie." In *L'Évangile selon Thomas et les textes de Nag Hammadi*, edited by Louis Painchaud and Paul-Hubert Poirier, 251–76. Quebec: Les Presses de l'Université Laval, 2007.

Leclercq, Jean, O.S.B. *The Love of Learning and the Desire for God*. Translated by Catharine Misrahi. New York: Fordham University Press, 1961.

Legros, Alain. *Essais sur poutres: peintures et inscriptions chez Montaigne*. Paris: Klincksieck, 2000.

Le Guern, Michel. *Pascal et Descartes*. Paris: A. G. Nizet, 1971.

Leutsch, Ernst von, and Friedrich Wilhelm Schneidewin, eds. *Corpus Paroemiographorum Graecorum*. Gottingen: Vandenhoeck et Ruprecht, 1893.

Levi, Anthony, S.J. *French Moralists: The Theory of the Passions, 1585–1649*. Oxford: Clarendon Press, 1964.

Levine, Caroline. *Forms: Whole, Rhythm, Hierarchy, Network.* Princeton: Princeton University Press, 2015.

Lewis, Mark Edward. *Writing and Authority in Early China.* Albany: State University of New York Press, 1999.

Lichtheim, Miriam. *Late-Egyptian Wisdom Literature in the International Context.* Göttingen: Vandenhoeck & Ruprecht, 1983.

Lilla, Salvatore Romano. *Clement of Alexandria: A Study in Christian Platonism and Gnosticism.* Oxford: Oxford University Press, 1971.

Lilti, Antoine. *Le monde des salons: sociabilité et mondanité à Paris au XVIIIe siècle.* Paris: Fayard, 2005.

Liu An. *The Huainanzi: A Guide to the Theory and Practice of Government in Early Han China.* Edited and translated by John S. Major, Sarah A. Queen, Andrew Seth Meyer, and Harold D. Roth. New York: Columbia University Press, 2010.

Liu Xie. *The Literary Mind and the Carving of Dragons: A Study of Thought and Pattern in Chinese Literature.* Translated and annotated by Vincent Yu-chung Shih. Hong Kong: Chinese University Press, 1983.

Li Zhi. *A Book to Burn and a Book to Keep (Hidden): Selected Writings.* Translated by Rebecca Handler-Spitz, Pauline Lee, and Haun Saussy. New York: Columbia University Press, 2016.

Loeb, Paul S. "Eternal Recurrence." In *Oxford Handbook of Nietzsche,* edited by John Richardson and Ken Gemes, 643–71. Oxford: Oxford University Press, 2013.

Long, A. A. *Greek Models of Mind and Self.* Cambridge, MA: Harvard University Press, 2015.

———. "Heraclitus on Measure and the Explicit Emergence of Rationality." In *Body and Soul in Ancient Philosophy,* edited by Dorothea Frede and Burkhard Reis, 87–109. Berlin: de Gruyter. 2009.

Lough, James, and Alex Stein, eds. *Short Flights: Thirty-Two Modern Writers Share Aphorisms of Insight, Inspiration, and Wit.* Tucson, AZ: Schaffner Press, 2015.

Löwith, Karl. *Nietzsche's Philosophy of the Eternal Recurrence of the Same.* Translated by J. Harvey Lomax. Berkeley: University of California Press, 1997.

Ludwin, Dawn M. *Blaise Pascal's Quest for the Ineffable.* New York: P. Lang, 2001.

Luiselli, Valeria. *Sidewalks.* London: Granta, 2010.

Mack, Peter. *Renaissance Argument: Valla and Agricola in the Traditions of Rhetoric and Dialectic.* Leiden: Brill, 1993.

Maclean, Ian. *Interpretation and Meaning in the Renaissance: The Case of Law.* Cambridge: Cambridge University Press, 1992.

———. "La Rochefoucauld, Little Learning and the Love of Truth." *Journal of the Warburg and Courtauld Institutes* 75 (2012): 296–317.

MacPhail, Eric. *Dancing around the Well: The Circulation of Commonplaces in Renaissance Humanism.* Leiden: Brill, 2014.

———. "The Submersion of Tradition: A Platonic Myth from Antiquity to the Renaissance." *Allegorica* 22 (2001): 47–67.

Makeham, John. "The Formation of *Lunyu* as a Book." *Monumenta Serica* 44 (1996): 1–24.

————. *Transmitters and Creators: Chinese Commentators and Commentaries on the Analects*. Cambridge, MA: Harvard University Asia Center, 2003.

Maleuvre, Didier. *The Horizon: A History of Our Infinite Longing*. Berkeley: University of California Press, 2011.

Mandela, Nelson. *Long Walk to Freedom*. New York: Little, Brown, 1994.

Mandelstam, Osip. *Selected Poems*. Translated by Clarence Brown and W. S. Merwin. New York: New York Review Books, 2004.

Mandeville, Scholastica. "The Rhetorical Tradition of the *Sententiae*, with a Study of Its Influence on the Prose of Sir Francis Bacon and of Sir Thomas Browne." PhD diss., St. Louis University, 1960.

Manetti, Giovanni. *Theories of the Sign in Classical Antiquity*. Bloomington: Indiana University Press, 1993.

Manguso, Sarah. "In Short: Thirty-six ways of looking at the aphorism." *Harper's*. September 2016. https://harpers.org/archive/2016/09/in-short

————. *300 Arguments: Essays*. Saint Paul, MN: Graywolf Press, 2017.

Mansfeld, Jaap. "Doxography of Ancient Philosophy." In *The Stanford Encyclopedia of Philosophy*, edited by Edward N. Zalta. Winter 2016. https://plato.stanford.edu/archives/win2016/entries/doxography-ancient

————. *Heresiography in Context: Hippolytus' Elenchos as a Source for Greek Philosophy*. Leiden: Brill, 1992.

————. "Myth, Science, Philosophy. A Question of Origins." In *Studies in the Historiography of Greek Philosophy*, edited by Jaap Mansfeld, 1–21. Maastricht: Van Gorcum, 1990.

Marcovich, Miroslav. *Hippolytus: Refutatio Omnium Haeresium*. Berlin: de Gruyter, 1986.

Marcus Aurelius. *Meditations*. Translated by Maxwell Staniforth. Baltimore: Penguin Books, 1964.

Marin, Louis. *La critique du discours: sur la "Logique de Port-Royal" et les "Pensées" de Pascal*. Paris: Editions de Minuit, 1975.

————. "'Pascal': Text, Author, Discourse." *Yale French Studies* 52 (1975): 129–51.

Mariner, Frank. "The Order of Disorder: The Problem of the Fragment in Pascal's *Pensées*." *Papers on French Seventeenth Century Literature* 20, no. 38 (1993): 171–82.

Marion, Jean-Luc. *God Without Being*. Translated by Thomas A. Carlson. Chicago: University of Chicago Press, 1991.

————. *Sur le prisme métaphysique de Descartes: constitution et limites de l'onto-théologie dans la pensée cartésienne*. Paris: Presses universitaires de France, 1986.

Marsden, Jill. "Nietzsche and the Art of the Aphorism." In *A Companion to Nietzsche*, edited by Keith Ansell Pearson, 22–37. London: Blackwell, 2006.

Martin, Kristen. "In Praise of the New Aphorism, No Longer Just for Great Men." *Literary Hub*. February 16, 2017. http://lithub.com/in-praise-of-the-new-aphorism-no-longer-just-for-great-men

Maurizio, Lisa. "Technopaegnia in Heraclitus and the Delphic Oracles: Shared Compositional Techniques." In *The Muse at Play: Riddles and Wordplay in Greek and*

*Latin Poetry,* edited by Jan Kwapisz, David Petrain, and Mikolaj Szymanski, 100–120. Berlin: de Gruyter, 2012.

McKenna, Antony. *De Pascal à Voltaire, 1670–1734.* 2 vols. Oxford: Voltaire Foundation, 1990.

———. *Entre Descartes et Gassendi: la première édition des 'Pensées' de Pascal.* Oxford: Voltaire Foundation, 1993.

McKirahan, Richard D. *Philosophy Before Socrates: An Introduction with Texts and Commentary.* Indianapolis: Hackett, 1994.

Melzer, Sara E. *Discourses of the Fall: A Study of Pascal's* Pensées. Berkeley: University of California Press, 1986.

Mesnard, Jean. *La culture du XVIIe siècle: enquêtes et synthèses.* Paris: Presses universitaires de France, 1992.

———. *Les Pensées de Pascal.* Paris: Société d'édition d'enseignement supérieur, 1976.

Meyer, Dirk. *Philosophy on Bamboo: Text and Production of Meaning in Early China.* Leiden: Brill, 2011.

Meyer, Marvin W. *The Nag Hammadi Scriptures.* New York: HarperOne, 2007.

———. *Secret Gospels: Essays on Thomas and the Secret Gospel of Mark.* Harrisburg, PA: Trinity Press International, 2003.

Michon, Hélène. *L'ordre du coeur: philosophie, théologie et mystique dans les 'Pensées' de Pascal.* Paris: H. Champion, 1996.

Miller, J. Hillis. "Aphorism as Instrument of Political Action in Nietzsche." *Parallax* 10, no. 3 (2004): 70–82.

Mizuno, Kogen. *Buddhist Sutras: Origin, Development, Transmission.* Tokyo: Kosei, 1982.

Montaigne, Michel de. *Complete Essays.* Translated by Donald Frame. Stanford: Stanford University Press, 1958.

Montandon, Alain. *Les Formes brèves.* Paris: Hachette, 1992.

Montinari, Mazzino. "The New Critical Edition of Nietzsche's Complete Works." *The Malahat Review* 24 (1973): 121–33.

———. "Nietzsche's Unpublished Writings from 1885–88, or, Textual Criticism and the Will to Power." In *Reading Nietzsche,* translated by Greg Whitlock, 80–102. Urbana: University of Illinois Press, 2003.

Morgan, Teresa. *Popular Morality in the Early Roman Empire.* Cambridge: Cambridge University Press, 2007.

Morson, Gary Saul. *The Long and Short of It: From Aphorism to Novel.* Stanford: Stanford University Press, 2012.

Moss, Ann. *Printed Commonplace-Books and the Structuring of Renaissance Thought.* Oxford: Clarendon Press, 1996.

Most, Glenn W. "Friedrich Nietzsche between Philosophy and Philology." *New Nietzsche Studies* 4, no. 1 (2000): 163–70.

———. "Heraclitus Fragment B123 DK." In *What Reason Promises: Essays on Reason, Nature and History,* edited by Susan Neiman, Peter Galison, and Wendy Doniger, 117–23. Berlin: de Gruyter, 2016.

———. "On Fragments." In *The Fragment: An Incomplete History*, edited by William Tronzo, 9–22. Los Angeles: Getty Research Institute, 2009.

———. "The Poetics of Early Greek Philosophy." In *The Cambridge Companion to Early Greek Philosophy*, edited by A. A. Long, 332–62. Cambridge: Cambridge University Press, 1999.

Mouraviev, Serge. "Le livre d'Héraclite 2500 ans après: L'état actuel de sa reconstruction." In *Nuevos ensayos sobre Heráclito*, edited by Enrique Hülsz Piccone, 11–73. México, D.F.: Universidad nacional autónoma de México, 2009.

N+1 Editors. "Please RT." *N+1*. Summer 2012. https://nplusonemag.com/issue-14/the-intellectual-situation/retweet

Nancy, Jean-Luc. *The Birth to Presence*. Translated by Brian Holmes. Stanford: Stanford University Press, 1993.

Nehamas, Alexander. *The Art of Living: Socratic Reflections from Plato to Foucault*. Sather Classical Lectures. Berkeley: University of California Press, 1998.

———. *Nietzsche, Life as Literature*. Cambridge, MA: Harvard University Press, 1985.

Nelson, Maggie. *Bluets*. Seattle: Wave Books, 2009.

Neumann, Gerhard. *Ideenparadiese: Untersuchungen zur Aphoristik von Lichtenberg, Novalis, Friedrich Schlegel und Goethe*. Munich: W. Fink, 1976.

Nietzsche, Friedrich Wilhelm. *Beyond Good and Evil: Prelude to a Philosophy of the Future*. Translated by Walter Kaufmann. New York: Vintage Books, 1989.

———. *The Birth of Tragedy and Other Writings*. Edited by Raymond Geuss and Ronald Speirs. Translated by Ronald Speirs. Cambridge: Cambridge University Press, 1999.

———. *Daybreak: Thoughts on the Prejudices of Morality*. Edited by Maudemarie Clark and Brian Leiter. Translated by R. J. Hollingdale. Cambridge: Cambridge University Press, 1997.

———. *The Gay Science: With a Prelude in Rhymes and an Appendix of Songs*. Translated by Walter Kaufmann. New York: Vintage, 1974.

———. *Human, All Too Human: A Book for Free Spirits*. Translated by R. J. Hollingdale. Cambridge: Cambridge University Press, 1986.

———. *On the Genealogy of Morals*. Translated by Walter Kaufmann. New York: Vintage Books, 1967.

———. *The Pre-Platonic Philosophers*. Translated by Greg Whitlock. Urbana: University of Illinois Press, 2001.

———. *Philosophy in the Tragic Age of the Greeks*. Translated by Marianne Cowan. Washington, DC: Regnery, 2012.

———. *Sämtliche Werke: Kritische Studienausgabe*. Edited by Giorgio Colli and Mazzino Montinari. 15 vols. Berlin: de Gruyter, 2009.

———. *Thus Spoke Zarathustra: A Book for All and None*. Translated by Walter Kaufmann. New York: Modern Library, 1995.

———. *Twilight of the Idols and the Anti-Christ*. Translated by R. J. Hollingdale. London: Penguin Books, 1990.

———. *Werke: Kritische Gesamtausgabe*. Edited by Giorgio Colli and Mazzino Montinari. 40 vols. Berlin: de Gruyter, 1967–.

———. *The Will to Power.* Translated and edited by Walter Kaufmann and R. J. Hollingdale. New York: Random House, 1967.

———. *Writings from the Late Notebooks.* Edited by Rüdiger Bittner. Translated by Kate Sturge. Cambridge: Cambridge University Press, 2003.

Norman, Judith. "Nietzsche and Early Romanticism." *Journal of the History of Ideas* 63, no. 3 (2002): 501–19.

Norman, K. R. *Pāli Literature: Including the Canonical Literature in Prakrit and Sanskrit of All the Hīnayāna Schools of Buddhism.* Wiesbaden: Harrassowitz, 1983.

Norman, Larry F. *The Shock of the Ancients: Literature and History in Early Modern France.* Chicago: University of Chicago Press, 2011.

North, Paul. *The Yield: Kafka's Atheological Reformation.* Stanford: Stanford University Press, 2015.

Novalis. *Blüthenstaub.* In *Schriften,* edited by Paul Kluckhohn and Richard Samuel, 2:421–70. Stuttgart: Kohlhammer, 1960.

Nussbaum, Martha C. "Psyche in Heraclitus." *Phronesis* 17 (1972): 1–16.

Nylan, Michael. *The Five "Confucian" Classics.* New Haven: Yale University Press, 2001.

Ong, Walter J. *Ramus, Method, and the Decay of Dialogue.* Chicago: University of Chicago Press, 1958.

Ortemann, Marie-Jeanne, ed. *Fragment(s), fragmentation, aphorisme poétique.* Nantes: Université de Nantes, 1998.

Osborne, Catherine. *Rethinking Early Greek Philosophy: Hippolytus of Rome and the Presocratics.* Ithaca, NY: Cornell University Press, 1987.

Otto, A. *Die Sprichwörter und sprichwörtlichen Redensarten der Römer.* Leipzig: Teubner, 1890.

Pagels, Elaine H. *Beyond Belief: The Secret Gospel of Thomas.* New York: Random House, 2003.

Panofsky, Erwin. *Renaissance and Renascences in Western Art.* New York: Harper Icon, 1972.

Parish, Richard. "Seventeenth-century Religious Writing." In *The Cambridge History of French Literature,* edited by William Burgwinkle, Nicholas Hammond, and Emma Wilson, 333–42. Cambridge: Cambridge University Press, 2011.

Parmentier, Bérengère. *Le Siècle des moralistes.* Paris: Éditions du Seuil, 2000.

Pascal, Blaise. *Pensées de M. Pascal sur la Religion et sur quelques autres sujets.* Port-Royal edition. Paris: Guillaume Desprez, 1669.

———. *Pensées de Pascal, Nouvelle édition, corrigée et augmentée.* Edited by Condorcet. London: 1776.

———. *Eloge et Pensées de Pascal.* Edited with commentary by Voltaire. 1778.

———. *Opuscules et Pensées.* Edited by Léon Brunschvicg. Paris: Hachette, 1897.

———. *Pensées.* Edited by Zacharie Tourneur. 2 vols. Paris: Éditions de Cluny, 1938.

———. *Pensées sur la Religion et sur quelques autres sujets.* Edited by Louis Lafuma. Paris: Delmas, 1951.

———. *Pensées.* Edited by Gérard Ferreyrolles and Philippe Sellier. Paris: Le Livre de Poche, 1976.

———. *Pensées.* Edited by Michel Le Guern. Paris: Gallimard, 2004.

————. *Pensées; Opuscules et lettres.* Edited by Philippe Sellier and Laurence Plazenet. Paris: Classiques Garnier, 2011.

————. *Pensées.* Translated by A. J. Krailsheimer. Harmondsworth: Penguin Books, 1966.

————. *Pensées and Other Writings.* Translated by Honor Levi and Anthony Levi. Oxford: Oxford University Press, 1995.

————. *Pensées.* Translated by Roger Ariew. Indianapolis: Hackett, 2005.

Patañjali. *The Yoga Sūtras of Patañjali.* Translated by Edwin F. Bryant. New York: North Point Press, 2009.

Paterson, Don. *Best Thought, Worst Thought.* Saint Paul, MN: Graywolf Press, 2008.

Patterson, Stephen J. *The Gospel of Thomas and Christian Origins: Essays on the Fifth Gospel.* Leiden: Brill, 2013.

————. "Wisdom in Q and *Thomas.*" In *In Search of Wisdom: Essays in Memory of John G. Gammie,* edited by Leo G. Perdue et al., 187–222. Louisville, KY: Westminster John Knox, 1993.

Patterson, Stephen J., James M. Robinson, and Hans-Gebhard Bethge. *The Fifth Gospel: The Gospel of Thomas Comes of Age.* London: T & T Clark, 2011.

Paulhan, Jean. "L'expérience du proverbe." In *Oeuvres complètes: L'art de la contradiction,* edited by Bernard Baillaud, 169–94. Paris: Gallimard, 2009.

————. "Sacred Language." In *The College of Sociology, 1937–39,* edited by Denis Hollier and translated by Betsy Wing, 304–21. Minneapolis: University of Minnesota Press, 1988.

Pelegrin, Benito, ed. *Les Formes brèves: actes du colloque international de la Baume-les-Aix, 26–27–28 novembre 1982.* Aix-en-Provence: Publications Université de Provence, 1984.

Pérouse, Marie. *L'invention des 'Pensées' de Pascal: les éditions de Port-Royal (1670–1678).* Paris: H. Champion, 2009.

Perry, Theodore Anthony. *The Moral Proverbs of Santob de Carrión: Jewish Wisdom in Christian Spain.* Princeton: Princeton University Press, 1987.

Pesic, Peter. "Proteus Rebound: Reconsidering the 'Torture of Nature.'" *Isis* 99, no. 2 (2008): 304–17.

————. "Wrestling with Proteus: Francis Bacon and the 'Torture' of Nature." *Isis* 90, no. 1 (1999): 81–94.

Petrarch, Francesco. *Letters on Familiar Matters (Rerum familiarium libri).* Translated by Aldo S. Bernardo. Baltimore: Johns Hopkins University Press, 1985.

————. *Petrarch's Remedies for Fortune Fair and Foul.* Translated by Conrad H. Rawski. Bloomington: Indiana University Press, 1991.

Phillips, Margaret Mann. *The 'Adages' of Erasmus: A Study with Translations.* Cambridge: Cambridge University Press, 1964.

Philo. *Selected Works.* Edited and translated by David Winston. New York: Paulist Press, 1981.

Pigman, G. W., III. "Versions of Imitation in the Renaissance." *Renaissance Quarterly* 33, no. 1 (1980): 1–32.

Piper, Ronald A. *Wisdom in the Q-Tradition: The Aphoristic Teaching of Jesus.* Cambridge: Cambridge University Press, 1989.

Pippin, Robert B. *Nietzsche, Psychology, and First Philosophy.* Chicago: University of Chicago Press, 2010.

Plato. *The Complete Works.* Edited by John M. Cooper and D. S. Hutchinson. Indianapolis: Hackett, 1997.

Pollock, Sheldon, Benjamin A. Elman, and Ku-ming Kevin Chang, eds. *World Philology.* Cambridge, MA: Harvard University Press, 2015.

Porter, James I. *Nietzsche and the Philology of the Future.* Stanford: Stanford University Press, 2000.

———. *The Sublime in Antiquity.* Cambridge: Cambridge University Press, 2016.

Pritchard, James B., ed. *The Ancient Near East: An Anthology of Texts and Pictures.* Princeton: Princeton University Press, 2011.

Proust, Marcel. *Remembrance of Things Past.* Translated by C. K. Scott Moncrieff and Terence Kilmartin. 3 vols. New York: Vintage Books, 1982.

Pugh, Anthony R. *The Composition of Pascal's Apologia.* Toronto: University of Toronto Press, 1984.

Purdy, Jedediah. "What I had lost was a country." *N+1.* December 20, 2016. https://nplusonemag.com/online-only/online-only/what-i-had-lost-was-a-country

al-Qadi al-Qudai. *A Treasury of Virtues: Sayings, Sermons, and Teachings of Ali, with the One Hundred Proverbs, Attributed to al-Jahiz.* Translated by Tahera Qutbuddin. New York: NYU Press, 2013.

Quignard, Pascal. *Une gêne technique à l'égard des fragments.* Paris: Editions Galilée, 1986.

Rambelli, Fabio. *Buddhist Materiality: A Cultural History of Objects in Japanese Buddhism.* Stanford: Stanford University Press, 2007.

Renou, Louis. *Histoire de la langue sanskrite.* Lyon: Éditions IAC, 1956.

———. "Sur le genre du Sûtra dans la littérature sanskrite." *Journal Asiatique* 251 (1963): 165–216.

Renou, Louis, and Jean Filliozat. *L'Inde classique; manuel des études indiennes.* Paris: Payot, 1947.

Ricci, Matteo. *On Friendship: One Hundred Maxims for a Chinese Prince.* Translated by Timothy Billings. New York: Columbia University Press, 2009.

Richardson, James. *Vectors.* Keene, NY: Ausable Press, 2001.

Rigoni, M. A., ed. *La brevità felice: Contributi alla teoria e alla storia dell'aforisma.* Venice: Marsilio, 2007.

Robinson, James M. "Logoi Sophon: On the Gattung of Q." In *Trajectories through Early Christianity,* edited by James M. Robinson and Helmut Koester, 71–113. Philadelphia: Fortress Press, 1971.

Rossi, Paolo. *Francis Bacon: From Magic to Science.* Chicago: University of Chicago Press, 1968.

———. *Naufragi senza spettatore.* Bologna: Il Mulino, 1995.

Roukhomovsky, Bernard. *Lire les formes brèves.* Paris: Nathan, 2001.

Ruby, Ryan. "The Long History of a Short Form." *Lapham's Quarterly*. May 9, 2016. www.laphamsquarterly.org/roundtable/long-history-short-form

Rummel, Erika. *The Humanist-Scholastic Debate in the Renaissance and Reformation.* Cambridge, MA: Harvard University Press, 1995.

Ruozzi, Gino, ed. *Scrittori italiani di aforismi.* 2 vols. Meridiani. Milan: Mondadori, 1994–96.

———. *Teoria e storia dell'aforisma.* Milan: Mondadori, 2004.

Russo, Joseph. "The Poetics of the Ancient Greek Proverb." *Journal of Folklore Research* 20, nos. 2/3 (1983): 121–30.

———. "Prose Genres for the Performance of Traditional Wisdom in Ancient Greece: Proverb, Maxim, Apothegm." In *Poet, Public, and Performance in Ancient Greece,* edited by Lowell Edmunds and Robert W. Wallace, 49–64. Baltimore: Johns Hopkins University Press, 1997.

Rütten, Thomas. "Hippocrates and the Construction of 'Progress' in Sixteenth- and Seventeenth-Century Medicine." In *Reinventing Hippocrates,* edited by David Cantor, 37–58. Aldershot: Ashgate, 2002.

Sablé, Madeleine de Souvré. *Maximes de Mme de Sablé (1678).* Edited by Damase Jouaust. Paris: Libr. des bibliophiles, 1870.

Safranski, Rüdiger. *Nietzsche: A Philosophical Biography.* Translated by Shelley Frisch. New York: Norton, 2002.

Saint-Cyran, Abbé de. *Maximes saintes et chrestiennes tirées des lettres de Messire Jean Duvergier de Hauranne.* Paris: Omont, 1703.

Sassi, Maria Michela. *The Beginnings of Philosophy in Greece.* Translated by Michele Asuni. Princeton: Princeton University Press, 2018.

Sato, Shozo. *Shodo: The Quiet Art of Japanese Zen Calligraphy; Learn the Wisdom of Zen through Traditional Brush Painting.* Translated by Alice Ogura Sato. Rutland, VT: Tuttle, 2014.

Saussy, Haun. *The Ethnography of Rhythm: Orality and Its Technologies.* New York: Fordham University Press, 2016.

Scarpari, Maurizio. *Il confucianesimo: i fondamenti e i testi.* Turin: Einaudi, 2010.

Schaberg, David. *A Patterned Past: Form and Thought in Early Chinese Historiography.* Cambridge, MA: Harvard University Asia Center, 2001.

Schaberg, William H. *The Nietzsche Canon: A Publication History and Bibliography.* Chicago: University of Chicago Press, 1995.

Schilleman, Matthew. "Typewriter Psyche: Henry James's Mechanical Mind." *Journal of Modern Literature* 36, no. 3 (2013): 14–30.

Schiller, Friedrich. "Letters on the Aesthetic Education of Man," translated by Elizabeth M. Wilkinson and L. A. Willoughby. In *Essays,* edited by Walter Hinderer and Daniel O. Dahlstrom, 86–178. The German Library, vol. 17. New York: Continuum, 1993.

Schlechta, Karl. *Der Fall Nietzsche.* Munich: Carl Hanser Verlag, 1959.

Schlegel, Friedrich. *"Athenäums" – Fragmente und andere Schriften.* Edited by Andreas Huyssen. Stuttgart: Reclam Verlag, 1986.

————. *Literary Notebooks, 1797–1801*. Translated by Hans Eichner. London: Athlone Press, 1957.

————. *Philosophical Fragments*. Translated by Peter Firchow. Foreword by Rodolphe Gasché. Minneapolis: University of Minnesota Press, 1991.

Schleiermacher, Friedrich. "Aphorisms on Hermeneutics from 1805, and 1809/10." Translated by Roland Haas and Jan Wojcik. *Cultural Hermeneutics* 4 (1997): 367–90.

————. *Hermeneutics and Criticism and Other Writings*. Translated by Andrew Bowie. New York: Cambridge University Press, 1998.

Schmaltz, Tad M. "What Has Cartesianism to Do with Jansenism?" *Journal of the History of Ideas* 60, no. 1 (1999): 37–56.

Schopenhauer, Arthur. *Essays and Aphorisms*. Edited and translated by R. J. Hollingdale. London: Penguin Books, 1970.

Scott, Michael. *Delphi: A History of the Center of the Ancient World*. Princeton: Princeton University Press, 2014.

Serjeantson, Richard. "Francis Bacon and the 'Interpretation of Nature' in the Late Renaissance." *Isis* 105, no. 4 (2014): 681–705.

Shapiro, Fred R., ed. *The Yale Book of Quotations*. New Haven: Yale University Press, 2006.

Shields, David, and Elizabeth Cooperman. *Life Is Short—Art Is Shorter: In Praise of Brevity*. Portland, OR: Hawthorn Books, 2014.

Sider, David. "The Fate of Heraclitus' Book in Later Antiquity." In *Nuevos ensayos sobre Heráclito*, edited by Enrique Hülsz Piccone, 443–58. México, D.F.: Universidad nacional autónoma de México, 2009.

Siskin, Clifford. *System: The Shaping of Modern Knowledge*. Cambridge, MA: MIT Press, 2016.

Sluiter, Ineke. "Obscurity." In *Canonical Texts and Scholarly Practices: A Global Comparative Approach*, edited by Anthony Grafton and Glenn W. Most, 34–51. Cambridge: Cambridge University Press, 2016.

Small, Robin. *Nietzsche and Rée: A Star Friendship*. Oxford: Clarendon Press, 2009.

Smith, Geoffrey S. *Guilt by Association: Heresy Catalogues in Early Christianity*. Oxford: Oxford University Press, 2015.

Smith, Henry. "Brevity in Pāṇini." *Journal of Indian Philosophy* 20, no. 1 (1992): 133–47.

Snider, Alvin. "Francis Bacon and the Authority of Aphorism." *Prose Studies* 11, no. 2 (1988): 60–71.

Sontag, Susan. *As Consciousness Is Harnessed to Flesh: Journals and Notebooks, 1964–1980*. Edited by David Rieff. New York: Farrar, Straus and Giroux, 2012.

Spicker, Friedemann. *Der Aphorismus: Begriff und Gattung von der Mitte des 18. Jahrhunderts bis 1912*. Berlin: de Gruyter, 1997.

Sprachman, Paul. "Aphorism." *Encyclopædia Iranica*. 2011. www.iranicaonline.org /articles/aphorism-short-sentences

Starobinski, Jean. *Montaigne in Motion*. Translated by Arthur Goldhammer. Chicago: University of Chicago Press, 1985.

Stegmaier, Werner. *Nietzsches Befreiung der Philosophie. Kontextuelle Interpretation des V. Buchs der "Fröhlichen Wissenschaft."* Berlin: de Gruyter, 2012.

Stephens, James. "Science and the Aphorism: Bacon's Theory of the Philosophical Style." *Speech Monographs* 37, no. 3 (1970): 157–71.

Stern, J. P. *Lichtenberg: A Doctrine of Scattered Occasions; Reconstructed from His Aphorisms and Reflections.* Bloomington: Indiana University Press, 1959.

Sternbach, Ludwik. *Subhāṣita, Gnomic, and Didactic Literature.* Wiesbaden: Harrassowitz, 1974.

Strobel, Eva. *Das "Pathos der Distanz." Nietzsches Entscheidung für den Aphorismenstil.* Würzburg: Königshausen & Neumann, 1998.

Stroumsa, Guy. *The End of Sacrifice: Religious Transformations in Late Antiquity.* Translated by Susan Emanuel. Chicago: University of Chicago Press, 2012.

———. *Hidden Wisdom: Esoteric Traditions and the Roots of Christian Mysticism.* Leiden: Brill, 1996.

———. *The Scriptural Universe of Ancient Christianity.* Cambridge, MA: Harvard University Press, 2017.

Struck, Peter T. *Birth of the Symbol: Ancient Readers at the Limits of Their Texts.* Princeton: Princeton University Press, 2004.

———. *Divination and Human Nature: A Cognitive History of Intuition in Classical Antiquity.* Princeton: Princeton University Press, 2016.

Summit, Jennifer. *Memory's Library: Medieval Books in Early Modern England.* Chicago: University of Chicago Press, 2008.

Szondi, Peter. *Introduction to Literary Hermeneutics.* Translated by Martha Woodmansee. Cambridge: Cambridge University Press, 1995.

Taylor, Benjamin. "Medieval Proverb Collections: The West European Tradition." *Journal of the Warburg and Courtauld Institutes* 55 (1992): 19–35.

Thoreau, Henry David. *Journal.* Edited by John C. Broderick. Princeton: Princeton University Press, 1981.

Tosi, Renzo. *Dizionario delle sentenze latine e greche: 10,000 citazioni dall'antichità al Rinascimento nell'originale e in traduzione con commento storico, letterario e filologico.* Milan: Biblioteca universale Rizzoli, 2000.

Tourrette, Éric. *Les formes brèves de la description morale: quatrains, maximes, remarques.* Paris: Champion, 2008.

Tronzo, William, ed. *The Fragment: An Incomplete History.* Los Angeles: Getty Research Institute, 2009.

Tufekci, Zeynep. *Twitter and Tear Gas: The Power and Fragility of Networked Protest.* New Haven: Yale University Press, 2017.

Turner, James. *Philology: The Forgotten Origins of the Modern Humanities.* Princeton: Princeton University Press, 2014.

Ungar, Steven. "Parts and Holes: Heraclitus / Nietzsche / Blanchot." *SubStance* 5, no. 14 (1976): 126–41.

Uro, Risto. *Thomas: Seeking the Historical Context of the Gospel of Thomas.* London: Clark, 2003.

Valantasis, Richard. *The Gospel of Thomas.* London: Routledge, 1997.

Valéry, Paul. *The Art of Poetry*. Translated by Denise Folliot. Princeton: Princeton University Press, 1958.

Valesio, Paolo. *Novantiqua: Rhetorics as a Contemporary Theory*. Bloomington: Indiana University Press, 1980.

Vallée, Gérard. *A Study in Anti-Gnostic Polemics: Irenaeus, Hippolytus, and Epiphanius*. Waterloo, Ont.: Wilfrid Laurier University Press, 1981.

Van Delft, Louis. *Les Moralistes. Une apologie*. Paris: Gallimard, 2008.

Van Den Abbeele, Georges. "Moralists and the Legacy of Cartesianism." In *A New History of French Literature*, edited by Denis Hollier, 327–34. Cambridge, MA: Harvard University Press, 1989.

Vasari, Giorgio. *Le Vite de' più eccellenti architetti, pittori, et scultori italiani*. Edited by Luciano Bellosi and Aldo Rossi. 2 vols. Turin: Einaudi, 1986.

Vauvenargues, Marquis de (Luc de Clapiers). *Réflexions et Maximes*. Edited by Samuel S. de Sacy. Paris: Le livre de poche, 1971.

Veidlinger, Daniel. "Sutta (Pāli / Theravada Canon)." *Oxford Bibliographies*. 2010. www.oxfordbibliographies.com/view/document/obo-9780195393521/obo-978 0195393521-0157.xml

Vernant, Jean-Pierre. *Myth and Thought among the Greeks*. Translated by Janet Lloyd and Jeff Fort. New York: Zone Books, 2006.

Vickers, Brian. "Bacon and Rhetoric." In *Cambridge Companion to Bacon*, edited by Markku Peltonen, 200–231. Cambridge: Cambridge University Press, 1996.

———. *Francis Bacon and Renaissance Prose*. Cambridge: Cambridge University Press, 1968.

———. "The Myth of Francis Bacon's 'Anti-Humanism.'" In *Humanism and Early Modern Philosophy*, edited by Jill Kraye and M. W. F. Stone, 135–58. London: Routledge, 2002.

Vlastos, Gregory. "On Heraclitus." *American Journal of Philology* 76, no. 4 (1955): 337–68.

Walther, Hans. *Proverbia sententiaeque latinitatis Medii Aevi: lateinische Sprichwörter und Sentenzen des Mittelalters in alphabetischer Anordnung*. Göttingen: Vandenhoeck & Ruprecht, 1963.

Weber, Max. *From Max Weber: Essays in Sociology*. Translated and edited by H. H. Gerth and C. Wright Mills. New York: Oxford University Press, 1946.

Weil, Simone. *Gravity and Grace*. Translated by Emma Crawford and Mario con der Ruhr. London: Routledge, 2004.

Weingarten, Oliver. "Recent Monographs on Confucius and Early Confucianism." *T'oung Pao* 97, nos. 1–3 (2011): 160–201.

West, M. L. *Early Greek Philosophy and the Orient*. Oxford: Clarendon Press, 1971.

———. *Iambi et elegi Graeci ante Alexandrum cantati*. Oxford: Clarendon Press, 1972.

Westerdale, Joel. *Nietzsche's Aphoristic Challenge*. Berlin: de Gruyter, 2013.

White, David Gordon. *The Yoga Sutra of Patanjali: A Biography*. Princeton: Princeton University Press, 2014.

Wilcox, John T. "That Exegesis of an Aphorism in *Genealogy* III: Reflections on the Scholarship." *Nietzsche-Studien* 27, no. 1 (1998): 448–62.

———. "What Aphorism Does Nietzsche Explicate in *Genealogy of Morals*, Essay III?" *Journal of the History of Philosophy* 35, no. 4 (1997): 593–610.

Williams, James G. *Those Who Ponder Proverbs: Aphoristic Thinking and Biblical Literature*. Sheffield: Almond Press, 1981.

Williams, R. John. *The Buddha in the Machine: Art, Technology, and the Meeting of East and West*. New Haven: Yale University Press, 2014.

Zhu, Xi (Chu Hsi). *Learning to Be a Sage: Selections from the Conversations of Master Chu, Arranged Topically*. Translated with a Commentary by Daniel K. Gardner. Berkeley: University of California Press, 1990.

Ziegler, Alan, ed. *Short: An International Anthology of Five Centuries of Short-Short Stories, Prose Poems, Brief Essays, and Other Short Prose Forms*. New York: Persea, 2014.

# INDEX

## A NOTE ON THE TYPE

This book has been composed in Adobe Text and Gotham. Adobe Text, designed by Robert Slimbach for Adobe, bridges the gap between fifteenth- and sixteenth-century calligraphic and eighteenth-century Modern styles. Gotham, inspired by New York street signs, was designed by Tobias Frere-Jones for Hoefler & Co.